Androgyny

*and the Denial
of Difference*

Feminist Issues: Practice, Politics, Theory

Kathleen M. Balutansky and Alison Booth, editors

Carol Siegel

*Lawrence among the Women: Wavering Boundaries
in Women's Literary Traditions*

Harriet Blodgett

*Capacious Hold-All: An Anthology of
Englishwomen's Diary Writings*

Joy Wiltenburg

*Disorderly Women and Female Power in the Street
Literature of Early Modern England and Germany*

Diane P. Freedman

*An Alchemy of Genres: Cross-Genre Writing
by American Feminist Poet-Critics*

Jean O'Barr and Mary Wyer

Engaging Feminism: Students Speak Up and Speak Out

Kari Weil

Androgny and the Denial of Difference

Androgyny
and the Denial of Difference

Kari Weil

University Press of Virginia

Charlottesville and
London

The University Press of Virginia
Copyright © 1992
by the Rector and Visitors
of the University of Virginia

First published 1992

Printed in the United States of America

Library of Congress Cataloging-in-Publication Data

Weil, Kari.
Androgyny and the denial of difference / Kari Weil.
p.   cm. — (Feminist issues)
Originally presented as the author's thesis (Ph. D.—Princeton
University, 1985) under the title: Veiling desire.
Includes bibliographical references (p.   ) and index.
ISBN 0-8139-1404-3 (cloth). — ISBN 0-8139-1405-1 (paper)
1. Androgyny (Psychology)—History.   2. Androgyny in
literature.   3. French literature—19th century—History and
criticism.   4. Feminist criticism.   I. Title.   II. Series: Feminist
issues (Charlottesville, Va.)
BF692.2.W45   1993
155.3'34—dc20   92-16774
                                                      CIP

For Mary and Leyla
and in memory of my father

Contents

Contents

Acknowledgments

THIS BOOK began as a dissertation at Princeton University under the direction of Suzanne Nash. For her encouragement and enthusiasm for this project, and for the invaluable critical insight with which she read and reread my words, I extend my deepest gratitude. I am also grateful to Sandra Bermann, Victor Brombert, and Ralph Freedman, who provided helpful comments on the dissertation. Many thanks to John Smith and Michael Roth for their close readings of portions of the expanded manuscript, and to Yvonne Reineke for her insightful response to my presentation of an early version of one chapter to the Department of Comparative Literature at the University of California at Irvine. I also wish to express my appreciation to members of the Graduate Colloquium in Women's Studies at Princeton, whose rigorous, feminist questioning helped shape my ideas at their inception. In particular I owe very special thanks to Mary Harper and Leyla Ezdinli, who have contributed more to this work than they know. Our discussions over the years have given new meaning to my understanding of scholarship and friendship and how they can come together.

Wake Forest University has been very generous with support for this project at various stages of research and production. I am grateful to the various committees of the university for granting this support; to Mickey King, who initially typed the manuscript onto the computer and who is much missed by the Department of Romance Languages; to Cathy Harris, who helped me through many computer nightmares; and to Byron Wells, who found ways to ease my teaching load and give me more time to complete the book. Cynthia Foote at the University Press of Virginia has been a remarkable editor, and I am grateful to her for putting up with my many inconsistencies.

Finally, my warmest thanks to my parents for their unfailing confidence in me and for teaching me the spirit of argument, to Pache who taught me to get back in the saddle, and to Michael who has made this ride an ever more interesting, exciting, and meaningful one. Difference will never be the same.

Parts of chapter 5 also appear as "Romantic Androgyny and Its Discontents: The Case of *Mademoiselle de Maupin*" in *Romanic Review* 77, no. 3, (May 1987): 348–58. Parts of chapters 4 and 6 also appear as "The Aesthetics of Androgyny in Balzac and Woolf, or The Difference of Difference," in *Critical Matrix* 1, no. 6 (1985): 1–24.

Androgyny
and the Denial
of Difference

Introduction

DURING the summer of 1984, in the aftermath of the hit runs of *Tootsie* and *Victor/Victoria,* and while Prince and Boy George were talked about from coast to coast, *Time* magazine published an article citing androgyny as the eleventh "megatrend" in American history. That article followed a special program of *Face the Nation* (July 8, 1984) in which Lesley Stahl brought Boy George and Jerry Falwell together specifically to discuss the explosion of androgyny and the resulting sexual fusion (or confusion, depending on how you perceived it). Of course, the explosion had been happening for some time. The year before, in a Sunday *New York Times* film review of, among others, *Tootsie* and *Victor/Victoria,* Mary Cantwell declared that "an extraordinary revolution in American sexual thinking" had taken place. And, four years before, in 1980, androgyny and revolution were brought together in a different (i.e., academic rather than popular) context, when Carolyn Heilbrun asked her readers to "recognize 'androgyny' as a step along a path that may be the most important, and is certainly the most revolutionary, traveled by humanity."[1]

While this androgynous trend is still around, most notably in celebrities like Michael Jackson, the exhilaration of a sexual liberation brought about by the "recognition" of androgyny, has all but vanished. A cursory look at the movies and figures of that megatrend reveals their liberatory potential to be, at best, limited; at worst, dangerously deceptive. While such movies depict a relaxing of gender stereotypes for men, allowing them to stretch the boundaries of masculinity by appropriating the best of "woman," they offer little in the way of new role models for women. Thus in *Tootsie,* while Julie (Jessica Lange) spends most of her time polishing her nails and shaving her legs, Michael Dorsey (Dustin Hoffman) proves through his newfound sensitivity, that a man can be a better woman than any woman could be. Even though *Victor/Victoria* depicts a female protagonist (Julie Andrews) whose male impersonations make inroads into exposing the myth of femininity as a construction of masculine fantasies, its conventional ending merely confirms that Victor was Victoria all along—a "real" woman whose principal desire is to please and marry a man.

That androgyny has often functioned as a conservative, if not a misogynistic, ideal is evident in the long and learned tradition of dual-sexed beings that can be traced at least as far back as the writings of Plato and Ovid. That tradition is one that brings together theosophical visions of man's original state with a system of aesthetics that could be called Platonic, or more generally, classical. Within this tradition, the androgyne is, above all, a figure of primordial totality and oneness, created out of a union of opposed forces. It is an especially privileged trope of the romantic period, carrying out the tasks set forth in German idealist philosophies for envisioning the union of subject and object and of spiritual and material worlds. Like the *schöne Seele* or beautiful soul, a predominant theme in eighteenth- and nineteenth-century literature, the androgyne functions as a figure of a privileged language in which sign is transparent to idea.[2] The androgyne is at once a real, empirical subject and an idealized abstraction, a figure of universal Man.[3] Defined as a union of masculine and feminine, the androgyne figures, furthermore, the dialectical synthesis of what is objectively known (identified as the masculine) and the unknown Other (identified as feminine) who will make that knowledge complete.

In aesthetic terms, the ideal of androgyny can be traced back to the statues of double-sexed beings created in ancient Greece. Again, romantic artists in particular turned to these sculptures as models and followed the precepts of the art historian J. J. Winckelmann, who praised the Greek representations of hermaphrodites as the highest form of art and the most pure manifestation of ideal beauty. (See chap. 4, below.) Finding these sculptures to be larger than life in their transcendence of sex, Winckelmann wrote that they were "pure" of any individual markings. Of course, *pure* in this sense meant Grecian and masculine, so that universal beauty was identified as Western and male. Such sculptures only represented male genitalia, never female, and the feminine element served only to soften and complement the masculine, not to challenge its privilege of representing Man.

In psychological terms, the androgyne has often been considered to be an archetype or a universal fantasy. More specifically, psychoanalysis equates androgyny with a repressed desire to return to the imaginary wholeness and self-sufficiency associated with the pre-Oedipal phase before sexual difference. The fantasy of the phallic mother is one manifestation of this desire that says that sexual difference is not an originary difference, that originally the sexes were the same—i.e., the same as man—and that woman became "different" as the result of a cut, hence of castration.[4] That cut is reminiscent of a parallel gesture that occurs in the myth of the androgyne recounted by Aristophanes in Plato's *Symposium* to explain the origin of love. Love (or desire) results when Zeus cuts the primal androgyne in two, sending each half in search of reunion with the other. This myth (which we shall look at more closely in chapter two), is central to the narratives we shall be looking at in this book, but also to narratives of psychoanalytic theory.

The similarities of psychoanalytic theories of the development of the sexed subject to the myth of the androgyne presented in the *Symposium* are striking, as are their misreadings of that myth. For Freud, as Samuel Weber remarks, Aristophanes' myth is confused with Plato's theory: hence, the " 'myth' turns out to be not a myth, 'of course,' but rather a theory, and Aristophanes merely the spokesman of Plato, the author of the *Symposium*." In fact, this myth/theory reappears in Freud's writings from the *Three Essays on the Theory of Sexuality* (1905) to *Beyond the Pleasure Principle* (1920). The *Three Essays* opens with reference to the "beautiful" description of the sexual instinct in the "poetic fable which tells how the original human beings were cut up into two halves—man and woman—and how these are always striving to unite again in love."[5] In this reference, Freud repeats a gesture common to a tradition of readers of Plato by neglecting to mention that Aristophanes describes *three* primal beings, not only one of a male and a female joined together, but also one of two females and two males, whose separation also instituted the beginning of homosexual love. Thus Plato's theory will not conflict with Freud's presentation of homosexuality and lesbianism as "deviations."

In *Beyond the Pleasure Principle* (1920), Freud returns to the myth with a different purpose. This time, it is not the metaphysical nature of love but the physical aspects of desire that interest him. He turns to Plato's Aristophanes for the only support he can find for his beliefs that "sexuality and the distinction between the sexes did not exist when life began," and that the sexual instincts are "conservative" in nature like all instincts: they "seek to restore an earlier state of things." After expressing his reservations about turning to such a "fantastic kind" of hypothesis, he proceeds to recount that myth and then give his own "scientific" version of it:

> Shall we follow the hint given us by the poet-philosopher, and venture upon the hypothesis that living substance at the time of its coming to life was torn apart into small particles, which have ever since endeavored to reunite through the sexual instincts? that these instincts, in which the chemical affinity of inanimate matter persisted, gradually succeeded, as they developed through the kingdom of protista, in overcoming the difficulties put in the way of that endeavor by an environment charged with dangerous stimuli—stimuli which compelled them to form a protective cortical layer? that these splintered fragments of living substance in this way attained a multicellular condition and finally transferred the instinct for reuniting, in the most highly concentrated form, to the germ-cells?—But here, I think, the moment has come for breaking off.[6]

With a change of characters and setting, Aristophanes' narrative of a fall from oneness into division, resulting in the search for reunion, becomes the catalyst for Freud's theory of ego formation. But Freud's scientific translation of Aristophanes' tale appears to contradict his very reason for citing it. If it is in "coming to life" that the living substance is "torn apart," then life begins in division, not wholeness. Such division, furthermore, is far more in keeping with Freud's theory of bisexuality, if not with what he understands elsewhere to be the infant's "polymorphous perversity."[7] Similarly, his mention of the "transference" of the sexual "instinct for reuniting" to the germ cells points to an inevitable displacement of sexual object that would render impossible any reunion with it. "Ventur[ing] to produce" this myth only because "it fulfills precisely the one condition whose fulfillment we desire," Freud seems to betray his own wish for a theory to fulfill his mythic faith in a unitary origin of desire before or beyond sexual difference—a state that his writing cannot substantiate.[8] No wonder he immediately becomes defensive, denying that he has any emotional stake in the matter or that anything other than the spirit of scientific inquiry led him to this hypothesis: "There is no reason, as it seems to me, why the emotional factor of conviction should enter into this question at all. It is surely possible to throw oneself into a line of thought and to follow it wherever it leads out of simple scientific curiosity."[9]

Within Freud's work the myth of the androgyne thus has a place analogous to the "dream of symmetry" that Luce Irigaray analyzes in his work to reveal its "blind spot." Taking Freud's essay "On Femininity" as her target, Irigaray demonstrates how his explanation of sexual difference and female sexual development is derived from a singular, masculine model of sexuality. "The *differentiation* into two sexes derives from the a priori assumption of the same." The little girl, as Irigaray writes, repeating Freud, "is a little man." Consequently, she is necessarily regarded as a man who is lacking (a penis) or is atrophied. Such a "desire of/for the same" as Irigaray calls it, confirms the male subject's place at the origin of sexuality as it also confers upon him the power to recognize himself and *his* other. "The same re-marking itself—more or less—would thus produce the other, whose function in the differentiation would be neglected, forgotten."[10] In positing one and the same origin for the sexes, Freud's text demonstrates what Irigaray calls a persistent "indifference" to the possibility of a specific female sexuality that is not assimilable to the male model.

This narcissistic structure is central to Lacan's theory of desire, as he explains in one of his frequent references to Aristophanes' myth. That myth, he says, is misleading because it masks desire for the lost totality of the self in a desire for the other: "Aristophanes' myth pictures the pursuit of the complement for us in a moving, and misleading, way, by articulating that it is the other, one's sexual other half, that the living being seeks in love. To this mythical representation of the mystery of love, the analytic experience substitutes the search by the subject, not of the sexual complement, but of the part of himself, lost forever, that is constituted by the fact that he is only a sexed living being, and that he is no longer immortal."[11] Like Freud,

Lacan turns to Aristophanes' androgyne to explain the origins of sexuality and desire. Indeed, the narrative structure of that myth is, as Kaja Silverman points out, central to Lacanian theory, wherein "the human subject derives from an original whole which was divided in half, and . . . its existence is dominated by the desire to recover its missing complement." The sense of loss or lack that results from that first division—which is the sexual division—pervades the Lacanian subject. "The real lack is what the living being loses, that part of himself *qua* living being, in reproducing himself through the way of sex."[12] To lose what Lacan calls the "lamella" and to have to be male or female, but not both, is to lose immortality. "The lamella is something extra-flat, which moves like the amoeba. It is just a little more complicated. But it goes everywhere. And it is something—I will tell you shortly why—that is related to what the sexed being loses in sexuality, it is, like the amoeba in relation to sexed beings, immortal—because it survives any division, any scissiparous intervention. And it can run around." If sexuality figures loss for Lacan, sexual union (and specifically heterosexual union) offers the one (false) hope of retrieving that origin. "It is through the lure that the sexed living being is induced into his sexual realization."[13]

Lacan has a second name for the lamella that problematizes its meaning, however. He calls the primal being, "to stress its joky side," the *hommelette*—a play on "omelet" (the primal egg already cracked and cooked), and "little man." In this term both the formal wholeness of the origin and its genderless or gender-balanced nature are refuted. Lacan states just before that the entire dialogue of the *Symposium* is a "practical joke," one whose starting point is Aristophanes' fable. The term *hommelette* bodies forth this joke that centers around the impossibility of ever knowing or describing the origin or, Lacan adds, the organ of love. Because of the displacements of the instincts to the drives, the only origin we can approach is the organ of the drive: "the organ of the drive is situated in relation to the true organ. In order to make this clear to you and in order to show that this is the only pole that, in the domain of sexuality, is within our grasp, capable of being apprehended, I will take the liberty of setting a myth before you— and in doing so I shall take as my starting point what is put into the mouth of Aristophanes on the subject of love in Plato's *Symposium*." The distance between the organ and the origin, Lacan suggests (like

the distance he describes elsewhere between the penis and the phallus), is comparable to the ironic distance between his rhetoric, or Aristophanes' rhetoric, and the origin/meaning it points to. *"You can
only find the treasure in the way I tell you,"* he writes (his emphasis),
and adds, "there is something comical about this way."[14] The joke is
also a joke about language and representation, about the impossible
task of trying to tell anything directly about love. It can only be
learned indirectly, in "the field of the other," a point well illustrated
by Aristophanes himself in the *Symposium*. "And when one of them
meets with his other half . . . yet they could not explain what they
desire of one another. For the other does not appear to be the desire of
the lover's intercourse, but of something else which the soul of either
evidently desires and cannot tell, and of which she has only a dark
and doubtful presentiment." They can only know what they desire
with the help of Hephaestus, the god of fire and metallurgy, who
expresses their desire for them with his linguistic tools—his metaphors of forging (if not of forgery). "Suppose Hephaestus, with his
instruments, to come to the pair who are lying side by side and to say
to them . . . 'Do you desire to be wholly one; always day and night to
be in one another's company? for if this is what you desire, I am ready
to melt you into one and let you grow together' . . . —there is not a
man of them who when he heard the proposal would deny or would
not acknowledge that this meeting and melting into one another, this
becoming one instead of two, was the very expression of his ancient
need."[15] Hephaestus's instruments remind us not only of the figurative nature of all language but also of its coerciveness. Desire, that is
to say, is expressed and recognized only in forms that bear the traces
of cultural and ideological mediation. Because desire derives its goals
from a preestablished "symbolic," but its energy from somatic drives,
it is, in Lacan's terms, "impossible."[16] Language functions only in the
absence of the object, it is the very inscription of loss of the object,
even as it offers the only tools for knowing and representing what it is
that was lost. Thus the lack that defines human subjectivity, for
Lacan, not only is physical, it is linguistic.

Lacan uses the sexually marked term *castration* to refer to this
state of lack that is shared by male and female subjects alike, just as
he uses the gendered term *hommelette* to refer to the primal man and
woman. We are all, as male and female, "castrated," he says, we all

lack the phallus—Lacan's privileged signifier for the loss incurred as we enter into language and the symbolic order. Feminists have, of course, criticized Lacan for this privileging of the masculine and for the phallo-centrism of his rhetoric. By investigating the theatrical nature of such rhetoric, however, the issues become more complex. Lacan deliberately flaunts his masculinity, parades it in an excessive and ironic manner that reveals his distance from it and shows that nobody has the phallus.[17] Moreover, insofar as he claims that "virile display itself appears as feminine," he performs his own bisexual masquerade wherein masculinity and femininity and the desires associated with each are identified as masks.[18]

The link between the notion of androgyny and problems of language and representation that is evident in both Freud and Lacan is paradigmatic of a thematic that is central to the literary works we shall be discussing. As they attempt to explain the origins of sexual desire and sexual difference through reference to the myth of the androgyne, they confront the inadequacies of the language they must use and which, in effect, only distances them from that origin. The presymbolic and presexual state associated with the androgyne, in other words, can only be envisioned from within what Lacan calls the symbolic, and with a language that is already marked by difference. Freud not only admits that "people are seldom impartial where ultimate things, the great problems of science and life, are concerned," he also suggests that the possible obscurity of his theory is due to "our being obliged to operate with the scientific terms, that is to say with the figurative language, peculiar to psychology (or, more precisely, depth psychology.)" Even as he offers a possible alternative to this language, he realizes that, in truth, no language would be less figurative. "We could not otherwise describe the processes in question at all, and indeed we could not have become aware of them. The deficiencies in our description would probably vanish if we were already in a position to replace the psychological terms by physiological or chemical ones. It is true that they too are only part of a figurative language; but it is one with which we have long been familiar and which is perhaps a simpler one as well."[19]

It is the partiality of language, the fact that it is always marked, and always sexually marked in the masculine, that Lacan's rhetoric appears to emphasize. In fact, sexuality and rhetoric are not simply related in Lacan, the former is displaced onto the latter so that, as Luce Irigaray states, "the sexes are now defined only as they are determined in and through language. Whose laws, it must not be forgotten, have been prescribed by male subjects for centuries." On the one hand, such displacement works to refute simplistic assumptions about the role of anatomy or biology in sexuality. On the other hand, it guards against addressing the body qua body, and in particular, the different difference that may be inscribed in the female body. By defining subjectivity as a relation of being or having the phallus, "regardless of the anatomical difference between the sexes,"[20] Lacan, like Freud, still posits only one, male, libido from which the feminine is claimed to be different or opposed. He thus returns to the old dream of symmetry.

That dream cannot see, or rather, it obstructs the perception of, a notion of sexual difference that does not arise from masculine sameness. This "hermaphroditic" difference, as I call it, is evident in both Freud and Lacan—as in Freud's notion of polymorphous perversity, or Lacan's lamella—even when, as in their recourse to idealist myths, they retreat from its pursuit. As Sarah Kofman claims, Freud will wave the theory of bisexuality, and its implications of the purely *speculative* character of masculine and feminine, to defend himself against accusations of antifeminism. But he must stop short of displaying his own femininity, "as he indulges in exposing the masculinity of his female colleagues. . . . And it is as though Freud were loudly proclaiming the universality of bisexuality in order better to disguise his silent disavowal of his own femininity, his paranoia."[21]

In this simultaneous attraction to and repulsion from the purely speculative and nonmetaphysical character of sexual difference, Freud and Lacan are typical of the writers we shall be looking at in the chapters that follow. I call this other difference *hermaphroditic,* despite the fact that this word is often considered to be a synonym for *androgynous.*[22] To distinguish between them is important, since *androgyne* and *hermaphrodite* have different histories and different psychical effects, having to do primarily with the status of the body.[23] In both the *O.E.D.* and *Webster's Third International Dictionary,* for instance, the definition of *hermaphrodite* refers immediately to the myth of Hermaphroditus and the physical joining of two bodies. That myth (which we shall examine in more detail in chapter two), presents the union of male and female as forever incomplete, two bodies competing with, rather than complementing, each other. Hermaphroditus is not a "whole" human, but "merely half a man." Similarly, medical and scientific manuals use the term *hermaphrodite* to describe an abnormal physiological state that combines male and female organs. In ancient Greece the actual birth of a hermaphrodite was regarded as a sign of divine anger that could be appeased only by destroying the "monster."[24]

At stake in the distinction I make between *androgyne* and *hermaphrodite* are two notions of sexual and textual difference. "Sexuality and textuality both depend on difference," writes Elizabeth Abel; but how is that difference spelled, with an *e* or with an *a?*[25] The Derridean spelling of "differ*a*nce," whose *a* makes the word into a verbal noun, brings together the two definitions of the French verb *différer*—"to differ" and "to defer"—in order to describe the process of signification whereby identity is constituted in language.[26] Identity, this spelling suggests, cannot be defined in itself or in terms of what it is in the present, but only in terms of what it differs from or what temporally it defers. Hence, what one is not is an element (although a repressed element) of one's own identity. What then about sexual identity and difference? Is there a stable line dividing the sexes, or is the division between male and female always rhetorically constituted on a shifting ground of criteria? How is difference to be understood in relation to androgyny—that which appears to do away with difference, or to move beyond it?

Derrida's critiques of Western metaphysics and the literary theories derived from them provide interesting and important perspectives on that tradition. Derrida traces a pervasive yearning and nostalgia for a "transcendental signified," for a single source of Truth and Beauty, something that could explain the desire and language we inherit.[27] Since classical Greece, the image of an androgyne has often served artists and philosophers as a means of representing or figuring this transcendent ideal. Many of the earliest Western cosmogonies posit an androgynous being as a vision of man's original, primordial nature before a fall from divine unity into alterity and difference. Such "first principles," have become the object of scrutiny for poststructuralist theories derived from Derridean philosophy. As Terry Eagleton writes, "first principles of this kind are commonly defined by what they exclude: they are part of the sort of 'binary opposition' beloved of structuralism." Eagleton's point is that the whole metaphysical system depends upon the logic and hierarchy of opposition, on the possibility of firmly drawing and maintaining the spatial and chronological dividing line between a first and second identity. How then does one understand the symbolic potential of the androgyne, a figure that, by definition, both asserts original difference (the male and female "halves" it unites), and claims to transcend that "most virulent" of binary oppositions by defining our origin as one?[28]

In what we have seen from the brief discussion of Freud and Lacan above, both the oneness of the origin posited by the androgyne and the difference it engenders through opposition are defined by the exclusion of an origin that is not organized by the phallus, in other words, by the exclusion of a "differ*ant*" sexual and textual body. Even when Freud acknowledges the irreducible specificity of female sexuality, as in his later works, he continues to take man as the model for sexuality.[29] Sexual difference is defined by Freud, explains Irigaray, "by giving *a priori* value to Sameness." In what follows, we shall be taking up Irigaray's suggestion to address the unquestioned philosophical and rhetorical presuppositions that such "systems" as Freud's rely upon in order to uncover this repressed or excluded body. One must examine, she writes, "the *operation of the 'grammar'* of each figure of discourse, its syntactic laws or requirements, its imaginary configurations, its metaphoric networks, and also, of course, what it does not articulate at the level of utterance: *its silences.*"[30] To examine the figure of the androgyne in this way is to discern the absent presence of another figure, that of the hermaphrodite, haunting the ideal of androgyny and its ordered, symmetrical opposition of male and female with the notion of an original confusion or chaos of sexes and desires. To bring this other figure onto the scene of representation, is to subvert the text's structure of opposition and its use as a paradigm for the creation of meaning and hierarchy. It is to dislodge the androgyne and the sexual, aesthetic, and racial hierarchies it establishes from the universal, revealing its givens to be constructions of patriarchal ideology and not the results of divine or natural law.

I have divided this book into three parts in order to address both the ubiquity of the figure of the androgyne—the first and third parts move between Plato and contemporary critical discourse—and the social and historical factors that enter into specific representations of this figure (hence the more contextualized analyses that make up the second and central part).

Part one is largely theoretical, focusing particularly on the distinction between androgyny and hermaphroditism. The first chapter clarifies this distinction by setting Aristophanes' description of the androgyne as the original, harmonious, and ideal state of man in the *Symposium* against Ovid's myth of Hermaphroditus in the *Metamorphoses*, wherein hermaphroditism itself constitutes the fallen state. The opposition between Plato and Ovid becomes less pronounced, however, as a closer reading of the *Symposium* unveils the narcissistic desires contaminating both Aristophanes' account of the origin of love and Socrates' vision of its ends—a vision of absolute beauty and oneness that Socrates attempts to enact in his own masquerade as androgyne. This reading of the androgyne draws especially from Luce Irigaray's deconstruction of the patriarchal "dream of symmetry" and its systematic effacement of (sexual) difference within a self-referential system of male subjectivity.

In the second chapter, the distinction between androgyne and hermaphrodite is set up in relation to key rhetorical categories in Roland Barthes and Friedrich Schlegel, and points to a similar practice and politics of sexualized rhetoric and rhetorical sex in poststructuralism and romanticism. As a figure of unmediated expression and projected fullness, the figure of the androgyne assumes the binary and oppositional structure of what Barthes calls antithesis and what Schlegel defines as simple irony. The hermaphrodite, on the other hand, situated in the realm of the physical, the visible, and the historically present, constitutes what Barthes calls "paradoxism" and Schlegel, the "irony of irony"—a figure that reveals both the instability of boundaries between categories of opposition such as masculine and feminine, and the self-serving function of their illusory symmetry. Hermaphroditism, moreover, like castration in Balzac's *Sarrasine,* is contagious, infecting all systems of representation and all representations of plenitude—aesthetic, linguistic, and sexual— with its own fundamental lack.

Part two is more historically oriented, focusing on fictionalized representations of the androgyne from a specific time period in nineteenth-century France, as they draw on a long philosophical and theosophical tradition and, specifically, as these representations borrow from the reformulation of that tradition in aesthetic terms by German thinkers of the eighteenth century. Chapter three traces the development of that tradition to its problematic resurgence in France under the July Monarchy, emphasizing how its gendered rhetoric was used to question and clarify complex aesthetic, social, and historical issues. Chapters four and five concentrate on two authors, Balzac and Gautier, and, in particular, on two novels, *Séraphîta* and *Mademoiselle de Maupin,* published within one year of each other, wherein the androgyne/hermaphrodite occupies a focal role. That role is first considered in relation to the poetic ideals each author defines elsewhere in critical and theoretical writings. Second, and against such idealizations, the ambivalence of this figure for Balzac and Gautier is demonstrated through close readings of those narratives, aided by deconstructive methods and feminist theory. While the figure projects a utopia of self-present and self-sufficient beauty, poetry, and love, its very figuration asserts a different aesthetics of fragmentation and incompletion that problematizes that idealism. Indeed, the very sexual articulation of the androgyne challenges the sufficiency of those ideals as it reveals them to be defined according to a single, male measure.

In part three, I examine the critical reception of the notion of androgyny, particularly as it has framed discussions of Virginia Woolf from Carolyn Heilbrun to Toril Moi. I indicate how this discourse has moved through claims to oneness, difference, and "differance" and how, more recently, similar terms shape arguments around the utopian possibilities of cyborgs, the technoandrogynes of our future. The book's conclusion emphasizes the extent to which this fantasy continues to order and consequently to ward off the reality of a hermaphroditic confusion. If I argue instead for taking pleasure in such a confusion of boundaries, I also argue, along with Donna Haraway, for a concurrent "responsibility in their construction," in order to ensure that even the hermaphrodite not always exhibit phallic proportions.[31]

Part I

1

Androgyny and the Origins of Love

Androgyne/Hermaphrodite

A S WE SAW in the Introduction, both Freud and Lacan turn to Aristophanes' myth of the primal androgyne in the *Symposium* to explain the origins of love. That gesture is a futile one, for in that myth the origins of androgyny are not only unclear, but are knowable only through their present-day, fallen state. Although it once identified an ideal being, the name *androgyne,* Aristophanes states, remains only as a term of abuse.

For Freud and Lacan, as for a whole tradition of readers of Aristophanes' tale, the origins of love coincide with the origins of sexual difference, although the relationship between these two origins is ambiguously defined. In explaining the origin of love, Aristophanes posits that sexual difference both results from and precedes desire. His well-known story begins with a depiction of "man's" original nature, which was dual, consisting of two bodies united into one spherically shaped being. These bodies could already be classified as one of three sexes: two men together, two women, or a union of man and woman called "androgynous"—thus indicating that sexual difference existed absolutely, from the beginning. Self-sufficient in their roundness, "with their back and sides forming a circle," consisting of two faces, two "privy members," four feet and hands, each of these primal beings could walk upright or roll and tumble with great speed. They were so mobile and mighty they "dared to scale heaven" and rival the gods.[1]

Love resulted, Aristophanes explains, from the fall from this primal state of wholeness into division. Jealous of the round and mighty humans, Zeus devised a plan to restrain their insolence and keep them in their proper, subservient place; he cut each in two, thereby reducing their strength and increasing their number. He then asked Apollo to sculpt a new form for each of the creatures. Apollo gathered the skin left hanging from Zeus's cut and smoothed out the wrinkles by pulling the skin from all sides and fastening it in a knot at the navel, the "memorial of the primeval state" (*Sym,* p. 145). Finally, he turned their faces around that they might "contemplate" their other, now severed half and "learn humility." From this initial division and from the profound feeling of incompleteness that it produced, desire and love were born, sending each of the newly created beings in search of his or her other half. "And the reason is that human nature was originally one and we were a whole, and pursuit of the whole is called love. . . . We must praise the god Love, who is our greatest benefactor, both leading us in this life back to our own nature and giving us hopes for the future, for he promises that if we are pious he will restore us to our original state and heal us and make us happy and blessed" (*Sym,* pp. 147–48).

Aristophanes' myth thus identifies the androgyne with an ideal, even an Edenic, state of being, a state of wholeness in which nothing is lacking. Visually, his story represents androgyny as perfect symmetry between two united halves. Structurally and thematically, his story recalls the separation of Eve from Adam (described as androgynous in certain versions of Genesis) and the biblical fall into disunity.[2] Both in Genesis and in Aristophanes' account, sexual division is regarded as the punishment for the fall. For Aristophanes it is also its remedy—the union of the two sexes through divinely inspired love is the route toward regaining salvation.

Aristophanes' account of the relation between desire and sexual difference can be contrasted to Ovid's tale of Hermaphroditus in book 2 of the *Metamorphoses.* Whereas for Aristophanes androgyny precedes the fall, Ovid's hermaphrodite embodies the fallen state, especially because s/he blurs the distinction between male and female. The myth of Salmacis and Hermaphroditus describes the negative consequences of desire, specifically of female desire, on sexual difference. Salmacis is the most passive and one might say feminine of the nymphs, for never would she join in the chase, preferring to comb her hair and gaze at her reflection in the water. When she catches sight of the beautiful Hermaphroditus stepping naked into her pond, however, desire transforms her into an aggressive hunter: "she was on fire with passion to possess his naked beauty." Unable to restrain herself, she attacks and, "like a squid which holds fast its prey," wraps herself around the struggling boy, and prays to the gods that they never be separated. Her prayer is granted: "when their limbs met in that clinging embrace the nymph and the boy were no longer two, but a single form, possessed of a dual nature, which could not be called male or female, but seemed to be at once both and neither." Much like Echo in the myth of Echo and Narcissus, Salmacis's body and name are totally effaced in the "enfeebled" figure that emerges from the pond, "but half a man." Beginning as a story of female desire, Ovid's myth ends as a tale of the fall of man, a fall from clear sexual division into sexual confusion.[3]

Unlike Aristophanes', Ovid's account tells us that at the origin of desire is, not wholeness, but an unstable and frightening confusion from which there emerges, not ideal love, but a power struggle between the sexes, each trying to establish a wholeness it never had. Salmacis's pursuit of oneness through union with Hermaphroditus results in her own effacement. Annihilated in name and body, Salmacis leaves a trace only in the effeminacy of which Hermaphroditus is hereafter accused. The resulting union does not produce wholeness; instead, it displaces the oppositions self/other and male/female between Salmacis and Hermaphroditus, to reveal their confused manifestation within Hermaphroditus. In fact this union seems to reveal what his name already implied, the replication of his mother and father, Hermes and Aphrodite, male and female, within his masculine body. In other words, Hermaphroditus's fallen state bodies forth the always already fused and confused relation of male and female.

In posing confusion at the origin of desire, furthermore, Ovid's tale suggests that the moral standard governing love is itself the result of a power struggle in which phallic desire has won out over any other type of love that does not conform to it. Having no interest in javelins, quivers, or other phallic instruments, Salmacis's gaze points toward an other, feminine eroticism and, no doubt, it is for this reason that she must be destroyed. Not penis envy, but a delight with herself precedes her desire to possess Hermaphroditus: "all she would do was bathe her lovely limbs in her own pool, frequently combing out her hair with a boxwood comb, and looking into the water, to see what hair style was becoming to her" (*M*, p. 102). Much as Freud will do, almost despite himself in his essay "On Narcissism" (1925), Ovid designates the origin of object love in ego love, suggesting, moreover, what may be a threatening idea to both, that the model of desire is not, or not only, the little boy, but also the little girl.

It is perhaps in the same vein of uncertainty over the morality of love that Freud equate's Aristophanes' account of desire in the *Symposium* with Plato's own thought. Socrates, who represents the moral force in the dialogue, is aware that Aristophanes' theory of love is modeled on a kind of narcissism and must be corrected: "you hear people say that lovers are seeking for their other half; but I say that they are seeking neither for the half of themselves, nor for the whole, unless the half or the whole be also a good. . . . For there is nothing men love but the good" (*Sym*, p. 164). Representing the force of morality, Socrates' speech and the divine ladder of love he describes are most often equated with the Platonic view. To identify Plato's position with Aristophanes as does Freud, is to expose an ambivalence in Plato that resembles the contradictory stance that Freud takes in his essay on narcissism. "'On Narcissism,'" writes Sarah Kofman, "thus indeed asserts the unsurpassable nature of narcissism, even if in the same text, for 'ethical' reasons, the love called objectal turns out to be preferred.[4]

In both Freud and Plato the effort to separate narcissism and object love is related to the construction of sexual difference and the need to distinguish other from same, female from male. But that difference is constructed according to a singular, phallic model of desire. Aristophanes' theory of the androgyne inscribes a symmetrical difference at the origin, *symmetry* meaning "of like measure," or "measured by the same standard."[5] In constructing a symmetrical difference between male and female, Aristophanes constructs a hierarchy and an ethics of the body that appears to erase the difference between his theory and Socrates'. In fact, the *Symposium*'s dialogue repeats Aristophanes' narrative structure and its progression from oneness to division and back to unity by alternately asserting that love is one, love is two—a good love and a bad love—or love is a dialectic of two culminating in a final one. That unity, however, like the androgynous unity that Socrates enacts (I would say embodies except for the fact that his apparent transcendence of the physical is part of his theatrics), collapses difference in the vision of truth and beauty to which love is said to lead. Indeed, it is above all in Socrates that we see the power of the philosophical logos to, in Luce Irigaray's terms, *"reduce all others to the economy of the Same.* The teleologically constructive project it takes on is always also a project of diversion, deflection, reduction of the other in the Same. And, in its greatest generality perhaps, from its power to *eradicate the difference between the sexes* in systems that are self-representative of a 'masculine subject.' "[6]

But Socrates does not have the last word in the *Symposium.* While his speech appears to resume and resolve the structural oppositions on which the dialogue builds its conception of ideal love, hermaphroditism—in the figure of Alcibiades—comes to disrupt that structure from within, and with the force of the paradoxism, it threatens to dispel the illusory permanence of the antitheses while revealing their self-serving functions.[7]

Androgyny in/and the *Symposium*

Narration, Roland Barthes writes in *S/Z*, is always modified by its object. "There is no question of an utterance on the one hand and on the other its uttering . . . what is told is the 'telling.' "[8] The story of the *Symposium* is framed by the story of its telling. The dialogue opens with a request to Apollodorus to rehearse the events that occurred one evening at Agathon's. Apollodorus admits that he had just told that story the day before in order to correct other versions already in circulation. Even so, he will not guarantee the accuracy of his own version, given that he was not himself at the party, and that his informant, whose version he must rely upon to the extent that he can recall it, was a "devoted admirer of Socrates" (*Sym* p. 122) and may, for all we know, have had reason to distort or to have a distorted perception of the events that took place. Foregrounded by this frame is the impossibility of arriving at the original story of the evening, each version being implicated in the act of its telling, limited by memory, motivated by desire. This narrative frame repeats a central concern of the *Symposium* itself—How is it possible to speak philosophically about love? How is it possible to extricate the discourse of desire from the (bodily) desire of its speaking subject(s)? Or are love and desire already two things?

Love is the proposed topic of discussion for the gathering that takes place at the house of Agathon—each of the invited guests is to take his turn at praising this god(ess). But some form of desire seems to be the motive force behind each of the speeches and, as such, is presented as the fabricator of rhetoric and fictions and not the purveyor of truth. Only Socrates pays heed to this problem that, he claims, contaminates all the other speeches but his own. When it is his turn, Socrates concedes with tempered irony that he mistakenly understood that the "topics of praise were to be true" when, in fact, the object was only to "appear to praise" love, thereby allowing each speaker to prove his merit either as rhetorician or as lover. His speech, he claims, will be different. "Spoken in any words and in any order which may happen to come into my mind at the time," it will be free of the rhetoric that has lent the other speeches the mere appearance of truth, and it will be outside of, if not above, the agonistic forces of desire: "for I do not praise in that way; no, indeed, I cannot. But if you like to hear the truth about love, I am ready to speak in my own manner, though I will not make myself ridiculous by entering into any rivalry with you" (*Sym*, p. 155). Placing himself on the side of love and truth, he accuses the others of self-promoting rhetoric.

Even before the symposium is under way, precautions are taken to guarantee serious, philosophical discussion: wine and the flute girl are banned, thereby eliminating whatever might influence the body and deter the working of the mind. This gesture of exclusion dramatizes the structural foundation of the ensuing speeches as they increasingly seek to distinguish physical, or earthly, desire from the form of spiritual or heavenly love that leads to the knowledge of truth. Founded upon the Platonic opposition of body and soul, this hierarchical polarity organizes a chain of associated oppositions: youth/age, beauty/goodness, rhetoric/truth, beloved/lover, and female/male, which grounds the discursive fellowship of guests and determines the hierarchy of shared values amongst the men. And yet as the image of the flute girl hints at a transgression of phallogocentric boundaries, her exclusion from the scene, like the ban on wine, sets the stage for her reappearance and for the return of a repressed Dionysian in the figure of Alcibiades. But let us first examine the progression of the dialogue.

Phaedrus begins the evening by praising love as the principle of greatest benefit to lover and beloved, to men and women alike—a principle that "ought to guide the whole life of those who intend to love nobly" (*Sym*, p. 42). When Pausanias takes his turn, he criticizes Phaedrus for not discriminating between kinds of love—the love born of the "common" and that of the "heavenly" Aphrodite. The first "is apt to be of women as well as of youths, and is of the body rather than the soul—the most foolish beings are the objects of this love," while the second "is derived from a mother in whose birth the female has no part,—she is from the male only; this is that love which is of youths, and the goddess being older, there is nothing of wantonness in her. Those who are inspired by this love turn to the male, and delight in him who is the more valiant and intelligent nature" (*Sym*, p. 133). Here "common" desire is projected elsewhere, onto the female and in particular onto the maternal body, in order to claim the superiority of the male and of "hom(m)osexual" desire.[9]

Following Pausanias, Eryximachus draws upon his skill as a physician to refine those distinctions, describing the healthy and unhealthy desires that may take place simultaneously within one body, and praising the art of the man who is able to "reconcile opposites" by curing the unhealthy or "converting one into the other" (*Sym*, p. 140), unhealth into health. Here, the introduction of healthy and unhealthy into the already established binary structure links the ethics of the body to that of the soul. It also provides a foreword on the reconciliation of opposites that Aristophanes' myth will describe. Reconciliation is not the playing out of differences, but rather, a conversion of difference, regarded as unhealthy, into the health of self or sameness. Indeed, Eryximachus's aims are clearly self-laudatory.

The very notion of bodily harmony (and bodily repression) that Eryximachus puts forth is mocked by Aristophanes, who, having been overcome by a bout of hiccups, is prevented from taking his rightful turn to speak before the doctor, and is cured only by a compensatory fit of sneezing. In accordance with his bodily disruptions, Aristophanes calls attention to the apparently less than philosophical or serious nature of his discourse, "I fear that in the speech which I am about to make, instead of others laughing with me, which is to the manner born of our muse and would be all the better, I shall only be laughed at by them" (*Sym*, p. 143). Aristophanes intends to be pedagogic and to "teach" the others "the power of Eros," which "they have not at all understood," but he fears the power of his audience to turn his narration against him and what he holds to be true. He thus attaches an ambiguous status to his speech that is heightened by his reliance on an essentially physical and materialist theory of desire, all the while that he supports the hierarchical separation of body and mind and their association with feminine and masculine respectively. "Men who are a section of that double nature which was once called Androgynous are lovers of women: adulterers are generally of this breed, and also adulterous women who lust after men. . . . But they who are a section of the male follow the male. . . . and these, when they grow up become our statesmen, and these only" (*Sym*, p. 146).

This distinction between physical love directed toward women with the aim of reproduction, and spiritual love directed toward men, and which produces statesmen, is also addressed by Socrates in the speech most often regarded as Platonic theory. His theory of love as a spiritual and intellectual force founds a system of aesthetics that will lead men (I use the masculine deliberately) to absolute beauty and truth. Yet at the same time, Socrates gives a central role to the fictional wise woman, Diotima of Mantinea, who was his "instructress in the art of love" (*Sym*, p. 159) and whose words he recites.

Unlike the flute girl, Diotima is thus allowed to partake in the symposium, but only rhetorically, that is, only as Socrates reports her words for her. Diotima is, in fact, necessary to Socrates in two ways. In the first place, because he learned of love from her in an intellectual exercise, his knowledge can be assured to be pure—unsullied by the force (or even the experience) of (physical) desire. Knowledge and desire, like truth and rhetoric, he can thus maintain, are separate. Second, he needs her as a "symbolic" other (and it is relevant that she is the only "fictional" character in the *Symposium*[10]) in order to guarantee the impartiality and absoluteness of the truth he describes. The nature of love, as he explains it through Diotima, is precisely one that identifies love and philosophy (or more precisely, lover and philosopher) in their pursuit of absolute unity and a singular vision of the world.

Once again, the starting point of his speech is a matter of distinctions. To prove his own knowledge of love, Socrates begins by demonstrating the ignorance lurking in the otherwise "magnificent" speech which Agathon has just given. While beautiful, his speech is only empty rhetoric because Agathon has not seen the difference between love and what love desires, which is to say between lover and beloved, subject and object: "then he and every one who desires, desires that which he has not already, and which is future and not present, and which he has not, and is not, and of which he is in want" (*Sym*, p. 158).

Such a separation, Socrates shows, is fundamental to the oppositions of body and soul, physical and material desire, that structure the shared value system of the *Symposium*'s participants. He reinforces the binarisms that are at the base of the other speeches, extending them to two other oppositions; rhetoric/truth, and ignorance/wisdom. It is the lover and not the beloved, Diotima explains, who will climb the ladder of philosophy and be admitted into the mysteries of Truth and Beauty (the beloved, like the beautiful, are presumably ignorant of their state). Diotima describes the stages through which the lover will pass, moving from ignorance to truth, from the physical to the spiritual, part to whole, until such time as all oppositions are reconciled in the sight of absolute beauty.

Although Diotima acts as Socrates' instructress, her role nevertheless points to the way in which, with regard to love, women are complicitous in their own exclusion.[11] The ladder does not admit women except insofar as the maternal function is appropriated by the male lover. "Those who are pregnant in the body only, betake themselves to women and beget children—this is the character of their love; their offspring, as they hope, will preserve their memory and give them the blessedness and immortality which they desire in the future. But souls which are pregnant—for there certainly are men who are more creative in their souls than in their bodies—conceive that which is proper for the soul to conceive or contain. And what are these conceptions—wisdom and virtue in general" (*Sym*, p. 168).

As John Brenkman explains in his reading of this text, what is excluded from this ladder is, not the feminine, but the maternal body. Socrates "secures the primacy of the spiritual One, and with it the suppression of materiality, difference, and language, not simply by denying the maternal as such but by assimilating it to the paternal. He removes maternity from the effects of materiality and the signifying mark."[12] Absolute beauty, in other words, is founded upon the repression of difference and its assimilation to the same: the conversion of female to male, and flesh to spirit.

Socrates' speech itself dramatizes this assimilation of maternal to paternal. Using a form of mimetic narrative that absolves him of responsibility for his words, he appropriates Diotima's knowledge for the masculine subject.[13] Placing himself in an analogous stance of ignorance and amazement before her, as Agathon had before him, Socrates "rehearses" before the others the words she once spoke to him. His performance thus enacts a reversal of positions whereby in assuming Diotima's role, Socrates becomes the teacher before his entourage. In this way the androgynous plenitude of the male-female relationship (itself an apparent reversal of gender hierarchies) and the transference of her wisdom to him are transformed instead into the highest of pedagogical relations, that of man to man.

Socrates thus poses as the primal androgyne in whom (sexual) difference is transcended and with it all forms of physical desire. Diotima's definition of love as the intermediary between man and God, in fact, defines Socrates. He is the example of a man in the process of becoming immortal by "making himself self-sufficient."[14] Always barefoot, his body proves impervious to hot or cold just as his mind is resistant to the effects of wine. Hunger is foreign to him, and he can bed beside a most beautiful man with no physical effect. In turning away from the inconstancy of the body (and in defiance of what Aristophanes had cited as Zeus's turning our heads in order that we contemplate the body of the other) Socrates approaches the state of remaining forever the same that is the prerogative of divinity. Indeed, his desire for immortality is one he has learned to satisfy on his own, through procreation without an other. Nonphysical, his love would thus appear to be the most narcissistic. The knowledge that awaits him at the top of the ladder is revealed to be knowledge forgotten and recollected, hence a truth that he has always possessed in himself. Even his brand of questioning, whereby he always has the answer, protects him from any real engagement with an other. Socrates' pursuit, in fact, is very much like that which Irigaray describes for Lacan, whose pleasure "could never be found in a relation.

Except in a relation to the same. The narcissistic pleasure that the master, believing himself to be unique, confuses with that of the One."[15]

Lacan himself no doubt refers to Socrates as the "precursor of psychoanalysis" because of the knowledge he is presumed to have and the way in which this knowledge engenders love in his subjects. In a reference to the *Symposium* Lacan hints, furthermore, that this knowledge and desirable stance is a function of his repression of the mark of sexual difference, or what we might call his androgynous pose. "It is because he [Alcibiades] has not seen Socrates' prick, if I may be permitted to follow Plato, who does not spare us the details, that Alcibiades the seducer exalts in him the 'agalma,' the marvel that he would like Socrates to cede to him in avowing his desire: the division of the subject that he bears within himself being admitted with great clarity on this occasion. . . . Such is the woman concealed behind her veil: it is the absence of the penis that turns her into the phallus, the object of desire."[16]

For Lacan, we may remember, the phallus only functions when veiled, which is to say in the absence of the penis and as its sign. Alcibiades spends some time describing the nature of Socrates' "veil,"— one that is neither like the flutes of the Silenus statues nor the instruments of Marsyas the satyr, both of which Alcibiades says he (Socrates) physically resembles. Socrates' own power, rather, is produced by "words only and do not require the flute," as if he veiled his own lack with pure symbolism, the sign of woman or woman as sign. He compares his words to the song of the Sirens, which invades the ears of its listeners only the better to reveal their own lack (the division of the subject Lacan refers to). Socrates, says Alcibiades, is the only man who has made him feel shame, made him want to run away and "shut [his] ears" (*Sym*, p. 177)—orifices that can be penetrated at will.[17] But his reaction is also to want to open up this master in the manner of the Silenus, and see "what is within" (*Sym*, p. 185).[18] In so doing, he pokes holes in his master's impervious self-sufficiency.

By referring to his master as a passive vessel to be opened and penetrated in its own right, Alcibiades unsettles the distinction between lover and beloved upon which the "heavenly ladder" is founded. Indeed, Alcibiades' story implies that that difference is rhetorical not philosophical—"to love is to want to be loved," is to depend upon the love and admiration of the beloved.[19] This dislocation of the lover-beloved opposition is figured in Alcibiades' very presence. Drunken, shouting, adorned "with a massive garland of ivy and violets" (*Sym*, p. 173), claiming to speak the truth, Alcibiades' physical appearance and the story he tells about Socrates make a mockery of the master. The sign of Aphrodite in the violets of his crown, the sign of Diony-sus—himself a God of sexual contradictions—in its ivy,[20] he makes a travesty of the Socrates-Diotima duo, as well as of Aristophanes' "halves." In Alcibiades, male and female, self and other, body and mind are intertwined into their confused and hermaphroditic para-doxism. Seating himself between Agathon and Socrates, and respond-ing to Agathon's earlier request that Dionysus judge which of the two is the wiser, he transfers the wreath from his own head first to Aga-thon's, then to Socrates's, indicating the interchangeability of their positions and infecting both with his own epicenism.

When asked to give his own speech about love, he avoids the abstract reasoning of the Socratic way and tells a story about his own experience of love for one man—Socrates—a particular story about his own experience of love. A lovelorn narrative, structured by the whims of intoxication and heavy with the physical pain of desire, it is a narrative that challenges the truth of pure reason and the logic of the heavenly ladder by undermining the distinctions that Socrates relies upon. He begins his speech with himself in the position of the beautiful beloved and Socrates in the position of lover, but by the end the roles have been reversed. In addition, his rhetoric emphasizes the physicality of his soul and of the love that, like a snake, has bitten it. His story thus contests the hierarchical opposition of mind and body, asserting that the body can provide another kind of knowledge and that his desire to "open up" Socrates is both sexual and epistemic.[21] Alcibiades reveals the implication of the subject's desire in the desire of and for the other; the desire to know what the other knows is necessary for the knowledge of what one desires.

Speaking as the drunken beloved, driven by bodily desires, Al-cibiades' speech could, as Brenkman acknowledges, be indicted by the very value system that structures the dialogue and be dismissed as pure entertainment if not as philosophy's hideous other. His relation to Socratic law is similar to that which Lacan defines as the relation of woman to the symbolic and to desire: "There is woman only as

excluded by the nature of things which is the nature of words"—
excluded by the very terms in which its whole is circumscribed. "To
the objection that this discourse is perhaps not all there is," writes
Irigaray, "the response will be that it is women who are 'not-all' [*pas-
toutes*]."[22] And yet, from the perspective of this feminine (w)hole,
Alcibiades could be seen to subvert the self-sufficiency of the whole
truth. Asked to interrupt the speech should Alcibiades "tell a lie,"
Socrates remains silent.

Alcibiades offers a truth of another sort, one that is inimical to
the truth of Socratic reasoning, whose absoluteness it denies. As
Martha Nussbaum writes: "we cannot simply add the love of Alcibiades to the ascent of Diotima; indeed we cannot have this love
and the kind of stable practical rationality, the orderly and respectful
goodness that she revealed to us."[23] To take the first step up her
ladder is to leave behind Alcibiades' kind of understanding, just as we
have seen it as leaving behind the maternal body—that which cannot
be assimilated to Socrates' singular vision. To follow Alcibiades'
vision is to grant other possible sources of truth—such as the enter-
taining flute girl—and to see why the production of philosophical
knowledge does indeed depend upon the exclusion and absence of a
feminine difference more unfathomable than Aristophanes' "other
half." Her "particular" difference may prove that knowledge produced to be purely rhetorical.

Rhetoric is indeed the issue, as Diotima herself suggests. Truth is
a kind of synechdoche, she teaches Socrates, so that the name that
appears to represent the whole instead names only a part, while the
other parts are unaccounted for by that name. " 'Why then,' she
rejoined, 'are not all men, Socrates, said to love, but only some of
them? whereas you say that all men are always loving the same
things.' 'I myself wonder,' I said, 'why this is.' 'There is nothing to
wonder at,' she replied; 'the reason is that one part of love is separated off and receives the name of the whole, but the other parts have
other names' " (*Sym*, p. 163).

Diotima's words anticipate Lacan's claim that desire is a metonymy. Metonymy—which as Jane Gallop explains, is often incor-
rectly, because metonymically, defined as the part standing for the
whole (this itself being only one aspect of metonymy)—"is a phallic
conceit, the part standing for the whole, standing for the hole."[24]

29

Socrates claims to speak the whole truth of love, to speak for himself and for his other half—Diotima, woman, the hole—but his vision is trapped within the "dream of symmetry" that judges all by one sexually "indifferent," and consequently phallic, measure. In contrast to Socrates, Alcibiades flaunts the asymmetry of unrepressed sexuality and the irresolvable difference within—being *in* difference. True, there is no attempt to represent woman's sexuality here, no sighting of the hole in the phallic system. And yet, the wine on Alcibiades' breath carries with it a feminine scent whose effect leaves Socrates speechless.

In an article entitled "Breaking the Bread," Elaine Marks writes, "Of all the many exclusions that have, until now, defined women's relation to culture, the most serious are the exclusions that keep us outside the desire for theory and the theory of desire."[25] Perhaps that outside is a strategic place from which to consider the relation not so much between women and theory as between theory and desire. Socrates, like the idealist theory of love that he institutes, makes Aristophanes' theory of origins into a theory of ends. In so doing, he skips over the stage of bodily investment and disregards the holes, protrusions, and paroxysms of the body. He converts the perceptible into the intelligible, the body into discourse, desire into theory. The androgyne he represents is theory's sublimated body.

Alcibiades uncovers or unveils this body, showing it to be a site of contradictory and uncontrollable drives, a site of pain as well as of pleasure. He also shows that while the androgyne may cover over the body's lack of wholeness, which is to say its desire if not its love, it also incurs a loss—a loss of pleasure: of pleasure, particularly, in the other's hermaphroditic body.

2

The Rhetoric of Androgyny

ROMANTIC TEXTS have long held a particular attraction for poststructuralist critics, perhaps because of their shared interest in questions of language and rhetoric. The affinity between romantic and poststructuralist discourses might also be explained by the way that such rhetorical questions are often articulated through questions of sexuality. It is in this connection that I bring together the writings of Friedrich Schlegel and Roland Barthes.

In *S/Z*, Barthes defines certain rhetorical figures with implicit reference to the body images and sexual dynamics represented in the novella of Balzac he analyzes. In Schlegel, a discursive mode, or more specifically a rhetoric of irony, is linked to the theme and figure of the androgyne. Just as rhetoric and sexuality are inseparable in Barthes, so Schlegel's theories of romantic irony, I will argue, must be examined in relation to his understanding of androgyny and of sexual difference. Structurally, both writers develop this link between rhetoric and sexuality through an elaboration of related binary couples. Thus, in Schlegel, one must distinguish between two levels of irony— one defined by opposition, the other defined by a more paradoxical and shifting relationship of terms. Barthes also distinguishes between two figures of difference—"antithesis," a figure of stable opposition, and "paradoxism," a figure of a more dynamic and unstable conflict. These rhetorical binarisms, in turn, inflect two notions of time, two economies, and two sexualities—male and female, to be sure, but also what I call androgynous and hermaphroditic. This binary structure results in a shared problematic for both writers. While one rhetorical mode presents male and female as opposed elements, the second mode, by undermining the nature of opposition itself, reveals a disturbing inseparability of the terms. The result is a paradoxical coupling of rhetorical modes and of sexualities that points to a fundamental indeterminacy of identity, whether linguistic or sexual. I shall consider the politics of this sexual indeterminacy at the end of the chapter.

Antithesis, Paradoxism, and Sexual Difference in Barthes

In *S/Z*, Roland Barthes describes the rhetorical figure of antithesis in terms that resonate with traditional descriptions of the androgyne as two opposed halves joined to form a completed whole. Let me begin, then, with Barthes's definition.

> The several hundred figures propounded by the art of rhetoric down through the centuries constitute a labor of classification intended to name, to lay the foundations for, the world. Among all these figures, one of the most stable is the Antithesis; its apparent function is to consecrate (and domesticate) by a name, by a meta-linguistic object, the division between opposites and the very irreducibility of this division. The antithesis separates for eternity; it thus refers to a nature of opposites, and this nature is untamed . . . the antithesis is the battle between two plenitudes set ritually face to face like two fully armed warriors; the Antithesis is the figure of the given opposition, eternal, eternally recurrent: the figure of the inexpiable.[1]

The antithesis, we can infer from this commentary on Balzac's *Sarrasine,* figures sexual difference like an androgyne—a whole created out of two joined but irreducibly divided halves. In Plato's *Symposium,* for instance, the androgyne, like the antithesis, exists from the beginning; it is eternal like its constituent parts—themselves "plenitudes," neither too much nor too little—bound together in an eternal struggle, never to be sundered. The antithesis is a figure of first things, a god-given transcendental signified whose opposed warriors found and delineate the world.

In *S/Z*, Barthes insists on the mutual implication of rhetoric and sexuality—that sex may function rhetorically and that the mastery of rhetoric, or of language in general, is not independent of mastery of the body. His description of antithesis is linked to an understanding of sexual difference as sexual opposition, a notion that, as he shows, comes under serious questioning in Balzac's novella *Sarrasine*. Like the figure of antithesis, the figure of the androgyne underscores, on the one hand, an irreducible division between male and female, and, on the other, the perfect union of these poles in what Barthes goes on to describe as a "harmoniously closed loop" (*S/Z*, p. 27). As we have seen in the *Symposium*, Aristophanes describes the androgyne as a union of two distinct bodies, with two faces, two "privy members," four feet and hands and their "back and sides forming a circle" (*Sym*, p. 144). That male and female exist as independently marked plenitudes is further emphasized by Aristophanes' assertion that the androgyne is but one of three original sexes, the other two consisting of all-male or all-female spheres. This is the original unity that comes to be divided by Zeus. Even as Aristophanes thus identifies the androgyne with an ideal state of being, however, he reminds us that this "double nature, which once had a real existence . . . is now lost," and that even its name " 'androgynous' is only preserved as a term of reproach" (*Sym*, pp. 143–44). Thus, androgyny is now only a degenerative state, and he warns against any representation of this ideal. To figure ideal androgyny is complicated by the fact that the androgyne is assumed to transcend, if not to exist prior to, the terms that define and constitute it, specifically the terms characterizing male and female.[2] Defined through this distinction, it reinscribes the sexual difference that it seeks to efface or to dissolve into a synthetic wholeness. It is thus like any *figura*, which, Erich Auerbach explains, depends for its successful functioning upon the negation of its figural pole—that which constitutes its concrete historical reality—so as to guarantee that the other pole will be "fulfilled" in some otherworldly realm.[3] In its alternation of male to female, the figure of the androgyne reflects a totality that it never encompasses in the present. S/he is always other than what is described and more complete in his/her absence than in his/her presence. Image of the ideal sex and text, s/he is a timeless poetic symbol brought to function within the temporality of prose fiction. But the difficulty of figuring this ideal is not only a linguistic problem. It is also a problem concerning the relation between rhetoric and sexuality—how sexual difference has been represented as a relation of antithesis that could lead naturally to an understanding of a transcendent and totalized being.

33

Barthes's interest in the binary opposition is evident throughout his work, particularly as such couples are related to ideologies of sexual difference and, by extension, totality. "The economy of contraries, the binary exchange, the *copula*" writes John Smyth in reference to Barthes, "joins antitheses (man/woman as well as subject/object) in a *natural* grammar of totalization."[4] The circumscribed antithesis, in other words, gives a natural appearance of wholeness. In his autobiographical *Roland Barthes by Roland Barthes,* Barthes writes of his erotic attraction to binarism as his delight with a figure that allowed him to say all. "For a certain time, he went into raptures over binarism; binarism became for him a kind of erotic object. This idea seemed to him inexhaustible, he could never exploit it enough. That one might say everything *with only one difference* produced a kind of joy in him, continuous astonishment. . . . Since intellectual things resemble erotic ones, in binarism what delighted him was a figure."[5]

Barthes is well known for organizing his works around binarisms such as pleasure/jouissance or studium/punctum, binarisms whose oppositional value, however, eventually breaks down. "There is always a vacillation," Barthes writes, "the distinction will not be the source of absolute classifications, the paradigm will falter, the meaning will be precarious, revocable, reversible, the discourse incomplete."[6] Binarisms establish a system of stable opposition and, hence, stable meaning through the other differences they conceal. The difference between entities, as Barbara Johnson succinctly puts it, results from "a repression of differences *within* entities, ways in which an entity differs from itself."[7] Antithesis itself, in other words, is a figure of repression—repression of what might disrupt the totality it projects.

Barthes's particular interest in Balzac's novella has to do with its very unstable representation of sexual difference. The hero, Sarrasine, shows a similar erotic attraction to binarisms, particularly as they categorize and contain sexual opposition—the difference between himself and Zambinella. He dreams of "her" as his Pygmalion, the ideal beauty to satisfy his artist's eye and sculptor's hands, the fragile woman who proves his manliness—"my strength to your shield" (*S/Z*, p. 244). Such binarisms, of course, support the narrative of androgynous fulfillment of which Sarrasine dreams, the happily-ever-after marriage with his other half, "woman herself" (p. 248).

Produced out of his ignorance of women and of those cultural practices that denature masculine and feminine—like the creation of castrati—such binarisms serve as his (temporary) defense against a more terrifying knowledge concerning women and sexual difference.

It is indeed a kind of totality that Zambinella is said to embody, but not the ideal totality we have been discussing. S/he is rather the "monster of Totality (Totality as monster)," to which Barthes refers elsewhere, a grotesque figure created out of excess and the surpassing of boundaries, especially those dividing the antithesis (*RB*, p. 190). In Zambinella the wall separating the sexes is transgressed, the assumption of male and female as separate, antithetical entities proven false. Even love is defiled, as contact with Zambinella leads, not to Sarrasine's self-completion, but to his own self-alienation and death. This monstrous creature thus embodies a different rhetorical figure, one that Barthes names paradoxism. "Every joining of two antithetical terms, every mixture, every conciliation—in short, every passage through the wall of the Antithesis—thus constitutes a transgression; to be sure, rhetoric can reinvent a figure designed to name the transgressive; this figure exists: it is the paradoxism (alliance of words): an unusual figure, it is the code's ultimate attempt to affect the inexpiable" (*S/Z*, p. 27). Not simply opposed to antithesis, paradoxism unsettles this "most stable" of figures, and, consequently, undoes "the most inflexible of barriers: that of meaning. . . . In copying woman, in assuming her position on the other side of the sexual barrier, the castrato will transgress morphology, grammar, discourse" (*S/Z*, pp. 65–66). It is in this sense that, for Barthes, castration becomes contagious in *Sarrasine,* infecting all systems of representation and all representations of plenitude—whether aesthetic, linguistic, or sexual—with its own fundamental lack.

The choice of the term *paradoxism* is itself significant. Derived from the term *paradox*—a linguistic and ideological state that is beyond (*para*), or contrary to, opinion (*doxa*)—it bears echoes of the physiological condition of paroxysm, a sudden attack of symptoms or a sudden convulsion (like Aristophanes' hiccups in the *Symposium,* which first prevent him from telling his story of the androgyne).[8] It is thus suggestive of the role of the body in language as in narrative, and hints that the ultimate lack of mastery over the one is related to the lack of mastery over the other. This physical and linguistic body is overlooked in the search for embodied meanings. Indeed, the androgynous ideal of totality demands this kind of mystical reading in which the body is present only as veil to an Isis-like presence beyond. To call attention to the body(ies) of the androgyne is to bring into focus another figure, one I would set in a vacillating opposition to it—like that of paradoxysm to antithesis—and that I would call the figure of the hermaphrodite.

The hermaphrodite occupies the space of the bodily. In ancient Greece, androgyny was an ideal immortalized in classical statuary, but the actual birth of a hermaphrodite was regarded as an evil omen from the Gods and required that the infant be put to death.[9] A physical anomaly, the hermaphrodite also belongs to the realm of the visible. The body of Herculine Barbin, the "French hermaphrodite" whose memoirs were published by Michel Foucault, is cut open for the medical gaze to analyze. That body is clearly a paradox in its countering of the opinion—the *doxa*—that everyone as Foucault puts it, has one "true sex" and that truth resides in the body.[10] The hermaphroditic body, like Zambinella's, is at once a body of excess and of lack, "both and neither" male and female, as Ovid explains in his tale of Hermaphroditus.[11] We might compare the difference between androgyne and hermaphrodite to another of Barthes's binarisms, that between "figuration" and "representation." Barthes defines *figuration* as "the way the erotic body appears . . . in the profile of the text" (*PT*, pp. 55–56), that appearance tied to no more than the desire incited in the reader. *Representation,* on the other hand, "is *embarrassed figuration,* encumbered with other meanings than that of desire: a space of alibis (reality, morality, likelihood, readability, truth, etc.)" (*PT*, p. 56). Androgyny, like figuration, is unmarked, an object of desire untainted by difference. The hermaphrodite, on the other hand, is positioned on the side of the representational; it is excessive, or lacking. But any figuration of the androgyne falls to the side of the representational and, indeed, to the "immediately ideological" (*PT*, p. 56). The hermaphrodite is the representation of the androgyne that cannot be otherwise figured.

For Barthes, the excessive element that disrupts representation and launches narrative is the body. In *S/Z*, paradoxism and the paradoxical body are also illustrated by reference to the body of

Sarrasine's narrator. In his window recess, with one leg inside, one leg outside, one warm and one cold, he straddles the "dance of life" and the "dance of death" (*S/Z*, p. 222):

> Mediation upsets the rhetorical—or paradigmatic—harmony of the Antithesis (AB/A/B/AB) and this difficulty arises not out of lack but out of an excess: there is one element *in excess* and this untoward supplement is the body (of the narrator). As supplement, the body is the site of the transgression effected by the narrative: it is at the level of the body that the two *inconciliabilia* of the Antithesis (outside and inside, cold and heat, death and life) are brought together, are made to touch, to mingle in the most amazing of figures in a composite substance (without *holding together*). . . . It is by way of this *excess* which enters the discourse after rhetoric has properly saturated it that something can be told and the narrative begin. (*S/Z*, p. 28)

Narration, Barthes tells us in his reading of Balzac, is the product of a specific narrator with a specific body, and that body is an effect of the act of narration. "The message is parametrically linked with its performance" (*S/Z*, p. 213). Hence, there is no disembodied narration, no androgynous totality. This is the important discovery at which Barthes arrives in *S/Z* and which creates for this work a paradoxical, if not a hermaphroditic, space in Barthes's own corpus. In this book Barthes intermingles semiotics and erotics, the system building of structuralism and the deconstructive drives of desire, while marking a turning point from one to the other. As bodies, pleasure and pain hold an increasingly prominent place in his writing, and as his writing thus embraces or performs a more "feminine" position, rhetoric becomes less important as an ideological tool and more so as an erotic one, wielded (often with difficulty) by the sexed self.

A similar siding with the "feminine" is evident in the work of the romantic thinker most associated with the theory of representation (*Darstellung*), Friedrich Schlegel. I turn to him, moreover, not only because of the importance of his theories of the "romantic" and of the novel as a romantic genre for the writers I shall treat later but also because his one and only novel focuses on an ideal of androgyny and addresses the issue not only of (not) representing the body, but of (not) representing sexual difference. Indeed, just as a kind of litotic excess leads to Barthes's figure of paradoxism (an excess of "not," of lack), so does it lead to Schlegel's figure of irony.

Friedrich Schlegel and Romantic Irony/Androgyny

The significance of the figure of the androgyne for German romanticism in general and for Friedrich Schlegel in particular has been widely acknowledged.[12] In many of Schlegel's critical essays and fragments, and also in his one novel, *Lucinde,* the image of a fusion of male and female into a more completed whole designates an ideal that is alternately political, psychological, and aesthetic. As Sara Friedrichsmeyer points out in her study of the androgyne in Schlegel, one can trace his shift away from republican concerns and toward a less directly political interest in aesthetics through the transformations of this figure in his writings from 1785 to 1800, the years when he was most actively engaged in questions of literary theory. Yet while Friedrichsmeyer thus points to changes, neither she nor other critics of the androgynous tradition in Germany consider this figure in relation to the theories of irony that were so much a part of his writing at this time. Conversely, critics of romantic irony have sidestepped any discussion of androgyny, or for that matter of sexual difference. Yet throughout Schlegel, irony and sexual difference are mutually implicated, like rhetoric and sexuality in Barthes.

The changes that occur in Schlegel's conception of androgyny from his essay "Uber die Diotima" (On Diotima, 1795) to *Lucinde* (1799), and that can be characterized in part by his increased attention to the body, to sexuality, and to eros, bear direct relation to his growing interest in the function of irony and his embracing of a certain kind of ironic stance as the writer's task. In what follows, then, I shall be underscoring the connections I see between romantic androgyny and romantic irony. One must be careful to discriminate between ironies here, however. On one level, like the understanding of antithesis developed by Barthes, androgyny and irony share a similar "ideal" structure based on the joining of opposed entities as a dialectical and progressive force. In other words, the ironic structure of androgyny can be seen as ideal only insofar as sexual difference is understood as sexual opposition. But on a second level, irony acts as no such progressive force. As Smyth too remarks with regard to Barthes, the "totalization" effected by the "economy of contraries (man/woman as well as subject/object) . . . is disrupted and interrupted by irony."[13] This undermining of the *copula* (the grammatical or logical link between two elements) is at once the product of the ironic consciousness and what goads it into a second-level "irony of irony" as Schlegel refers to it, a fragile and vertiginous stance that needs simultaneously to disavow the knowledge of sexual difference that it fearfully reveals. The irony of irony is that "copulation" cannot repair but can only displace division, setting asunder male and female through the fragmentation of their presumed plenitude. The irony of androgyny is its erotic coupling with hermaphroditism.

Schlegel's interest in androgyny as a personal and social ideal is already in evidence in his essay "On Diotima." Diotima, Socrates' instructress in love in the *Symposium,* is presented as an image not only of "beautiful femininity" but even more so of "completed humanity" (*vollendete Menschheit*).[14] Diotima's ideas, Schlegel writes, are as thorough as they are "perceptive" (*scharfsinnig*), and as "definite" (*bestimmt*) as they are "tender" (*zart*). His objective in focusing on Diotima in this way is to challenge the view, prevalent amongst his contemporaries, of masculine and feminine as distinct and absolute categories. Such thinking, he warns, is an obstruction of moral freedom, specifically the freedom to direct both masculine and feminine to a higher order, in which they are integrated. The destiny (*Bestimmung*—which Schlegel uses in contrast to nature or necessity) of both sexes, he says, should be "a single endeavor" (OD, p. 20). One must "subordinate sex to the species without destroying it" (OD, p. 92), writes Schlegel, emphasizing that androgyny is a spiritual state that overlooks the physical and sexual nature of male and female. Indeed, after arguing that Diotima is a model of completed humanity, Schlegel goes to some length to try to disprove the commonly held opinion that she was a courtesan—a profession that, presumably, would be incongruous with her holistic image.

In 1799, Schlegel returned to the notion of androgyny in a letter to his lover, Dorothea Veit, published as "Uber die Philosophie, an Dorothea" (On philosophy, to Dorothea), in which he engages in a discussion of women's education and the role that philosophy should play in it. Refuting the idea that a spiritual education would destroy women's femininity, Schlegel writes that philosophy is "indispensable" for women, because only through it can they reach religion, their "only virtue."[15] Philosophy must do for women what poetry must do for men—make them more "human" by developing their nature beyond the "hindrance" of sex: "In actuality, masculinity and femininity, as they are usually taken and carried out, are the most dangerous hindrances to humanity, which, according to the old sage, is indigenous to the middle and can only be a harmonious whole that allows for no separation" (OP, p. 44). Referring to classical ideas of proportion, he claims that "the balance of human beings is only attained by the presence of opposites" (ibid.), and, furthermore, that the worth of men and women "must be judged according to the same scale" (OP, p. 45).

While Schlegel thus believes in a common destiny for the sexes, he nevertheless asserts that men and women do begin their journeys with different "natures." For women, in particular, this nature is located in the body, although here he is reluctant to go into specifics. "Do not fear that I will approach you with anatomy. I will leave to a future Fontanelle or Algarotti the task of decently and elegantly presenting the special secret of the difference between the sexes to the ladies. One does not need to go to much trouble to find that the female constitution is completely aimed toward the beautiful purpose [*Zweck*] of motherliness (OP, pp. 45–46)." Schlegel distinguishes between the purpose of femininity that is located in the body and related to her "domestic" (*Hauslich*) nature and condition, and her destiny (*Bestimmung*), which he defines as the path "which the voice of God points to in ourselves" (OP, p. 43) and which will take her beyond her nature. Once he does so, however, he is brought to acknowledge her deficiency with regard to the moral and aesthetic standards used to judge humanity. According to idealist notions of the nature of beauty as free and purposive but without purpose, women's singular purpose makes her less beautiful—at least in the eyes of the "priests of art."[16] "The female body is completely aimed toward the beautiful purpose of motherliness. And for that reason, excuses must be made to women for the priests of art if they tend to give the prize of beauty to the masculine figure" (OP, p. 46). However, the question arises, or rather Schlegel imagines Dorothea pointing (albeit indirectly) to a consequent misrepresentation of feminine desire, " 'But how,' you would say, 'can this gluttonous sex then not delight in the kaleidoscope or the smell of a rose, without immediately thinking of the fruit which is to become ripe in their goblet?" (ibid.). Implicit in his roundabout response to this question is both the acknowledgment of a different moral and aesthetic standard governing the development of the sexes and, consequently, the impossibility for women's fulfillment.

> But if the masculine figure is richer, more independent, more artificial and more superior, then I would like to find the feminine figure *more human*. Godliness and "animalness" are far more isolated in the most beautiful male. Both are completely melted together in the female, as in humanity itself. And therefore, I find it to be very true that only the beauty of the female can actually be the highest—because what is human is the highest everywhere, and is higher than what is godly. Perhaps some theorists of femininity have assumed this—to demand expressionless beauty as the most important duty of feminine bodies and to emphatically admonish the fulfillment of it. (OP, p. 46)

In raising the issue of the body, Schlegel contradicts his faith in a common, androgynous destiny for the sexes, and in one, single standard that can account for their respective worth.

The disruptive force of the body that subverts any simple understanding of sexual difference as opposition becomes more apparent in *Lucinde*. To understand that force, however, one must first understand the disruptive force of irony in narration to which it is linked. Schlegel is widely recognized as the major theorist of what would come to be called romantic irony. For him, irony is a defining element of romantic literature, in that it indicates not so much a rhetorical turn of phrase as a philosophical attitude toward writing (poetry) and the world. "Philosophy is the real homeland of irony. . . . Only poetry can also reach the heights of philosophy in this way, and only poetry does not restrict itself to isolated ironical passages, as rhetoric does."[17]

Irony for Schlegel is an assertion of literary self-consciousness either on the part of the author/narrator, or on the part of the work itself. The aim of all writing, and of romantic writing in particular for Schlegel, is to reflect upon and describe itself as it reflects upon and

41

describes its object. It thus engages both subjective and objective processes:

> There is a kind of poetry whose essence lies in the relation between ideal and real, and which therefore, by analogy to philosophical jargon, should be called transcendental poetry. It begins as satire in the absolute difference of ideal and real, hovers in between as elegy, and ends as idyll with the absolute identity of the two. But just as we wouldn't think much of an uncritical transcendental philosophy that doesn't represent the producer along with the product and contain at the same time within the system of transcendental thoughts a description of transcendental thinking: so too this sort of poetry should unite the transcendental raw materials and preliminaries of a theory of poetic creativity. . . . In all its descriptions, this poetry should describe itself, and always be simultaneously poetry and the poetry of poetry. (*AF* 238, p. 195)

In a note of 1797, Schlegel defines *irony* as "permanent parabasis"—an endless narrative interruption or intrusion of the narrator by which the work comments upon itself.[18] Critics of Schlegel have disputed whether or not this form of self-consciousness is a positive or a negative force in narrative. In the majority are those like René Bourgeois, Gary Handwerk, and Peter Szondi, who regard such a form of ironic self-consciousness as a necessary component and a preparation for self-transcendence. They regard such irony as a dialectical and progressive force, a contradictory moment of suspension and sublation, or *Aufhebung,* prefiguring a future unity of subject and object, spiritual and material worlds. Bourgeois writes that "irony is above all a philosophical faculty that allows for the realization of a synthesis between ideal and real in one movement," and later, as a form of "poetic reflection [that] makes poetry progress."[19] While calling attention to a temporal disjunction between real and ideal, Szondi, nevertheless, writes of irony as that which offers the glimpse of their future resolution.

> It is clear, then, that in the romantic conception of irony the subject is the isolated man who has become his own object, from whom the ability to act has been taken away by consciousness. He longs for unity and infinity; the world appears to him riven and finite. Irony, then, is his attempt to endure a painfully difficult position by means of a renunciation and an inversion of

values. . . . He cannot overcome the negativity of his situation through an action leading to a reconciliation of the contingent and the necessary. Nevertheless, by anticipating the future unity in which he believes, he declares this negativity to be temporary, whereby it is both preserved and reevaluated.[20]

Against such readings are those of Paul de Man and, to a certain extent, Lilian Furst, who, in terms that support Hegel's attack on Schlegel, find that romantic irony offers no such progressive force, but only the infinite regress of the unhappy consciousness. "Schlegel makes clear," states de Man,

> that the effect of this intrusion is not a heightened realism, an affirmation of the priority of a historical over a fictional act, but that it has the very opposite aim and effect: it serves to prevent the all too readily mystified reader from confusing fact and fiction and from forgetting the essential negativity of the fiction. The problem is familiar to students of point of view in a fictional narrative, in the distinction they have learned to make between the persona of the author and the persona of the fictional narrator. The moment when this difference is asserted is precisely the moment when the author does not return to the world. He asserts instead the ironic necessity of not becoming the dupe of his own irony and discovers that there is no way back from his fictional self to his actual self.[21]

The entrance of irony thus creates an endless process of doubling ("dédoublement" in de Man's terms), an irremediable division between the ironized, empirical self and the ironizing, linguistic self that must in turn be ironized or risk being duped by his own irony.

These two ways of reading romantic irony arise from the fact that there are at least two levels of irony at work in Schlegel's writing and two kinds or levels of irony that he tries at various times to define. The difference between the two, furthermore, resembles the difference Barthes establishes between antithesis and paradoxism. The first level relies on the structure of antithesis and sees irony in terms of opposition—to say the opposite of what one means or intends. Such is, of course, the traditional definition of irony. A French encyclopedia of 1765 defines *irony* as "a figure of speech by which one wants to convey the opposite of what one says";[22] the *O.E.D.* calls it "a figure of speech in which the intended meaning is the opposite of that expressed by the words used." Such a definition assumes that meaning itself is stable and can be controlled by the ironist. Schlegel takes this a step further, however, in positing that opposition within a dialectical scheme. "An idea is a concept perfected to the point of irony, an absolute synthesis of absolute antitheses, the continual self-creating interchange of two conflicting thoughts" (*CF* 121, p. 128). It is this first form of irony, understood as a synthesis of opposing forces, that is directly linked to Schlegel's ideal of romantic literature as "progressive," and eternally "becoming," such as he states in the well-known Fragment 116:

> Romantic poetry is a progressive, universal poetry. Its aim isn't merely to reunite all the separated species of poetry and put poetry in touch with philosophy and rhetoric. It tries to and should mix and fuse poetry and prose, inspiration and criticism, the poetry of art and the poetry of nature; and make poetry lively and sociable, and life and society poetical. . . . It alone can become, like the epic, a mirror of the whole circumambient world, an image of the age. And it can also—more than any other form—hover at the midpoint between the portrayed and the portrayer, free of all real and ideal self-interest, on the wings of poetic reflection, and can raise that reflection again and again to a higher power, can multiply it in an endless succession of mirrors. . . . The romantic kind of poetry is still in the state of becoming; that, in fact, is its real essence: that it should forever be becoming and never be perfected. . . . The romantic kind of poetry is the only one that is more than a kind, that is, as it were, poetry itself: for in a certain sense all poetry is or should be romantic. (*AF* 116, pp. 175–76)

Romantic poetry, then, is ironic because of its dialectical fusion of two antithetical plenitudes, leading to an even higher synthesis.

A second form of irony is structured, not by antithesis, but by what Schlegel will call alternately paradox or chaos. "Irony is the form of paradox. Paradox is everything simultaneously good and great" (*CF* 48, p. 149). Paradox involves a relation between elements that are different but not oppositional. As Furst writes, the more subtle form of irony "says not so much the *opposite* to what is meant as something *other than* is stated."[23] For Schlegel, as for Barthes, the paradoxical relation appears to undermine the subject's sense of mastery or control over meaning by revealing the subjectivity and insufficiency of his categories. Paradox slips into the structureless concept of chaos precisely because, in the absence of opposition, there can be no dialectical synthesis of parts to give order and purpose to the difference between them. "Irony is the clear consciousness of eternal agility, of an infinitely teeming chaos" (*I* 69, p. 247). Nor can this consciousness afford the subject any real consolation, since it initiates that infinite regress of masks by which the ironist attempts to protect himself from being the dupe of his own irony.[24] As de Man explains, "the ironic language splits the subject into an empirical self that exists in a state of inauthenticity and a self that exists only in the form of a language that asserts the knowledge of this inauthenticity. This does not, however make it into an authentic language, for to know inauthenticity is not the same as to be authentic."[25] Here, becoming and consciousness are irreparably split, undermining any progressive direction for either.

Schlegel's most extensive treatment of this second form of irony is a short essay written in 1798 and entitled "Über die Unverständlichkeit" (On incomprehensibility).[26] In this essay irony is addressed in terms of a subject's control over language and meaning, and consequently as a question of the possibility for real communication. Chaos is a linguistic phenomenon, a chaos of language and signs. "I wanted to demonstrate that words often understand themselves better than do those who use them, wanted to point out that there must be a connection of some secret brotherhood among philosophical words that, like a host of spirits too soon aroused, bring everything into confusion in their writings and exert the invisible power of the World Spirit on even those who try to deny it" (OI, p. 260). Schlegel muses on the possibility of what he calls a "real language," which would free us from the worry over words and would force attention to the origin, the "power and source of all activity" (ibid.). Yet as his elaboration of this "real language" slips to a discussion of alchemist's gold, he identifies it with an economic and semiotic system of exchange that is severed from any origin, and whose value is one of exchange or commodification rather than of meaning.

> Only a very short while ago this thought of a real language occurred to me again and a glorious prospect opened up before my mind's eye. In the nineteenth century, so Girtanner assures us, in the nineteenth century man will be able to make gold; and isn't it now more than mere conjecture that the nineteenth century is

shortly going to begin? With laudable confidence and some huffing and puffing, the worthy man says: "Every chemist, every artist will make gold. . . ."

I saw the whole thing from another point of view. I had often secretly admired the objectivity of gold, I might say even worshipped it. . . . wherever there is a little enlightenment and education, silver and gold are comprehensible and through them everything else. When it comes to pass that every artist possesses these materials in sufficient quantity, then he will be allowed only to write his works in bas-relief, with gold letters on silver tablets. Who would want to reject so beautifully printed a book with the vulgar remark that it doesn't make any sense? (OI, p. 261)

Implicated in this gold standard is the fundamentally ironic nature of language that can only exacerbate and never resolve the "indissoluble antagonism between the absolute and the relative, between the impossibility and the necessity of complete communication" (OI, p. 265).

The economic metaphor in "On Incomprehensibility" is similar to the rhetorical associations between language and money that Barthes calls attention to in Balzac's *Sarrasine*. The shift from a feudal to a bourgeois economy, he explains, is symbolized by the status of Parisian gold—not the "index" of an origin (whether land, inheritance, blood, etc.), it functions speculatively as a "sign" within a system of equivalences without origin. More importantly for my purposes, and why I bring Schlegel and Barthes together, is that both also raise the issue of the sign's economic functioning in relation to questions of sexuality, if not of sexual difference. Thus, for Barthes, the loss or lack of languages' indexical value is compared to the castrato's "lack," and inability to procreate: "Parisian indifference to the origin of money equates symbolically with the non-origin of money; a money that has no smell is money withdrawn from the basic order of the index, from the consecration of origin, this money is as empty as being-castrated: for Parisian Gold, what corresponds to the physiological impossibility of procreating is the impossibility of having an origin" (*S/Z*, p. 40).

Whereas Barthes thus identifies paradoxism with the emptiness of signs and castration, Schlegel calls attention to the infinite fullness of language by associating the highest of ironies, the "irony of irony," with a state of rampant procreativity over which one lacks all control.

> Finally there is the irony of irony. . . . For example, if one speaks of irony without using it, as I have just done; if one speaks of irony ironically without in the process being aware of having fallen into a far more noticeable irony; if one can't disentangle oneself from irony anymore, as seems to be happening in this essay on incomprehensibility. . . .
>
> What gods will rescue us from all these ironies? The only solution is to find an irony that might be able to swallow up all these big and little ironies and leave no trace of them at all. . . . But even this would only be a short-term solution. I fear if I understand correctly what destiny seems to be hinting at, *then soon there will arise a new generation of little ironies.* (OI, p. 267, my emphasis)

This fertility is not the fullness of androgyny, not a joining of two plenitudes, but a confluence of masculine and feminine that blurs the distinction between them. The irony of irony is that one loses all ability to designate the difference between the ironic and the nonironic, between rhetoric and truth, (sexual) performance and (sexual) identity. This loss of control results, in fact, in a breakdown of difference, bringing questions of language in touch with questions of the body by feminizing the (male/ironic) subject through the association of his state with the female reproductive process, regarded as a form of productivity over which one is powerless.

The irony of irony, like paradoxism, is thus a figure that can only be characterized as hermaphroditic, not androgynous. A figure of antithesis, the androgyne depends upon a stable opposition between male and female, and on knowing the difference. But the irony of irony, or the irony of androgyny, reveals the hermaphrodite within the androgyne—the constantly shifting lines of difference that rhetoric alone maintains—and hence, the impossibility of knowing the difference.

This mutual implication of philosophy, rhetoric, and the sexed body is most evident in *Lucinde* (1799). In this novel the "romantic" (in the popular sense) is clearly tied to the ironic, and romantic irony functions in a performative mode related to the role of sexuality and the body. From this work it would thus appear to be that the changes in the conception of irony that critics have located at the turn of the eighteenth century are not only connected to changes in the understanding of self-identity and self-definition (as many have shown with regard to Schlegel), but also reveal a new concern for sexual definition and the relation of sexual identity to self-identity.

Lucinde is Schlegel's one attempt to demonstrate his theory of the novel as "a romantic book" that is fundamentally ironic. In this work, unlike his earlier essays "On Diotima" and "On Philosophy," Schlegel also considers humanity in its embodiment with all the physical impulses that implies. Within the novel, the narrator comments on the importance of addressing matters of sex and the body and criticizes the character of Diotima, whom Schlegel formerly praised, for advancing a teleology of sublimation. Thus, she no longer presents the image of full humanity, but only half the story. "Inspired Diotima revealed to Socrates only the moiety of love. Love is not merely the quiet longing for eternity: it is also the holy enjoyment of a lovely presence It is not merely a mixture, a transition from mortal to immortal: rather it is the total union of both" (*L*, p. 106). Indeed, Schlegel's emphasis on bodily presence in this novel brought charges of scandal and even pornography upon its publication.

Schlegel pursued some of the less scandalous and more theoretical issues raised by *Lucinde* in his "Brief über den Roman" (Letter about the novel), published the following year. The letter consists of a commentary on that novel at the same time that it extends its self-critical process, exemplifying Schlegel's claim that "a theory of the novel would have to be itself a novel." "What is best in the best of novels is nothing but a more or less veiled confession of the author, the profit of his experience, the quintessence of his originality."[27] Both the letter and the novel are at once poetic and prosaic, fictional and historical, confessional and philosophical, and *Lucinde*'s subtitle, *Bekenntnisse eines Ungeschickten* (Confessions of a blunderer) calls attention also to its combination of confession and irony. The ironic structure central to both works, furthermore, is predicated on a dialogic and oppositional relation between the male narrator and a woman (Lucinde, in the novel, and Amalia, the "dear lady" to whom the "Letter" is addressed) through which the self is posited and critiqued—a dialogue, however, in which she never, or only rarely, speaks. Or, to put it another way, the relationship between the narrator and the woman he addresses is the model for an ironic relationship that can be seen alternately as "progressive" or chaotic: progressive if their relationship is one of complementarity leading to a higher, more complete form of self-knowledge; chaotic if, coupled with her difference that is neither complementary nor opposite, he comes to see only the false ground on which he has come to know his own self-identity and sexual identity. The letter thus reasserts the ironic structure of the novel without clarifying how to read it or how to understand the sexual relation represented within it.

Lucinde opens under the sign of an androgynous union of male and female as a beautiful synthesis of opposing forces—past/present, body/mind, sensuality/spirituality—and, thus as emblematic of romantic poetry itself:

> I didn't yearn only for your lips or your eyes or your body. It was, rather, a romantic confusion of all these things, a wonderful mixture of the most various memories and yearnings. All the mysteries of male and female frivolity seemed to hover about me as suddenly your real presence and the gleam of blooming happiness on your face inflamed my lonely self. Wit and rapture alternated between us and became the common pulse of our united life and we embraced each other with as much wantonness as religion. . . . I didn't simply enjoy but felt and enjoyed the enjoyment itself. (*L*, p. 44)

It is through Lucinde that Julius is brought to that state of self-consciousness where he not only "enjoys" but is aware of that enjoyment. Projecting his self onto her, he comes to assume a romantic/ironic stance of self-criticism, and even at times of self-parody, presented as a progressive process of self-transcendence and a means toward self-completion. "A large tear falls on this sacred page that I've found here in place of you. How honestly and simply you've expressed the old, daring thought of my most cherished and secret intention. In you it's come to fruition and I'm not afraid to admire and love myself in such a mirror" (*L*, p. 46). Julius is first attracted to Lucinde because of a "wonderful similarity" between the two that allows them to share "unspoken questions and answers," their voices "merging into one" in song (*L*, p. 98). The emphasis is less on merging masculine and feminine within the individual, which we saw in "On Diotima," than on drawing a firm distinction between men and women that will organize the sexual relation and union between them. While an androgynous union is thus the model for their relationship, their love acts also as an individualizing force that separates and delineates entities out of the "great chaos of conflicting forms." "Not hate, as the wise men say, but love, separates living creatures, and shapes the world; and only in love's light can you find this and observe it. Only in the answer of its 'you' can every 'I' wholly feel its boundless unity" (*L,* p. 106). It is as if their similarity allows for a more emphatic articulation of their difference as opposition.[28] I/you, subject/object, male/female are safeguarded as distinct and opposed entities in this love.

> "Can't people even talk to each other without first thinking about whether they're men or women?"
> "That could easily turn out rather badly. At best you would have an interesting club. . . . But the finest and the best part would always be lacking—what's always the spirit and soul of good society. . . . It would really be boorish to speak with a charming girl as if she were some sexless amphibian." (*L,* p. 75)

On one level, then, the relationship between Julius and Lucinde proves the sexes to be distinct and oppositional. Contemplating his beloved, Julius becomes aware of his male self in its "wholeness," "confident of being able to act as a man among men" (*L,* p. 112). Against her passive nature, he acquires an aesthetic consciousness whereby "his life now came to be a work of art for him. . . . A light entered his soul: he saw and surveyed all the parts of his life and the structure of the whole clearly and truly because he stood at its center" (*L,* p. 102). Lucinde, too, is an artist, but one whose works display a "wildness," an unlabored and unthought quality that lend "limited value as works of art" (*L,* p. 97). She is nature to his culture—her painting regarded as a simple reflection of her mood, (*L,* p. 97) and her creativity destined, not for spiritual progeny as Julius's is, but for physical procreation—thus allowing him to "dwell in nature's paradise" (*L,* p. 107) through her. "Women," Schlegel tells us in the *Ideas,* "have less need for the poetry of poets because their very essence is poetry" (*I* 127, p. 253). In *Lucinde* he says something similar with regard to love—that women have little need for it because their very essence is love. Recalling Diotima's ladder of love in the *Symposium,* Julius describes a tripartite ascent to "the summit of life" whereby "humanity has reached perfection" (*L,* p. 59). It is a journey that men take, guided by the love of an eternal feminine who has no need for growth. "There are none among them [women] who are uninitiated; for everyone of them already contains love completely within herself, a love of whose inexhaustible essence we youths are forever learning and understanding only a little more" (*L,* p. 60). Hence, education (*Bildung*) like that of Julius, which occupies the central and longest chapter in the novel, is an exclusively male process. In love, as in art, women are deprived of the becoming and of the consciousness that is necessary for transcendence, deprived of it, perhaps, so that men may define themselves by it all the more. "All mankind should really be divided into only two separate classes, the creative and the created [*den Bildenden und den Gebildeten*], the male and the female" (*L,* p. 108).

A similar opposition to that of the creative and the created comes into play in what is the most explicitly philosophical chapter of *Lucinde*—and, hence, potentially the most ironic, given Schlegel's association of philosophy and irony—entitled "A Reflection." Here, the application of terminology concerning the definite and the indefinite, borrowed primarily from J. G. Fichte, has the structure of a gendered antithesis. The chapter is a reflection on reflection, on thought thinking itself, and a representation of the reflexive moment of irony whereby the self looks at and defines itself from the distant position of the other.[29] "The mind has this peculiarity, that next to itself it loves to think about something it can think about forever. Hence the life of the cultivated [*Gebildeten*] and meditative man is a continual cultivation [*Bilden*] and meditation on the lovely riddle of his destiny [*Bestimmung*]. He is continually defining [*bestimmt*] it anew for himself, for that is precisely his whole destiny [*Bestimmung*], to be defined and to define [*bestimmt zu werden und zu bestimmen*]. Only in the search does the human mind find the secret that it seeks" (*L,* p. 119). The interplay of *Bilden* and *Bestimmen*— what is formed or cultivated versus what is destined, necessary— reinforces the ambiguity of *Bestimmung* itself, referring both to destiny and to the process of (self-)definition, the act by which the self transcends destiny. The roles of creative and created are both assumed by the self in this process that demands both self-creation and self-destruction (definition and redefinition). And here again, that opposition is explicitly gendered in such a way that the interplay of "symmetrical" forces allegorically describes the androgynous wholeness of the universe, if not simply the act of sexual intercourse. "But what, then, is the definer or the defined itself? For the man it is the anonymous. And what is the anonymous for the woman? The indefinite. . . . The definite and the indefinite and the whole wealth of their definite and indefinite relations: that is the one and the all, the strangest and yet the simplest, the simplest and yet the best. The universe itself is only a plaything of the definite and the indefinite; the real definition of the definable is an allegorical miniature of the warp and woof of everflowing creation" (*L*, pp. 119–20). The man is definite but nameless (*namenlos*), an identity in search of itself and of its definition that will be found in his relation with the other, the woman.[30] She, on the other hand, is indefinite, which is to say without identity, for her role is to reveal what man is, and not to impose that identity or define/create it for him, just as the light, *lux*, of Lucinde's name is not the direct light of the sun, but rather, the reflecting and reflected light of the moon. Only in the play of this "universal antithesis" will individuality find its "final shape and perfection." We find here, then, a deliberate gendering of the process of the self-becoming or self-realization of Spirit, if not an attempt to take sexual difference into account in that dialectic of finite and infinite, of particular and universal, of morality (freedom) and nature. Schlegel ironically posits sexual intercourse between male and female as the embodiment or objectification of Spirit, and hence as a spiritual act leading toward the ultimate stage of manifest Religion.[31]

And yet the representation of that act simultaneously invalidates the progressive model of knowledge it claims to sustain. In the end, it is not a Hegelian telos but a Nietzschean play that love enforces—a play of much "seriousness," to be sure. In his comments on this section de Man points to the way that philosophical and sexual codes are confused, so that what reads like a philosophical argument becomes a "reflection" on sexual intercourse. "It's not just that there is a philosophical code and then another code describing sexual activities. These two codes are radically incompatible with each other. They interrupt, they disrupt, each other in such a fundamental way that this very possibility of disruption represents a threat to all assumptions one has about what a text should be."[32] Such a threat, he says, was enough to establish a whole tradition of studies to "defuse" both Schlegel and his irony. It seems, however, that de Man is himself defusing Schlegel in his explanation of this threat as "textual." One of the ironies of the reflexive structure of irony is the reversibility and hence the loss of distinction between the opposed positions that ground that structure. Thus we see how in approaching the perfectly definite and its clarity with regard to the world and the individual self—"Now everything is clear!"—Julius loses his self in that reflection, to become, as it were, the indefinite. "Plunging deeper into this individuality, my reflection pursued such an individualistic turn that it soon ended and forgot itself" (*L*, p. 120).

More than textual, irony is threatening to the knowledge of the self and the knowledge of the other, to the self-definition and to the *sexual* definition that the self achieves through the other. To the extent that Julius seeks his whole, male self in relation to Lucinde, he must fail, and fail especially because Lucinde is not the "other" he imagines and requires. She is something other than what he has created, as she informs him in one of the few moments when words are allowed her: "I am not, my Julius, the sanctified person you describe even though I might like to sing laments like the nightingale, and though I am, as I deeply feel, consecrated to the night alone. You are that person. When the turmoil has died down and nothing mean or common distracts your noble soul, then you see reflected in me— in me who am forever yours—the marvelous flower of your imagination" (*L*, p. 126).

Lucinde's response is one of several moments disrupting the antithetical structure of sexual difference and love. For Schlegel, love—which is always heterosexual love—is, like irony, a serious game. To "play at loving" (*L*, p. 73), Julius asserts earlier in the novel, it is necessary to establish sexual difference—to have assurance of an opposition between male and female. But it is that opposition that the game of love proves false, or purely rhetorical. This we see already in the second section of the novel, which interrupts the first, disrupts the progressive vision of androgyny presented as the book opens with an ironic view of the love game as a performance of exchangeable roles.

How could distance make us more distant, since for us the present is, as it were, too present. We have to lessen and cool the consuming fire with playful good humor, and therefore the wittiest of all the shapes and situations of happiness is for us also the loveliest. One above all is wittiest and most beautiful: when we exchange roles and in childish high spirits compete to see who can mimic the other more convincingly, whether you are better at imitating the protective intensity of the man, or I the appealing devotion of the woman. But are you aware that this sweet game still has quite other attractions for me than its own—and not simply the voluptuousness of exhaustion or the anticipation of revenge. I see here a wonderful, deeply meaningful [*sinnreich*] allegory of the development of man and woman to full and complete humanity. There is much in it—and what is in it certainly doesn't rise up as quickly as I do when I am overcome by you. (*L,* p. 49) [Es liegt viel darin, und was darin liegt, steht gewiß nicht so schell auf wie ich, wenn ich dir unterliege.[33]]

Here, in fact, are two different theories of love based on two different presentations of love's relationship to time and two different understandings of allegory.[34] On the one hand, love is progressive, where men and women move dialectically toward a goal that will be the transcendence of sexual difference, their disembodiment in "complete humanity." But the love game, in fact, allows for no such spiritual end. What "liegt . . . darin"—literally, "lies in the allegory"—is a body that is much more concerned with its physical erection and with reversing the positions of who's on top and who "lies under" (*unterliegen*), than with any kind of spiritual ascent.

What is revealed in the love game is the existence of an insuperable temporality and distance between self and other whose efforts toward union lead only to an infinite regress of mimetic reflection. Irony, like love, is thus both means and obstacle to absolute self-consciousness. The dynamics of love reveal and repeat the moment of irony as a "permanent parabasis"—one that disrupts the narrative of human development by undoing the coherence of sexual opposition on which it is based. As a means toward the union of self and other, love leads only to recognition of a sexual masquerade that takes the place of a "relation" between the sexes. If Lucinde's role is to play mirror to Julius—or in other words to be the phallus and signifier of his desire—she also undermines the aesthetic vision through which he defines himself, revealing it to be no more than an effect of her role-playing.

It should not be surprising that in *Lucinde* even the *schöne Seele,* or beautiful soul—what for Schiller and Goethe figures the spirit that knows and is in conformity with itself—is here revealed to be a mask. In the chapter entitled "Allegory of Impudence," the beautiful soul is one of many allegorical figures personified as woman. At one point in the chapter, Impudence seizes the beautiful soul by the face and declares, "That's only a mask . . . you're not the Beautiful Soul but at best Daintiness, and sometimes Coquetry as well" (*L,* p. 56). For Schlegel, as for Hegel, the beautiful soul is thus an "unhappy consciousness." Hegel describes the beautiful soul as "unhinged," "disordered," and in more feminine terms, as one who "wastes itself in yearning, and pines away in consumption." Like Schlegel's "indefinite," she is, Hegel explains, without "concrete reality," in need of an actor (Schlegel's "anonymous definite") to "externalize itself and turn into something actual," but refuses to risk her purity with embodiment.[35] For Schlegel too, knowledge of the spirit must come through the body. But that body is always already a mask, a falseness with which there can be no reconciliation. She is not one element of a dialectic leading to Religion, but the very mockery of Religion, as of truth and beauty. This is the conjecture that Philippe Lacoue-Labarthe and Jean-Luc Nancy put forward, recalling the threat that Schlegel's irony posed to the Hegelian system.

> And perhaps at bottom it is a "stroke" of irony to refer to such a metaphysics of art as "religion." Unless irony itself, by a supplementary turn (by an imperceptible movement of reflection), were the mockery of what should be understood by "religion." . . . And what if "religion" should be understood in the proper meaning of the word? As *re-ligion,* the possibility of "linking together"? Or as a means, like (and in the "same" position as) the future Hegelian *Aufhebung,* of linking the indefinite series of oppositions—of art and religion, paganism and Christianity, man and woman, work and artist, philosophy and poetry, etc.,—as parts of the Same in general?[36]

Where Hegel rejects the disruptive force of irony, Schlegel accepts it, not in the place of the dialectic, but coupled to it in a hermaphroditic embrace.

Rhetoric and Body Politics

In *Lucinde,* the *schöne Seele* is thus a figure of the text and of writing that is both means and obstacle to the Spirit. There can be no knowledge of the transcendent, androgynous Spirit, and hence no self-knowledge except as embodied in the letter that particularizes, sexualizes. The novel's subtitle reminds us that *Bekenntnis*—confession in the religious sense of avowal of spirit—takes place in the body, a clumsy, unmanageable entity—*das Ungeschick* (translated as "the blunderer"). Beckoned to announce that "The time has come. . . . The inner being of God may be revealed and described" (*L,* p. 57), the narrator finds himself speechless, unable to profess a thing. At the same time another voice says to him:

> You mustn't try to communicate the immortal fire in its pure and raw form. . . . Create, discover, transform, and retain the world and its eternal forms in the perpetual variation of new marriages and divorces. Veil and bind the spirit in the letter. The real letter is all-powerful; it's the true magic wand. It is the letter with which the irresistible will of that great magician, Fantasy, touches the sublime chaos of all-encompassing nature, touches it and calls the infinite word to light, the word that is an image and a mirror of the divine spirit, and that mortals call the universe. (*L,* p. 58)

The passage should remind us of what Schlegel says in "On Incomprehensibility" about words understanding themselves better than those who use them do. The letter touches the spirit, brings it to light, to experience, but only as it also veils or conceals it. All-powerful, the letter itself can never be completely mastered, and instead reveals the finiteness and limitation of the subject who attempts to control it.[37]

It is this vulnerable, "feminine" body, the body that can be impregnated (with "a new generation of little ironies"—OI, p. 267), or "pricked" in Barthes's terms, that Schlegel, like Barthes, celebrates. And his celebration goes hand in hand with the valorization of a form of writing that is fragmented (both have entitled their aphorisms as

"Fragments"), untotalizable, chaotic. "It's equally fatal for the mind to have a system as to have none. It will simply have to combine the two" (*AF* 53, p. 167). *Lucinde* is such a combination, an apparently random juxtaposition of chapters placed symmetrically around a central story of *Bildung,* framing and challenging that chapter's teleological or progressive shape.

In a similar fashion Schlegel and Barthes move between (if not from) a systematic application of binarisms and (if not to) a flirtation with a third term that undoes the system. This is also their approach to sexual difference, on the one hand, structured by absolute antitheses leading to androgyny as a trope of wholeness, and, on the other hand, presented as a chaotic performance of external masks leading only to more masks behind. I hesitate to put this move into any kind of progressive scheme for reasons that should be apparent by now and despite what might appear to be the more modernist and feminist stance of this latter position.[38] Barthes's emphasis on the performative nature of sexuality and his understanding of sexuality as "plural" rather than binary has been an effective tool in the feminist war on essentialism. So too, Schlegel's play with sexual masquerade can be seen as part of his own continuing critique of masculine and feminine as restricting categories that must not be regarded as absolutes. Within the context of *Lucinde,* such play recognizes the asymmetrical and, hence, illusory nature of sexual opposition, defined always from the standpoint of a finite (male) subject—thereby denying the other any plenitudinous nature. But is the subject of the masquerade delivered from this sexist irony? Does the masking instability mask a different, problematic stability?

In *Roland Barthes by Roland Barthes,* Barthes questions his attraction to the plural: "Who knows if this insistence on the plural is not a way of denying sexual duality? The opposition of the sexes must not be a law of Nature; therefore, the confrontations and paradigms must be dissolved, both the meanings and the sexes must be pluralized: meaning will tend toward its multiplication, its dispersion (in the theory of the Text), and sex will be taken into no typology (there will be, for example, only *homosexualities,* whose plural will baffle any constituted, centered discourse, to the point where it seems to him virtually pointless to talk about it)" (*RB,* p. 69). As Naomi Schor comments, "denied sexual difference shades into sexual indifference," into one sexuality, a "hom(m)osexuality" where the concept of a specifically feminine desire has no place. Jane Gallop is even more critical, seeing Barthes's move to a poststructuralist position as a deliberate attempt to reinscribe the differences that such a position taught were no longer man's to proclaim:

> Barthes' move from the classic domination of scientific structuralism to the cleverer and more subtle mechanisms which characterize a certain post-structuralist embrace of what undercuts mastery as the last hope of some masterful position in a world in which the sons of Descartes, the sons of a certain Western European tradition of subjugating the secondary body to a disembodied consciousness, are less and less able to maintain that domination, a domination which historically depended on other sexes, classes, and races to embody the body as well as care for the Master's body so he would not have to be concerned with it, so he could consider himself disembodied, autonomous, and free to will.[39]

The poststructuralist is thus not so far from the romantic ironist—both embrace their own vulnerability, their so-called femininity as the ultimate effort to prove, if nothing else, their intellectual prowess, the virility of their consciousness, and their distinction from Others who cannot do so. "They don't know what they're saying, which is all the difference between them and me."[40]

In Schlegel, the choice between sexual difference as sexual opposition or as mimetic play offers a similar retreat from considering the possibility of either a specific feminine sexuality or female desire—a retreat too from considering women as historical actors, even if that means accepting history as an agentless force (we may not be too far from Barthes's death of the author). While, in his time, a relatively secure background of non-European others might still appear to embody the body thereby allowing (European) Man to stand for humanity, and to be defined in terms of freedom, of self-consciousness and the ability to represent himself to himself, it was increasingly less sure that woman was part of that background.[41] Schlegel's final embrace of an overpowering and endless "generation of little ironies" can, thus, also be read as a last hope of gaining some mastery over the feminine by means of appropriating it—containing the erotics between the ironizing and ironized within the (male) self and the play between author-narrator.[42]

This sexual politics of irony will be played out in the narrative politics of the nineteenth century, particularly in France. The contest between idealism and realism as representational modes, I would suggest, developed partly as a battle between the ironized and the ironizing. Perhaps the feminization and consequent discrediting of idealism, a mode that appears to be beyond or void of irony, and the concomitant valorization of realism—"the masculine mode"—has to do with the triumph of irony as what affirms and legitimates the (male) right to authorship, even while undermining the authority of that position?[43] Vulnerability in men has often had its charm. Maybe that is why feminists are still accused of having no sense of humor.

Part II

3

The Aesthetics of Romantic Androgyny

From Platonic to Romantic Ideal

IN PART ONE, I established a distinction between two terms, *androgyne* and *hermaphrodite*, that, although they are often considered synonymous, have very different connotations. *Androgyne* suggests a spiritual or psychological state of wholeness and balance arrived at through the joining of masculine and feminine conceived of as complementary and symmetrically opposed. *Hermaphrodite,* on the other hand, calls attention to the visible and physiological fact of two differently sexed but noncomplementary bodies brought together in an unrelieved process of joining and splitting that manifests the irreparable divisions wrought by desire. In Plato the androgyne is said to exist at the beginning, before division and before desire; s/he is a figure of origins, of fullness, and of presence. Ovid's hermaphrodite, on the other hand, results from a transformation; s/he is a figure of the displacement of origin and is the locus of generative play.

Since Plato, the androgyne has often figured a kind of transcendental signified—a single source of truth and beauty that founds the forces of language and desire we inherit, while remaining outside of and untainted by the play of linguistic and sexual difference. But as the *Symposium* illustrates the impossibility of tracing such origins, we also find that such purity is not "original," but the result of exclusion and repression. Plato's myth, for example, comes down to us with the androgyne's homosexual kin banished, its bawdy context eliminated along with Aristophanes's hiccups. From the Renaissance to the present, as Jean Libis tells us, philosophical commentaries on the myth have displayed a common prudishness, turning the opportunity to discuss sexuality to an occasion to consider our transcendental origins instead.[1] And insofar as it is man's origin that they seek to disclose, it is above all female sexuality that they avoid discussing.

This sexual avoidance is evident throughout the androgynous tradition following Plato. In both Saint Paul and the Gospel of John, androgyny is considered one of the characteristics of spiritual perfection.[2] In Gnostic and Kabbalistic doctrines accounts are given of man's original state as androgynous and as having fallen into sexual differentiation like Plato's androgyne: "Adam and Eve were made back to back, joined at the shoulders; then God divided them with an axe stroke, cutting them in two."[3] Similarly, the Zohar, the fundamental book of Jewish Kabbalism tells of Adam Kadman, the "Man of emanation [who] was both male and female from the side of both Father and Mother."[4] Androgyny, here again, signals a transcendence of the physical world. Primal man is described only as light, emanating from a single source. This idea becomes central to versions of hermetic and emanation philosophy during the Renaissance. According to Paracelsus, the world is an emanation from the first principle of simple and eternal unity, called the "Mysterium Magnum." Abrams describes the primal Adam, "who represented in himself the cosmic whole—had a non-physical body and was androgyne, but his fall plunged him into the gross material world of separated and conflicting physical and sexual elements, in which each individual part attempts to be self-sufficient." This fall, nevertheless, had a positive outcome in establishing the first step in a process of respiritualization. Christ, the God-man, made possible the reunion of separate parts and their return to the source. A similar process takes place in alchemical theory and practice, whereby the philosopher's stone—understood, like Christ, to be androgynous—expedites the alchemist's task of transmuting base metals into their primordial perfection as gold.[5] Thus, the hermetic tradition combined a body of Platonic philosophy with a new science of alchemy. Joining craft and creed in its search for origins, the hermetic tradition recreates that tension between the myths of Plato and Ovid. The principle of transformation, as Abrams describes it, is the principle of the *Metamorphoses,* of artificially re-created origins that remove us even further from the original presence they are meant to reveal.

Traces of emanation philosophy reappear in the seventeenth

century, particularly in the German mystical-theosophical writings. Jacob Boehme, the most influential theosophist of this period, brings together alchemy, Christian faith, and biblical history in a neat philosophical system wherein the androgyne plays a central role. As Libis explains, Boehme's androgyne is described as a "negative of sexuality," the image of immortal man before his perfect state was disrupted by desire—"a knowledge inappropriate to his nature"— and before he "thus materialized."[6] Man's fall and mortality is thus blamed on erotic lust. The effect of the fall, according to Boehme, was the separation of the divine virgin, Sophia, from primal man, an event that established the prioritizing of male over female and the view of the female as erring and less essential.[7] This asymmetrical relation between the sexes is also evident in Boehme's Trinity, where the second person, man's sought counterpart, is associated with the philosopher's stone or androgyne and at the same time with Sophia, the feminine essence. As Ronald Gray explains:

> Man himself was isolated and in need of a feminine or divine counterpart, but the search for this counterpart was always represented as a search not merely for a woman, but for a hermaphrodite. This led, as always, to an extreme confusion of terms. At one moment the Stone might be referred to as a Virgin, at another it would clearly be intended to represent Christ, and yet again it would represent both male and female. In so far as the stone represented the One and All, it was male and female, and could bear all possible names, but in so far as it perfected the male nature of the seeker it was female."[8]

In Boehme, then, the ideal of the androgyne alternated with that of the *Ewig Weibliche*, or eternal feminine, as an image for perfecting man, making him into that "one and all" that the "mere" woman could never represent.

Similar themes are prominent in the writings of those mystics who, following Boehme, most influenced the romantics. Swedenborg (1688–1772) insisted on the material world's impurity and the need to separate from it. His notion of marriage, as Balzac presents it, reiterates Boehme's sexual hierarchy: "The Lord took beauty and elegance from the life of man and transported it into woman. When man is not reunited with that beauty, he is severe, sad, and unsociable, when he is reunited with it, he is joyous, he is complete." Saint-Martin (1743–1803), to whom Balzac refers in the Preface to the Livre Mystique as "the last great mystical writer," also regarded man's fall as a descent into materiality and envisioned his salvation as a process of androgynation that would guard against carnal knowledge by respiritualizing the body.[9] The process is a matter of overcoming desire for (or fear of) woman (as "the sex") by appropriating her qualities, thereby making her separate, bodily existence unnecessary. According to Jacques Borel, Saint Martin believed himself to be "rescued" from the fate of marriage and saved from his own weaknesses, but only to realize that man originally contained woman and must rediscover that androgynous state by rediscovering her: "reintegration demands that we give birth to an eternal virgin in our soul by bringing back our original body."[10] In each of these systems, women have no place as subjects of desire, or subjects to be perfected by man, and desire for them is said always to be desire for the virgin—a theme that becomes prominent both in German romanticism and in fin-de-siècle poetry.

An essential inspiration behind the German Pietist movement in the seventeenth century, Boehme also influenced the widespread resurgence of the theme of androgyny during the early stages of German romanticism, which was particularly evident in the work of Novalis, Wilhelm von Humboldt, and Franz von Baader. At this time, with the increasing trend toward categorization of thought, the theme moves out of the discourse of philosophy and into that of literature and history. Versions of universal history (*Universalgeschichte*) formulated by such writers as Leibniz, Herder, and Schiller were secular in their emphasis on human progress, while, structurally, they paralleled biblical notions of the fall from a simple and androgynous unity into division, complexity, and sexual bondage.[11] Responding to Rousseau's paradox of civilization that emphasized the conflict between cultural advancement and moral happiness or goodness, these theories correlated an image of androgynous primal man with a vision of man in the future, who would not only retrieve his original happy state but would be brought to an even higher level of existence through the intervening faculty of his free will. Thus history took the shape of a spiral whereby the movement of return to a lost golden age was simultaneously a movement of progress and advancement. Hegel's narrative of the human Spirit is paradigmatic of this structure found in history and literature alike. In Novalis's *Heinrich von Ofterdingen,* for instance, man's educational journey always takes him back home (*immer nach Hause*), where, reunited with nature, represented as feminine, he rediscovers his original wholeness.[12] Here, as in Boehme, the image of the androgyne embodies a mystical notion of love that heals division while leading us back to the primeval paradise. What motivates and sustains this historical process is desire for the feminine—whether as nature, the virgin, the bride of Christ or the New Jerusalem—a desire that legitimates her absence as desiring subject.

This subordination of the feminine is evident as well in the new discipline of art history and its mapping of a return to the origins of beauty. J. J. Winckelmann's *History of Ancient Art* (1764) charts the decline of art since classical Greece. For him, the Greek statues of hermaphrodites are models of "ideal beauty." Bringing together the most beautiful parts of men and women into a form that transcends both male and female, their beauty dissolves all particularity of features into a harmonious wholeness. In these sculptures, therefore, art's mastery over nature is uncontested. "Art went still farther; it united the beauties and attributes of both sexes in the figures of hermaphrodites. The great number of hermaphrodites, differing in size and position, shows that artists sought to express in the mixed nature of the two sexes an image of higher beauty; this image was ideal."[13]

Praising how these statues transcend the particularity of sex, Winckelmann's sensuous descriptions nevertheless confirm that they all have "male organs of generation" and thus are essentially masculine figures whose virile, classical features have been softened by the incorporation of feminine characteristics. Indeed, he suggests that the closest models for such sculptures were eunuchs, "those equivocal beauties effected by the removal of the seminal vessels—in which the masculine characteristics approximated, in the superior delicacy of the limbs, and in the greater plumpness and roundness generally, to the softness of the female sex."[14] Once again, the image of androgynous and full humanity prescribes a subservient role for the feminine.

Androgyny and the Erotics of Progress in Nineteenth-Century France

As the popularity of the androgynous figure spread to France during the height of the romantic movement, it moved out of the realm of pure ideas and entered practical treatises concerning the social order and social "progress." The prominence of the image of the androgyne in nineteenth-century France has been noted by critics and particularly by A. J. L. Busst, whose "Image of the Androgyne in the Nineteenth Century" is the most thorough study on the subject. Busst describes two opposed roles for the figure: an optimistic and utopian function in the early part of the century, projecting total unity and equilibrium; and its pessimistic, erotic presentations among decadents, who stress its sexual ambiguity. Busst's study is learned and insightful, but in concentrating on this major dichotomy, he oversimplifies both positive and negative categories. Indeed, he is forced to admit that Balzac's androgyne does not fit neatly into either slot. It is precisely this refusal of either/or categories and the forced consideration of a both/and way of thinking that makes the androgyne/hermaphrodite such a provocative figure for this period in France.

Much of the mystical theorizing seen in German romanticism is carried on also in France in the work of the so-called gentle mystic of Lyon, Pierre-Simon Ballanche (1776–1847). His work treats similar questions about the unity and nature of mankind (*L'homme cosmogonique*), but in a more specifically historical context where the androgyne becomes for the first time, as Busst states, "a vast social symbol."[15] That symbol's presentation, however, problematizes the Platonic view of essential unity and identity that Ballanche supports. His system privileges history and social progress over equilibrium, so that the symbol of the androgyne as promising restitution of original unity in the future is used to confirm the present necessity for inequality. Thus, in the *Vision d'Hébal* (1831), the social roles of male and female are determined by the fall, and the cosmogonic division into sexes structures further social divisions and polarities. "And the division of sexes will be the emblem of the division of castes and classes in primitive human institutions. . . . And all the instructors of peoples will have the feeling of that division, which is that between the active principle and the passive principle."[16]

Reflecting this division, humanity is divided into active "initia-tors" and passive "initiates," so that the masculine principle may rehabilitate the feminine principle, God having revealed His divine laws to the initiators. Gradually, as divine knowledge is made known to the masculine and as, in turn, the masculine instructs and initiates the feminine, social, racial, and geographical distinctions will disap-pear, and eventually the original unity of masculine and feminine, active and passive, spirit and flesh, will be retrieved. "From that cos-mogonic event, the degeneration and the rehabilitation—a dogma so profoundly buried in the mystery of origins, results the separation of the sexes, the designations of castes and of classes, the distinctive character of the races. . . . The passive sex will thus without doubt arrive at equality with the active sex, because it belongs to the same original essence."[17]

Ballanche's system both repeats and develops the temporal ten-sion I have described between androgyne and hermaphrodite: "What is true in eternity, is not necessarily true in time."[18] Certainly this tension is already present in German theories of *Universalgeshichte,* but in France it reaches a critical point. After 1789 France is facing a lost past in very concrete terms, and words like *eternity, time,* and *history* are assuming new significance. Indeed, what becomes appar-ent in Ballanche is also true for much of French romanticism. The increasing tempo of change in all realms of present experience in-creases the need to believe in an eternal realm and those eternal ideals that are being challenged. Despite his projections of unity and equal-ity, what Ballanche endorses is a divinely ordained social, political, religious, and even aesthetic hierarchy, which is to say, a rejection of the changes in thought forced on society by the French Revolution, the increasing secularization of ideas, and the slow demise of the aristocracy's power.

Ballanche is no exception in this respect. Ambivalence about historical change is a common response to the political uncertainties and disappointments of the early part of the century. Symbolizations of the androgyne like his project a future effacement of distinctions, but only as they reinscribe those differences between sex and class challenged by history. The revolution of 1789 and the Napoleonic Code dislodged class, family, and sex status, offering property rights not previously known to nonnobility and to unmarried women.

Although religious orthodoxy had praised "woman" as the Virgin Mother or condemned her as seductive Eve, a proliferation of biological and medical theories busily produced secular, empirical knowledge of her nature.[19] What seems especially representative in Ballanche's writing, moreover, is the use of a sexual metaphor, supporting Molino's statement that by the nineteenth century "masculine and feminine become a fundamental category of the world and of reflection."[20] The writings of Michelet, for example, offer evidence of a similar use of sexualized rhetoric. As Barthes has demonstrated, the discourse on sex—more rightly seen as the discourse on woman—is fundamental to Michelet's representation of historical process and progress. "Based on the alliance of the two sexes, the People gradually becomes in Michelet a superior means of knowledge. Quite like Woman, and in virtually the same direction, the People is above History, it opens Nature and grants access to the supernatural goal of a paradisal, reconciled humanity. The conjunction of adverse sexes into a third and complete ultra-sex represents the abolition of all contraries, the magical restoration of a seamless world which is no longer torn between contradictory postulations."[21] Michelet's scheme combines the mystic's *coincidentia oppositorum*[22] with a Hegelian dialectic, and motivates both by desire for the androgyne/woman; s/he, of course, is positioned outside the system, and outside the historical process. A similar rhetoric is evident in utopian socialist attempts to alter the relationship between the sexes. Beginning with the Saint-Simonians, and carried on to a greater extent in Enfantin's search for the female messiah, the questions of sexual equality and woman's social role were central issues by 1831. What is clear, nevertheless, is that the question of sexuality—whether it is posed by liberal or conservative, orthodox or heterodox—becomes the question of woman, defined by man as his specular opposite. The image of the androgyne and eventual joining of the sexes describes a historical process whereby man will be perfected and completed by union with the feminine, woman having no function as historical actor.[23] In history, as in literature and art, such archetypal oppositions thus function conservatively, and a figure like the androgyne explores change while providing reactionary coherence against the threat of disorder.[24]

Social change was a threat to the status of the artist as well, who found it increasingly difficult to make claims to a sacred or privileged position. The nature of art and the art world were also becoming secularized and works of art were considered commodities rather than gifts from the gods. The diminishing stratification of class and sex did have noticeable economic effect by the 1830s. Moreover, the breakup of large concentrations of wealth and property under Napoleon brought about the slow demise of "les grandes dames" who had supported the artist. A French version of the eternal feminine or *Ewig Weibliche* positioned women as emblems or bearers of spiritual and aristocratic values in a bourgeois and materialistic world. As a result the artist him/herself was seen as a sort of androgyne, at once "womanly" in his/her dreams and aesthetic tastes and forced to act like a man in the materialistic, masculine world of the literary marketplace.[25]

Returning to Ballanche we see that there is a specifically aesthetic or poetic nostalgia associated with the androgyne. Man's present language is regarded in *La Vision d'Hébal* as imperfect communication and a result of his fallen state. "God has no need of a sign to know himself; the subjective and objective faculties are not separated in absolute existence. Man, a successive being, needs a sign to understand his own intelligence. In him the subjective faculty and the objective faculty are not simultaneous. From this results, for him, the necessity of the word."[26] In contrast to Man's word, the androgyne, *l'homme cosmogonique,* image of original and immortal man, reflects the original language of divine communication, the word as fully present and unmediated, "the word of truth."[27] As Busst writes, poetry for Ballanche is "essentially the language of collective humanity, of the cosmogonic man, that abolishes divisions brought by the fall and the entry of man into time and space. . . . "The poet dominates from on high the epoch in which he lives and inundates it with light: the future is also in his thought; from a single point of view he embraces all human generations and the intimate cause of events within the secrets of Providence."[28]

This privileging of poetry takes on greater significance in light both of the debates over the origin of language carried on in France and Germany in the eighteenth century and of German aesthetic philosophies that gave a preeminent role to art and to the artist in furthering human progress. Ballanche brings Herder and the Port Royale grammarians together by envisioning poetic language as a

divine gift, while at the same time making it an instrument of "initiation" and human progress.[29] Bridging the gap between the religious
and the secular, between the divinely inspired and the scientifically
determined, poetry serves a dialectical function similar to that which
Kant and Hegel ascribe to the aesthetic realm.

Thus the romantic image of the androgyne was transmitted from
Germany along with the idealist philosophies of the beautiful, known
especially through the works of Mme. de Staël and Victor Cousin.[30]
This is not surprising, since the image itself already suggested a
coincidence of opposites (*coincidentia oppositorum*), bringing together the antithetical realms of the universal and the particular or
the objective and the subjective. Furthermore, the narratives associated with the androgyne lead directly to the poetic ideal projected in
Schelling's *The Ages of the World* (1811). Art or poetry, he claims,
can redeem man from the Fall, allowing him once again to see the
connection between the spiritual and physical worlds. "There will no
longer be any difference between the world of thought and the world
of reality. There will be one world, and the peace of the golden age
will make itself known for the first time in the harmonious union of
all sciences. . . . Perhaps he will yet come who is to sing the great
heroic poem, comprehending in spirit what was, what is, what will
be, the kind of poem attributed to the seers of yore."[31]

Balzac and Gautier: Toward a Modernist Poetics

It is with a similar ideal of art and poetry that Balzac and Gautier
associate the androgyne. The significance of this figure for each
author is related to a poetics or a theory of fiction defined in polem-
ical and idealizing terms. The principle of "unité de composition"
was fundamental to Balzac's concept of art long before he publicized
and explained it in the *Avant Propos* to the *Comédie humaine* of
1842. A principle of creativity, it links artist to God, sees the work of
art as governed by the same laws according to which God created the
universe. A principle of reception or readership, it offers those who
are gifted and know the laws (the *Princes d'Art* as they are called in
Séraphîta) the possibility of penetrating to the source, and of seeing,
in each moment of the text, the reflection not only of the whole
oeuvre of the author but also of the divine text.

Less concerned with truth than with beauty, Gautier displays an aesthetic attitude that spurns his social milieu. In his prefaces, he describes the ideal artwork as complete in itself and achieved only through a disinterested attention to the beautiful, independent from concerns of morality, progress, and society. Universal truth is reflected in a Kantian idea of "beauty without purpose" and in art that exists for its own sake, *l'art pour l'art*.

That both authors published works focusing on the image of the androgyne within a year of each other—*Séraphîta* was published in 1835, *Mademoiselle de Maupin* in 1834—attests to this figure's popularity even as it also says something about the transitional nature of this time period in general. What is evident in both Balzac and Gautier is the persistence of classical values, the need to hold on to certain objective notions of unity, harmony, and organicity as defining the work of art. At the same time these values are combined with a romantic insistence on the role of subjectivity and the individual consciousness in the creative function. Seen from this perspective, their artistic projects carry out tasks set forth in German idealist philosophies but with significant differences. On the one hand, they put far greater emphasis on the place of the particular, whether in terms of historical situation, as in Balzac, or in terms of the object's concrete sensuality, as in Gautier. In this respect then, their work parallels Hegel's effort to break out of the Kantian entrapment in a subjective and an ahistorical framework.

Of course, Balzac and Gautier consider themselves to be artists first, not theoreticians. Their aesthetic theories are found in journals read by other artists (whether poets, painters, or writers) or, most often, in prefaces to the fictional writing that such theories serve, a point often overlooked in the case of the Preface to *Mademoiselle de Maupin*. It is difficult to distinguish the artist's voice from the voice of the critic-theorist in these prefaces, because in making claims for art, he is making claims for his own work and putting himself as artist under scrutiny. An ironic distance is discernible, similar to the ironic voice(s) heard in the narratives that follow. As a figure for the ideal text, the androgyne participates in this irony, accentuating authorial self-consciousness with a sex consciousness related to the historical situations of these two authors.

The popularity of the androgyne for artists during the 1830s in

France indicates that the political and religious malaise of the period is also an aesthetic malaise; and just as one could consider the divine right of kings to be ironized by the reign of a bourgeois monarch, so art's truth or beauty is ironically represented in this semireal, semimythical figure. Irony itself, that with which Ballanche associates man's fallen language, is veiled, but is integral to the androgyne who simultaneously stands for those universal ideals and obscures them with the markings of particular desire.[32] Under the July Monarchy writers were increasingly aware of their changing role in society, and their works incorporated a good deal of criticism against it, specifically in the form of criticism against the bourgeois. Yet, to the extent that the writer depended on this bourgeois and especially on the bourgeoise as readers, such criticism also developed into a self-critical and self-referential questioning of his craft.[33] A double movement is thus evident, to prove the writer's distinctness from his society but also his ability to speak for his reader, to share his or her language and desires—a task of new measure in the 1830s, given the explosion of readership. Frequent allusions to the artist's proximity to the divine text or to a reality verified in positivist terms are conspicuous evidence of the writer's need to valorize or authorize his fictions for his reader. The desire to speak for both self and other, artist and bourgeois, man and woman, and to join these perceived poles into an androgynous language of full communication is undercut by the fear that his discourse might just as easily alienate the other—the bourgeois, the woman—or might prove the limitations of his knowledge of that other and, for that matter, of himself.

Thus the androgyne is associated in the texts of Balzac and Gautier with a desire for a certain degree zero writing, innocent of any markings of class or sex, transparent to truth and beauty. Characterized by metaphors of radiant light and crystalline purity borrowed from mysticism and alchemy, the androgyne inhabits worlds or texts that, like *Séraphîta* and *Mademoiselle de Maupin* seem to turn away from the growing impulse toward realism, as if the visible real world were mere veil of the more profound and more romantic ideals of truth and beauty. But what is always apparent also in this figure is the already marked ideals it represents, and which must, consequently, be veiled. A figure of absolutes, the androgyne is also a figure of inconsistency. It expresses the duplicitous nature of the language and narratives with which we conceive and express absolutes.

This figure's ambivalence is most apparent in its fictional contexts. Image of the ideal text and referred to as a creation or a masterpiece, s/he is also a figure of textuality. As the figure projects an ideal of unity and wholeness, its narrative representation inevitably undermines the arrival at that ideal and remains fragmented and incomplete. We might venture to say that the androgyne performs a continuing act of deconstruction on the text itself, destabilizing at all levels the center and boundaries of identity and presence. Like the symbol of the Ouraboros, the circular serpent eating its tail that in hermetic philosophy symbolized a cosmic process of androgynation, we see that beneath the appearance of an "independent, absolute and self-sufficient organism," the androgyne reveals itself and its text to be a creature of unrest and of necessary incompletion.[34]

Surrounding this figure is a question of origins, origins of man, of his creativity, and, in particular, of language. The latter had been a heated issue during the eighteenth century, with the growing interest in philology and language's role in the progress of civilization. By considering language in secular and purely linguistic terms, the new philology posed a threat to religion, resulting in reactionary measures under Napoleon.[35] Such skeptical and revolutionary thought was effectively repressed for fear of its dangerous repercussions on the social and political order of things.[36] At this point, moreover, the shifting political situation left room for those issues to resurface, if in a less philosophical, less systematic, and more subtle fashion. Sidestepping the more positivist methods of philology and the metaphysical underpinnings of philosophy (but indirectly implicating them), much of the literature of this time betrays a skeptical attitude toward language itself and toward what and how language represents.

In the texts of Balzac and Gautier, language's origin and function is questioned through a complex relationship between words (or writing) and clothes as they pertain to the central figure of the androgyne. Valorization for this thematic, furthermore, can be found in the Bible and in traditional notions of the fall. We saw in Ballanche, that the fall of the androgyne into sexuality also constitutes a fall in language. With consciousness, a division occurred between subject and object, and man became conscious of a separation within himself at the moment he became conscious of (and desirous of) the other (the other half of the former androgynous whole). Thus, consciousness brought the need for a medium of communication. As we see in Genesis, it also created the need for clothing. "And the eyes of them were opened, and they knew that they were naked; and they sewed fig leaves together, and made themselves aprons" (Genesis 3:7). Indeed, God's clothing of Adam and Eve is simultaneous with Adam's naming of Eve. "And Adam called his wife's name Eve; because she was the mother of all living. Unto Adam also and to his wife did the Lord God make them coats of skins, and clothed them" (20:21).

The covering of the body is a symbolic manifestation of the covering of ideas with words. Words act upon ideas as clothes act upon the body—they restrict, they mask, but they also reveal. That is to say, there is a strict system of propriety, of codes, which determines the rules both of clothing and of language. The moral imperative invested in this system is set forth in Deuteronomy, where the first rule is about gender distinction. "The woman shall not wear that which pertaineth unto a man, neither shall a man put on a woman's garment: for all that do so are an abomination unto the Lord thy God" (22:5). These habits of the first garden are not so different from those of what Philippe Perrot calls the nineteenth century's "Garden of Fashion" where "a sexual dimorphism . . . imposed itself as never before."[37] Drawing on Veblen's theories of the leisure class, Perrot points out that this polarization of men's and women's wardrobe was exacerbated with the growing prominence of the bourgeoisie around 1830. Women became the "sign" of all that the man's gray suit could no longer show. "Henceforth, what man is no longer—bedecked and coquettish—woman becomes doubly. A new role is assigned to her: from now on displaying the luxurious dress of the Ancien Régime, she alone is to illustrate by proxy and by means of this wealth, the glory of the father, the husband, the lover, his social status and his financial power." Serving to preserve otherwise fading distinctions of class, her "deviant" costumes, as Perrot calls them, served also to reinforce a diminishing sexual distinction—since they deviated only from the masculine norm. Tocqueville's paradox that Perrot recalls, "to the decrease in concrete disparities corresponds an unleashing of the desire to distinguish oneself from the other," is as true with regard to sex as to class.[38]

Susan Brownmiller has commented on the reason for God's attention to dress. "Naked as He created them, Adam and Eve could not be mistaken. Dressed in fig leaves and animal skins after they came to know shame, their gender differences were partially obscured. A sex-distinctive dress code (a loin cloth for Adam, a sarong for Eve; a striped tie for Adam, a pair of high heels for Eve) created an emblematic polarity that satisfied a societal need for un-ambiguous division, neat categories and stable order."[39] Brownmiller's reasoning supports Michel Foucault's demonstration that modern Western societies show a "persistent" if not a "stubborn" need for a "true" sex. Sex is linked in discourse, he writes, to "the revelation of truth, the overturning of global laws, the proclamation of a new day to come, and the promise of a certain felicity."[40] With regard to the discourse on sex and the search for the truth, the androgyne must be considered as both catalyst and obstacle. In the narratives we will consider, s/he inspires a "will to truth" about the central character's sexual identity, and expectations of a narrative structure that will develop progressively from falsehood to truth and from ambiguity to clarity with regard to his/her (sexual) identity. In each case, however, we find that at the end of our narrative journeys with their surprise turns and perorations, identity is both proffered and revoked, not because the character's truth is a higher one, beyond sex, although this is what Balzac tells his reader to believe. The very notion of a prior and original truth and the neat divisions and stable order derived from the "history of sexuality," appear to be unfounded. Thus, in these fictions we can also discern a resisting discourse and resisting narrative structure that derives from what Foucault would call a "stubborn will to non-knowledge."[41]

In terms of clothing, then, the problem posed by the androgyne is not that his/her true appearance can only exist in a realm without veils, beyond the divisions between high heels and ties, but that whatever s/he does wear now, even if it is nudity, defines his/her identity as something s/he was not before. Conventional codes lose all legibility. On one level this often playful thematics of clothing amounts to no more than an act of mild protest against social convention. On a second level, the attempt to reveal the origin of language by metaphorically trying to undress the androgyne and unveil his/her true sexual identity paradoxically uncovers the metaphoric or veiled nature of all language. Thus the impulse toward revealing a full and totalized meaning of truth and beauty is thwarted by the narrative means to that end. Concern for ultimate referents slips to unending concern for the signifying process. The ideals of wholeness and self-completion associated with the androgyne are upheld, but also give way to a more modernist, hermaphroditic aesthetic of unstable meaning and fragmented identity.

While both Séraphîta and Maupin share an ideal status, the ways each figure betrays or undermines that ideal expose significant weaknesses in the author's ideological systems. Thus, for Balzac, language or the sign is not simply transparent or "representational" as bourgeois ideology and theories of realism would have it. Its fragmented or plural nature is apparent in moments of his work that are at once troubling and exciting in their self-conscious awareness. For Gautier signification is also troubling, but in a different way: not because of the sign's opacity, but rather because of its status as something borrowed, worn, and never wholly one's own. In Gautier, language and art unsettle the boundaries between self and other, artist and the masses, that they are created to secure—a matter that is most obvious in the shifting ground between male and female.

The status of woman in these texts constitutes a threat to the "feminine" and androgynous ideals alike. Resistant to her prescribed role, s/he is paradigmatic of the writing process and its constant doing, undoing, and redoing. The alternation between woman and androgyne reveals the false symmetry upon which poetic notions of wholeness have been constituted. The whole, writes Irigaray, is always "circumscribed and determined in and by *his* discourse."[42] As a result the androgyne challenges the Platonic and patriarchal tradition in which s/he is inscribed as ideal, by revealing an otherness that that tradition's discourse must exclude or repress. We shall examine both the ideal and the challenge in the next two chapters.

4

Balzac's Androgyne:
Ideal Sex, Ideal Text

BALZAC'S *Comédie humaine* is filled with characters described as having various mixtures of masculine and feminine traits. There is, however, only one androgyne, Séraphîtüs/a. This uniqueness is significant and essential to the thematic structure of the grand work that Balzac outlines in his many prefaces. In his Avant Propos to the *Comedie humaine* (1842) for example, he explains the theory of synthetic unity that is said to govern biological life: "There is only one animal. . . . The animal is a principle that takes its exterior form, or to be more exact, the differences of its form, in the milieus where it is called upon to develop."[1] Séraphîtüs/a is that formal idea, that one animal from which the other creatures who people the *Comédie humaine* are derived. S/he is a figure of origins, of Man before his separation from self or from God. S/he also, as we shall see, embodies the ideal of an original, unmediated poetry, one that precedes the linguistic differences that humans have to contend with. S/he is the eternal hymn itself, expressed "neither with words, nor with looks, nor with gestures, nor by any of the signs that men use to communicate their thoughts, but as the soul speaks to itself" (*Sér*, 7:607).

The uniqueness of the androgyne is also related to the fact that for Balzac, virtue itself has only one form. "Virtue is absolute," he writes in the Preface to *Père Goriot,* "it is one and indivisible, as was the republic, while vice is multiform" (*PG*, 2:611). The androgynous seraph is one of Balzac's most virtuous, indeed, most ideal characters, and the novel named for him/her Balzac conceived as his most ideal, or so he indicates in a letter of November 1833: "Sunday I was at

Bra's, the sculptor, there I saw the most beautiful masterpiece ever to exist. . . . It is 'Marie holding the Christ Child adored by two angels.' . . . There I conceived of the most beautiful book . . . a small volume for which *Louis Lambert* would be the preface, a work entitled *Séraphîta*. Séraphîta would be the two natures in one like Fragoletta, with the difference that I see this creature as an angel that has arrived at its last transformation and breaking through its envelope to ascend to heaven."[2] In this creature both male and female, Balzac has created an image of ideal love, of love that, as it transcends linguistic difference, also transcends sexual difference, thereby leading to the noncarnal love of God. Séraphîta, consequently, is not only a figure of origins but a figure of ends.

The idealism of this novel did not pass unnoticed among Balzac's contemporaries. Théophile Gautier was one of the first to praise *Séraphîta* as his most beautiful and poetic work: "Never has Balzac come nearer, never will he be nearer ideal beauty than in this book: the ascension on the mountain has something ethereal, something supernatural, something luminous that lifts you from the earth."[3] More recently the idealism of the novel has led some critics to see it as a separate work, outside the oeuvre of the man known to most as the father of French realism.[4] In this text of 1835, which, along with *Les Proscrits* (The Exiles) (1831) and *Louis Lambert* (1832), made up the *Livre mystique,* the focus shifts away from the social intrigues and details of contemporary life that preoccupied his *Scènes de la vie privée* and shorter *Etudes philosophiques,* in order to express and expose the "religious thought that is cast as the soul of the work" (Preface to *LM,* 7:606). The narrative concern is not realist representation but, rather, the apprehension and translation of divine truth. "It will be the book for those souls who like to lose themselves in infinite images."[5] Balzac's declared intent is to write an idealist work, if not the most ideal of idealist novels—where idealism verges on the fantastic and also the horrific. The aesthetic and moral criteria for the manifestation of the ideal in art, established by Hippolyte Taine toward the end of the century, are evident in the extreme in *Séraphîta.* The title character, said to be the very soul and essence of humanity, is a universal type. S/he is also a clear manifestation of moral goodness—his/her desires directed only to God and the spiritual world.[6]

Why Balzac should conceive of this idealist novel in 1833 and

why that novel should focus on the androgyne are complicated questions I don't intend fully to answer, but to ask them together brings us
to the gendering of aesthetic categories in the nineteenth century and
the sexual politics behind them. It was only one year earlier, in 1832,
that George Sand published *Indiana,* the novel in which, according to
Naomi Schor, her distinctive idealist mode emerged "from the matrix
of Balzacian realism." According to Sand, moreover, she and Balzac had conversations regarding their diverse poetics, conversations
in which Balzac labeled Sand's approach as specifically "woman's
work." ... "You seek man as he should be; I take him as he is. Believe
me, we are both right. Our paths meet in the end. I love exceptional
people too; I *am* one. Besides, I need them—to set off my vulgar
people—and I never sacrifice them needlessly. But these vulgar people interest me more than they do you. I magnify and idealize them in
reverse, in their ugliness or folly. I give their deformities frightening
or grotesque proportions. That you could never do, and you do well
not to gaze too closely on the beings who give you nightmares. Idealize only toward the lovely and the beautiful: that is woman's work."[7]
If Balzac regarded such idealization toward the beautiful as what
women do, he also took that work upon himself in *Séraphîta*. Séraphîta's androgyny, we may conclude, like his/her frightening beauty,
is a commentary on the gendering of genre, and the novel's mixture of
genres is a reflection of Balzac's "exceptional" ability to master both
men's and women's work.[8]

In his many prefaces, Balzac addresses in clear, but often contradictory, terms such questions regarding the writer's task. On the one
hand, Balzac claims in his Avant Propos of 1842 to be no more than a
"secretary" who merely records the events society displays before
him. Similar realist claims are made in the Preface to the *Livre
mystique,* where he writes that as author he must absent himself so as
to remain faithful to the object(s) he represents: "Please note, I ask of
you, that the author has nowhere spoken in his own name: he sees
something and describes it, he finds a feeling and translates it. ... In
this work each will be what he is" (7:606).

Against the objective demands of the realist, we find appeals for
the symbolic and transcendent aims of the idealist, especially in a
series of articles entitled "Des Artistes," published in *La Silhouette* in
1830. "For artists, in short," he writes, "the world outside is noth-

ing." Indeed, the tenor of those articles resounds with romantic idealism in which the artist is praised, not for his replication of observed experience, but for his revelation of other worlds and abstractions of universal truths. For Balzac, the artist is caught between two realms that he must bridge and unite: "He walks with his head in the clouds, his feet on the ground."[9] This is also the way he describes his ethereal book, *Séraphîta,* whose feet, he apologetically tells his reader, have been placed "in the mud of the globe" (*LM*, 7:608).[10]

The sexual politics of aesthetics and the importance of mastering the idealist genre was made clear to Balzac in a letter he received in February of 1832, sent by a woman who signed her name only as *L'Etrangère*—the stranger. Linking representational modes to the representation of women, this avid reader of Balzac admitted her dislike for the new turn his work was taking and asked the author to "give up the ironic or skeptical portraits whose point of departure is the debasing of woman or the negation of the noble and pure role that belongs to her once she understands the mission that heaven has asked her to fulfill here on earth."[11] Reminding Balzac of the desires of his female readership, the letter also marked the beginning of a long-distance love affair that lasted eighteen years, ending in his marriage to Madame Eveline Hanska (the aristocratic name the correspondent eventually revealed to him), five months before his death. In many ways this Polish countess was to become Balzac's ideal reader and judge. *Séraphîta* is dedicated to her, and the books' divinely inspired and "feminine" nature—indicated by the use of the feminine form in the title—is Balzac's answer to her request. But the androgynous nature of the book and the title character also suggests that the way to move beyond irony would be to transcend the physical world and in so doing to move beyond sexual difference.

This effort is already in evidence in *Louis Lambert, Séraphîta*'s "preface," as Balzac calls it, especially in its attempt to reconcile "internal" and "external" man (*l'homme intérieur* and *l'homme extérieur,* as they are referred to in both works), terms Balzac attributes to Swedenborg (*Sér*, 7:341). As in *Séraphîta,* in this work the finite discourses of science and philosophy, identified as masculine, are juxtaposed with the infinite languages of faith and the imagination, identified as feminine, in the effort to transcend their difference. Louis's double nature, however, results in schizophrenia. The reiteration of that doubleness in the relationship between Louis and his inseparable narrator-friend manifests a process of narrative self-criticism and self-irony that, reminiscent of Diderot's *Neveu de Rameau,* leaves no room for resolution. As preface to *Séraphîta, Louis Lambert* enacts a state of self-separation whose reparation is attendant upon that final work. Hence, in *Séraphîta,* that ironic structure dissolves into a narrative mode that is both allegorical and symbolic; a mode that acknowledges a disjuncture between the temporal world of the flesh and the world of the spirit but also envisions its resolution in the projection of an absolute self or transcendent hero. Séraphîta appears to be that poetic figure Baudelaire dream of in "De l'Essence du rire" (On the essence of laughter) and who according to de Man exists "beyond the realm of irony."[12] "If in these ultracivilized nations," Baudelaire writes, "one intelligence, driven by a superior ambition, wants to cross the limits of human pride, and boldly thrust himself toward pure poetry, in that poetry, limpid and profound like nature, laughter will be lacking, like in the soul of the Sage." If this is indeed Séraphîta's role, then the progression from *Louis Lambert* to that novel reiterates the "regression of critical insight" that de Man sees in the transition from an eighteenth-century ironic novel in the Schlegelian sense, to nineteenth-century realism's "leap out of language into faith."[13]

Séraphîta, as I have stated, is not a realist novel, or rather it is a strange combination of realist and idealist modes and of narrative and philosophical investigation. This androgynous, or more appropriately (as we shall see), hermaphroditic combination, I suggest, is Balzac's means of simultaneously giving in to the beautiful illusions of a mystical faith, while maintaining his distance from it—the same ironic distance he maintained from the woman who inspired it. The irony, here, or perhaps, as I discussed in chapter 2, the irony of irony, remembering his conversation with Sand, is that more than any of his previous works, *Séraphîta* will give him nightmares. Here, Balzac's mastery is most in jeopardy: "It's a work whose making is crushing and terrible—I have spent, I spend, day and night at it. I do, I undo, I redo, but in a few days all will be said: either I will have grown, or the Parisians won't understand."[14] What is most apparent in this "ideal" work is Balzac's struggle with the faith that underlies both realist and idealist modes—his faith in representation.

The image of a fusion or marriage of male and female as a

representation of unmediated expression is not unique to Balzac. It is as much a constant for the mystical tradition to which he refers in his prefaces as it is for romantic fiction.[15] Yet, any reader of the *Comédie humaine* with its plethora of torturesome marriages and instances of failed communication between men and women knows that the fusion of male and female differences is, at best, a fleeting dream. The androgyne too, emerges as an ambivalent figure, indicating more than a skeptical attitude toward love on the part of the author. It is symptomatic of a more profound and pervasive skepticism toward the very possibility of universal ideals—especially those shared between lines of class and sex—and their representation in art.

Between Mysticism and the Marketplace

There is another way to understand Balzac's attraction to idealism in the novel, and more specifically to mysticism, the tradition that inspired his androgynous creation. *Séraphîta* is the third of the trilogy of novels making up the *Livre mystique*. Here Balzac sets out to "plunge into the infinite chasms opened by the Mystics," and to introduce the French to this religious system that is no more than "the pure principle of Christianity" (*LM*, 7:607). In this trilogy and particularly in its third part, Balzac attempts to reaffirm certain Platonic ideals of Love, Beauty, and Truth for a materialist society overcome with doubt, a society that saw art only as a commodity and denied the artist any transcendent function. Hovering like Hermes between heaven and hell, interpreting the word of God like Moses, Séraphîta is the figure of the artist who can negotiate two worlds, while affirming the divine source of creation.

One of the more disturbing realities for the nineteenth-century artist was the increasing tendency and necessity to quantify art in terms of monetary return. Balzac saw his own works relegated to the status of commodities, as publishers described him as a "frivolous storyteller" or an "entertainer."[16] In press articles from 1830 to 1841, furthermore, Balzac acted as the chief spokesman for writers' rights, responding to the confusing question of literary property and asking for the protection of ownership for this new public commodity. Thus, in contrast to his claims that "all is God-given" and that the writer merely imposes a form on a preexistent idea, he was forced to deal with consumer issues of writing and to propose a value for the text that is not transcendent but negotiable: "Let's talk capital, then, let's talk money! Let's materialize, quantify thought in this century that prides itself on being the century of positive ideas." Forced to deal in two separate spheres, that of the marketplace (the new agon where men proved their worth) and the spiritual and increasingly feminine world of emotions and ideas—intelligence being, Balzac writes, "a woman taller than the count of Tours was big"[17]—the artist is thus androgyne as well.

Inspired by Bra and the writings of the mystics, *Séraphîta* was conceived in opposition to the marketplace of reading. But even s/he, the book and the character, whose divine countenance is purported to break through his/her carnal and linguistic envelope, is finally to be accounted for as "a thing" with exchange value. "Here it is this thing" (*ce quelque chose*) (*Sér,* 7:326) he writes in the dedication of *Séraphîta,* and in the Preface to the trilogy he admits to having tried to "make it [Séraphîta] attractive like a modern novel" and to having deliberately placed his/her feet in the mud to boost the work's popularity" (*LM,* 7:608) and attract more readers.

The aims of the *Livre mystique* are thus in conflict with what Balzac understands to be the status of literature in the nineteenth century. But this is not only because of a "materiality" imposed from outside. Balzac is increasingly aware of a materiality inherent to his own language, obscuring its transcendental aims with problems of communication between text and reader. "At a time when literature courts the masses," he realized that it is not possible to write only for "a few faithfuls," but neither could he count on the masses to share his ideals and desires.[18] Why, he thus deplores in the book's dedication, "couldn't this work belong exclusively to those noble minds who . . . are protected from the pettiness of the world by solitude? they would know how to inscribe the melodious measure that is missing." (*LM,* 7:326). Throughout the *Livre mystique* and particularly in its first volume, *Les Proscrits,* where Dr. Siger and the stranger alone understand each other, mysticism is thematized as a language of initiates that is incomprehensible to everyone else. Similar to Hegel's skeptical attitude to the *schöne Seele* discussed in chapter 2, however, Balzac is critical of this language that prefers romantic solipsism to "embodiment" and to engagement in the marketplace of ideas. "What mysticism has lacked up to the present is form, poetry" (*LM,* 7:607). This is the mission he undertakes in *Séraphîta*—to "incarnate . . . the most incomprehensible doctrine," to give it "a head, a heart, bones" (Preface to *LM,* 7:608). And in so doing, he asks forgiveness. To make such a language understandable for the masses is to attempt to translate the infinite into the finite, to debase the poetry of the spirit and distort its truths (we may recall Schlegel's warnings about binding the spirit in the letter).[19] "If you could imagine the thousands of propositions that give birth to each other in Swedenborg like waves; if you could figure the endless lands that these authors present; if you would compare the mind trying to put that ocean of furious sentences in the limits of logic to the eye trying to perceive a light in the shadows, you would appreciate the authors' efforts to give a body to that doctrine and to put it within reach of French thoughtlessness" (*LM,* 7:607).

Séraphîta is exemplary of the nineteenth-century novel's effort to "secularize—and thus revivify—the "spiritual," for a materialist age.[20] Balzac's use of a symbol of ideal (heterosexual) love is analogous to Saint-Simonian and Fourierist attempts to revitalize Christianity with images of an androgynous god. But his faith that "the pleasures of love are only a means to arrive at that union, that fusion of souls," or that, once incarnated, angels would be able to "lift us on their white wings to that sphere where . . . pleasures are thoughts," which is to say his faith in the respiritualization of love and word following its embodiment is open to question.[21]

In 1832, Balzac published a letter to Charles Nodier responding to his article "On Human Palingenesis and the Resurrection," in which Nodier praised the beauty and significance of mystical truths for the Christian world. In the letter Balzac displays his own ambiguity toward the mystical tradition as he criticizes Nodier and the mystics for their otherworldly focus. "In the name of the ravishing things of which you are one of the most passionate admirers, in the name of visible flowers, pretty insects, the thousand elegant masterpieces of botany and zoology," he tries to redirect Nodier's attention to the beauties of this world. He addresses Nodier's notion of the double nature, recalling Swedenborg's "interior" and "exterior" man," but translates it into more common psychological terms: "So Buffon's 'homo duplex' will be the point of departure or the common end of a thousand related observations about the possible separation of the two natures, the two actions, of word and act, of the interior and exterior man, forever coupled, forever separated within us."[22] Such considerations of incessant separation and coupling of selves reverberates with both the eroticism and the unstable temporality we saw in Schlegel's *Lucinde*.

From the beginning of the letter, Balzac's skepticism is tied to the possibilities of misreading. Wondering whether Nodier's enthusiasm might be ironic, he guards himself against being duped by it in the same way that he was taken in by Swedenborg and Saint-Martin: "To certain persons, your article would seem to be nothing but a fantastic mockery in which you, a second Mathanasias, freely spent the treasures of your profound erudition, amusing yourself with embroidering a mean edge of delicately worked and colored flowers, a fairy's trick, a delicious dream of a poet seeing brown cows in his cinders, and laughing at his illusions at the moment that others begin to participate in them."[23] Calling attention to the poetic qualities of mystical language, Balzac reveals part of his attraction to, and mistrust of, the mystics. The seductive power and apparent logic of this language lies in its affective nature, in the talismanic charm of its words and images that overpower without explaining.[24] One can read a thousand pages by any one of its writers, he says in the Preface, without getting a thing. Yet, it is "grandiose poetry." Mystics seem able to "name something unnamed," to define the undefined and perhaps indefinable. Skeptical of Nodier's language, Balzac admits, in closing, his own vulnerability to it. "Couldn't you now victoriously dissolve my doubts and, maybe, convince me of ignorance? . . . Accept the good memories of a traveler who can't cover the same territory as you have without admiring the poetry you have sown there.[25]

For Balzac, the mystical tradition is paradigmatic of a textual enterprise whose success is derived from what Martin Kanes defines as the "word event." Words function, "not as a means of self-discovery," but as a "source of external power"—weapons used by Balzacian characters and narrators alike.[26] Already in *Les Proscrits*, metaphors of weaponry describe the power Dr. Siger derives from his citation of the Scriptures. Similarly, the Preface to the *Livre mystique* describes the sacred language of the mystics with metaphors of a light that blinds rather than illuminates. The power of such language is to create a following, to inspire faith in a worldview—like the sign that created the Catholic religion instead of revealing it. "When Saint-Pierre showed the keys of Paradise and the baby Jesus in a virgin's arms, the crowd understood and the Catholic religion was brought into existence" (*LM,* 7:607).

Such word power has more immediate and practical use than one might first suspect, given the rise of an immensely varied reading public whose learning and vocabulary could not be taken for granted. As "mysticism taken as true, personified," the double nature of the androgyne projects the ideal meeting ground of author and reader, but only insofar as s/he annuls the transcendent origins of meaning. As mysticism "personified," Séraphîta is the Word made flesh, but only insofar as s/he makes clear the very fleshiness of words: "the most incomprehensible doctrine . . . has a head, a heart, bones" (*LM,* 7:608). Indeed, even before readership can be considered, this incarnation turns against his/her creator to daunt his optimism with the reflection of his own linguistic and semantic uncertainties. "The conception of this thundering *Séraphîta* has worn me out. . . . For two days she has whipped me."[27] Like the "word-event," *Séraphîta* may act as a weapon, but Balzac cannot determine who is the assailant and who the victim.

The problematic nature of this text becomes most evident in the correspondence between Balzac and the Contessa Eveline Hanska. *Séraphîta* was inspired by her, he says, written for the most part by her side, and dedicated to her in anticipation of a return that, if not monetary, cannot be said either to partake simply of the spiritual "purity" projected in the text. Balzac's efforts to move beyond such a personal and even sexual object of desire to the universal and spiritual depiction of love (of God, Truth, . . .) is evident in the allegorical and utopian mode of the novel. Indeed, the particular and timely attraction this aristocratic and wealthy woman must have had for the aspiring author is absent. And yet the rhetorical fabric of the text implicates the novel in the very physical and material forces that the androgynous seraph is intended to resist. Even the dedication to Mme. Hanska focuses on the ambiguities between that "figure dreamed of by you as by me since childhood" and this "thing" whose physicality impedes transcendence.

The relationship between Balzac and *L'Etrangère,* a pious woman and devoted follower of the mystics, also sheds new light on Balzac's attraction to mysticism. The mystic's language, which is at once exceedingly spiritual and highly erotic, provided a conveniently ambiguous means of courting this countess whom he called both "my angel" and "my soul," offering under the disguise of a divine and ineffable love what might, in reality, be an all-too-personal and therefore unspeakable desire. "My completely virile imagination, having never been prostituted or used up," he writes in a letter of March 1833, "is my enemy, is still made for a heart that is young, pure, and violent with repressed desires."[31] With her, that is, he finds a way at once to express and to veil his desires, if not to redirect them to his work. At times, he sees Eveline as his ideal reader—one like the stranger of *Les Proscrits,* who understands Dr. Siger because he already speaks his language even though it is incomprehensible to the rest of his audience. "Through love you have guessed the delicious language of love," he writes to her, and mortal men will be blind to it: "What you want becomes a quality of my soul. I need make no effort to do what you want.—What you want, I want. However, don't you feel the necessity of putting a veil on our love, a thick veil. What am I saying, who in the world could suspect its nature. Angels, because men!"[29] *Séraphîta* is the symbol of this love and a symbol of an ideal language between man and woman or author and reader. "Séraphîta is the two of us, let's spread our wings with one and the same movement"—or so he tried to persuade her. In fact, Balzac puts a great deal of effort into assuring Eva, if not seducing her into believing, that their desires are one and the same.[30] But Balzac could not always count on such agreement. Even as her first letter flattered him with the attention of a feminine readership that was becoming increasingly important to the publishing world, it also awakened him to the moral and ethical responsibilities that a portion of that readership demanded of the author and, consequently, to certain differences in their outlooks. The countess expressed her particular displeasure over the depiction of women in his most recent novel, *La Peau de chagrin* (*The wild ass's skin*), where the author forgot "the delicacy of feeling, the refined nuances" of the female characters in his previous works.[31] Such fear of her possible misunderstanding or dislike makes the writing process excruciating. She as well as the book that "belongs to her" become torturous for him, "tyrannical." "Finishing this work is killing and crushing me. I have a fever every day."[32] For his own health he is forced to put *Séraphîta* aside for weeks at a time, "abort" the birth as he says, a metaphor that alerts his readers to the gender struggles also at play.

Striving for a language of immediacy and fullness, Balzac is made aware that the distance between him and his beloved is more than geographical. "I wish you could be me for an instant to know how you are loved," he writes, and he tries to convince her that he can love "both as a woman loves and as a man loves." It is almost as if he must prove that he can love like a woman, or better yet, be one, in order to prove that he can know (and therefore represent) women and women's feelings. "Only artists are worthy of women because they are partly women". "Am I not a bit of a woman . . . ?" he asks when he describes how he shall offer the manuscript of *Séraphîta* to her, calling attention, furthermore, to the body of the book rather than its embodied message. Balzac imagines the manuscript lavishly swaddled in the cloth from a dress that Eva wore with him in Geneva. "The manuscript of *Séraphîta* . . . will be thickly bound with the gray cloth that slid so well across the floor. Am I not a bit of a woman, huh, my pet? haven't I found a lovely use for that which you wanted to destroy, and a memory. . . . Celestial book of love, covered in love and earthly pleasures as complete as it is possible to have here below."[33]

As Balzac's correspondence to Mme. Hanska adopts a mystical rhetoric focusing on the purifying and spiritual properties of love, so he appears to imagine a role for her like that he envisions for *Séraphîta*.[34] She is a creature of his imagination, someone he can love from a distance without having to test her reality. "I love you too much already without having seen you." The feminine form of the novel's title signals, moreover, a conflation of androgyne and eternal feminine like that in Boehme, revealing both images as veilings of a specifically male dream. Eva, that is to say, is the ideal and eternal feminine insofar as she fulfills Balzac's need, is, as he puts it, "the realization of that ambition of love. . . . Oh, my dear Eve, let me shorten your name, that way it will say better that you are the whole sex for me, the only woman in the world, you alone fulfill it, like the first woman for the first man." And again, "Eva, Eva of love, my beautiful and noble mistress, my kind, naive servant, my great sovereign, my fairy, my flower, yes you enlighten all! . . . Oh, your letters! they ravish me, they move me, what a soul, what a heart, what a dear mind, you complete all my ambitions, and I told Mme. de Benny yesterday that you were, you, 'the Unknown' of Geneva and Neuchâtel, the realization of the ambitious program that I had made for a woman." As the embodiment of all women, she can also act as a mirror, reflecting the woman he claims to harbor in himself, legitimating his artistic ambition to understand and represent women. "My one passion . . . has made me observe women, study, know and cherish them, without any other compensation than that of being understood at a distance by great and noble hearts." But this great and noble heart, this ideal woman, is his invention. "You are a more beautiful, kinder me," he writes, adding later, "You are really myself."[35] If, as Alice Jardine and others have shown, "the space 'outside of' the conscious subject has always connoted the feminine in the history of Western thought," the androgyne connotes the ultimate taming and appropriating of that space by and for the male subject.[36]

In his explanation of Balzac's attraction to the myth of the androgyne, Albert Béguin writes that "the myth of the Androgyne is only in appearance a negation of love, and it is contradictory to explain it by an ascetic wish, or worse yet, by a homosexual dream. Its profound significance—and what must have attracted Balzac's mind— . . . depends on that nostalgia for a return to the lost Unity that so many images of all times express."[37] While love is indeed central to this myth, I must take issue with Béguin. On the one hand, the particular kind of love involved, like the notion of lost unity, *is* dependent on a certain asceticism, one that the distance between Eva and Balzac supported. "Oh, you don't know what it is to have three years of chastity thrusting at any moment at your heart, making it jump, and at your head, making it throb! If I weren't sober and if I didn't work, this purity would drive me crazy."[38] The process of writing becomes a substitute for the object of desire, diverting sexual energies into the textual project. As a figure of unity, of a plenary language of love, the androgyne insists on the text as sublimated desire and the writing process as the work neither of divine inspiration nor of diligent and perceptive observation, but of a narcissistic and solipsistic enterprise.[39] One could say that it is, indeed, a ho(m)mosexual desire, a desire for the same, for the self-same.[40] "How, then can there be love, or pleasure of the other? Except by speaking to oneself about it? . . . Surrounding, adorning, engulfing, interpellating oneself with the Other, in order to speak oneself: the language of love. Speaking to oneself about it with the Other in discourse, in order to speak love to oneself."[41]

It is precisely the necessary solipsism of such a language, "the soul speaking to itself," that *Séraphîta* reveals. Knowing the rest of the Balzacian oeuvre—works like *Sarrasine,* which he had already written, and *La Fille aux yeux d'or* (The girl with the golden eyes), which he was writing simultaneously—one wonders what commitment he had to this figure who demanded an effacement of sex as of language. What attraction could the androgyne hold for the artist characterized by Gautier as "loving the woman of today and not a pale statue," whose life seemed dedicated to this world and to the writing of it? That Balzac's profession of chastity to Mme. Hanska was itself a lie is perhaps some indication of his sincerity.[42] Might the double nature be no more than a veil of duplicity in this most ideal of works?

A Disrupted Dream of Symmetry

In his commentary on *Séraphîta,* Hippolyte Taine recognized the loftiness of the novel's aspirations, but criticized it for its failure to live up to the expectations it aroused and for its ungainly mix of opposed forms of writing. "Here are the fairies and beliefs where his genius leads him. To express them, he abused the novel, like Shakespeare did drama, imposing on it more than it could bear. . . . Many tire of it and reject *Séraphîta* and *Louis Lambert* as dreams that are painful to read; they would like a less novelistic philosophy, or less philosophical novels. They find they are neither sufficiently instructed, nor sufficiently amused. They demand more interest or more proofs."[43]

Albert Béguin also says that *Séraphîta* failed to live up to Balzac's spiritual aspirations, but he sees this, paradoxically, as the mark of his greatness. "Balzac's greatness—as soon as one considers his work the mythic translation of his spiritual life and the answer to the needs of a religious soul—is in the exact faithfulness to his verified knowledge. His greatness is in his failure, just as his truth breaks through his errors."[44] Béguin sees failure thematized within the novel itself (in the failure of the young couple, Minna and Wilfred, to follow Séraphîta out of the material world), and thus as evidence of Balzac's awareness of the limits of his own spirituality and religious imagination.

Taking a cue from Béguin and Taine, I, too, find the "failure" of *Séraphîta* and the way the novel disappoints the reader to be significant, though for different reasons. In my view, it indicates a breakdown of the aesthetic ideals outlined in the Avant Propos of 1842 and in the Preface to the *Livre mystique* and thus of the ideals that we have seen to be projected in the central androgynous figure. From this perspective, moreover, the ungainly jumble of genres can be related to a disorder of gender—a breakdown in the "old dream of symmetry" between male and female in the very image of their symmetrical and harmonious fusion.[45]

Séraphîta suffers from an excessive "invasion of the story (*le récit*) by the telling (*le discours*)" that Gérard Genette calls attention to in much of *La Comédie humaine*.[46] At the center of the novel is a lengthy and tedious philosophical debate, which begins to overpower the *drame* and seems "on the verge of suffocating the events [it is] meant to explain." Where the *récit* begins to lose its "pertinence" to the work, explains Genette, what is at stake is the very shape and status of what is reputed to be the "traditional" novel.[47]

In *Séraphîta*, explanation—or better yet, interpretation—takes the place of event: each of the characters trying to explain how they see and understand the androgyne, just as Séraphîta/us explains to them how they are unable to understand or to read him/her. In this work, which was considered Balzac's most spiritual, moreover, it is not only the traditional novel that is at stake but the ontology of the work of art. Here the oppressive *discours* is not at the service of the *vraisemblable*, the representation of day-to-day life, but of the *vrai*, life in its original principle and in its relation to the absolutes of love, beauty, truth. Here, then, truth is upstaged by its telling, by its various interpretations and contradictory languages.[48] It is not the naked truth that the reader witnesses, but only the many veils of its representation that, as in the "unknown masterpiece," obscure and ultimately destroy what they are meant to represent.[49] What is at stake, consequently, is the possibility for that fusion and unity that the androgyne as symbol reflects, and, similarly, the possibility for a clear or exact expression (*l'expression nette*) that faithfully serves "thought" or "truth."

Séraphîta, text and character, confronts both reader and author with the blind spot in the androgynous dream, the way its sexual symmetry prioritizes a masculine perspective. Within the text, for example, the distinction between the explanatory *discours* and the narrative *récit* is associated with the distinction between masculine and feminine. The male role, represented by Dr. Becker or Wilfred, is to read, to theorize, and thereby, to penetrate to the source of truth: "His completely thorough studies of a point of science dig like a drill" (*Sér*, 7:329). The feminine role, on the contrary, is to spin yarns (ibid.), implying her fabrication of clothes as well as of tales: "Isn't it on that winged fairy that young girls should sail?" (*Sér*, 7:363). What Genette calls the "oppressive discourse" thus points also to a privileging of the masculine and of the interior—the source and logos—over feminine exteriority and the veils of truth. The opposition of masculine and feminine in Balzac's fiction becomes a purely rhetorical relation that conceals the more intimate relationship of male and female as weavers of textual fictions and woven figures within those fictions.

The dream of symmetry to which I alluded at the outset is the foundation for the paternal myth that pervades the *Comédie humaine*.[50] As an image of primordial man, man in his original and unruptured relation to poetry or the word, the androgyne is at the source of creation and of the trinity of Father-God-Artist that, as many critics have shown, Balzac calls upon to authorize his fictional universe. Christopher Prendergast explains the trinity as that of "the master of the house, the master of the universe, the master of the text—three roles which combine in Balzac's imagination to evoke an ideal of transcendent and omnipotent control. Above all they are different incarnations of the master of the word; the word of the father, the word of God, the word of the artist are so many forms of the dream of the paternal discourse, a discourse grasped not just as a social language of command and prohibition, but as source of nomination itself, origin of what is known and named as reality."[51] In naming the androgyne, Balzac realizes this dream and thereby names the origin of Man. The androgyne, in turn, in his/her attempts to return to that origin, and to overcome a "fallen" body and a fallen language, doubles for the authorial presence in the *Comédie humaine*. S/he provides a symbol for his aesthetic aims of unity and coherence and for his social and personal quest to depict a universal object of desire beyond differences of class and sex.

If the Balzacian oeuvre so emphatically stages the father, it also undermines his authority, and along with him the principles of authorship Balzac clings to so fervently.[52] It is in the context of this mythic paternal discourse that the "failures" of the androgynous dream of *Séraphîta* will become most significant. Already the title's feminine suffix disrupts the symmetry of the double nature, indicating that s/he is conceived not by a transcendent mind, but by a (hetero-)sexed (male) body, and in a language whose own sexual markings are only too apparent.

At first look, Séraphîta performs the androgyne's traditional function as both social and aesthetic symbol. S/he incarnates an image of "Man's" original, pristine state. Born in the mountains of Norway, beyond the borders of the European market and above the tree line, s/he is removed from the sullied air and the tainted practices of the social world. Having dropped the family title of baron, s/he is pure of the signs of social status. A creature, we are told, of irresistible beauty, his/her attractiveness goes beyond the merely physical. Indeed, we learn that his/her struggle to be free of the material world has all but freed him/her of a body and left in its place a brilliant and captivating luminescence, "a vivid flash, the only expression that could render the animation of his/her face, the appearance of his/her being" (*Sér,* 7:331).[53] S/he glows, not from the reflection of glittering gold that stimulates Parisian society, but from an "internal light," a "look of gold [that] rivalled the rays of the sun . . . (s/he) seemed not to receive but to give off light" (ibid.). No one has ever seen him/her nude, and s/he is said to be without any "exterior senses." "All interior" and "all intelligence," s/he is covered only by a wrap that "resembled a woman's robe as much as a man's coat" (*Sér,* 7:334), thus defying a sexed body underneath.

In fusing male and female, Séraphîta does not confuse the delineation between the sexes. There is, in other words, a clear separation between the feminine half—associated with the earth, physical grace, and devotion—and the masculine half, manifest in the mind's moral force and the visionary's (*voyant*) penetrating eye. The existence of male and female in the androgyne thus reflects, on the one hand, the *coincidentia oppositorum* or existence of opposed forces in nature— "Life, is it not the combat of two forces?" (*Sér*, 7:329), asks the narrator—and on the other hand, the necessary division of these forces in the social world. Thus Seraphîta's two lovers occupy two opposed realms. Minna's place is by the hearth, for she is "the most authentic model of the woman destined for earthly works" (*Sér*, 7:338) Wilfred, by contrast, has set out to conquer the world of the mind. His "nature aspired to the light," and since birth, "study increased his intelligence, meditation sharpened his thought, and the sciences expanded his understanding" (*Sér*, 7:350).

A similar opposition between Minna and her father reveals a comfortable and secure family structure. The pastor has his place at one end of the parlor, immersed in clouds of pipe smoke and the "fantastic whirlwind" of ideas written before him. "On the other side of the stove," unaware of his smoke that envelops her as well, Minna counts "the threads of her napkin or the stitches of her stocking." A fantasy brought to life, the narrator tells us that "many homes have the appearance of a dream, the occasional flash of pleasure seems to hide ruins beneath the cold smile of luxury; but this parlor was sublimely real, harmonious in color, and inspired patriarchal ideas of a complete and contemplative life (*Sér*, 7:338). In this parlor there is no mother and no room for the unnatural acts committed by the daughters of Goriot or Grandet.

As a creature incorporating two "natures," Séraphîta is also seen to partake of two worlds. S/he assumes "the aerial pose that sublime painters have always given to the Messengers from on high" (*Sér*, 7:336) and, like Hermes, acts as a medium of divine revelation—a guide to the higher spheres of the spirit. Rejecting the "too crude love" (*Sér*, 7:333) of both Minna and Wilfred, his/her function is to reveal to them a purer form of love and, in so doing, to lead them to God. His/her effect on those who come in contact with him/her is precisely to "transport" them to other worlds, to "superior worlds" (*Sér*, 7:369). Both Minna and Wilfred attest to the strange power Séraphîta exerts over them and the heretofore unknown worlds and feelings that s/he opens up, even though they are unable to relate the content of those experiences when they leave him/her. What they do describe, however, is no less than the Schillerian experience of the sublime, that perilous position at the edge of an abyss where opposing extremes and absolutes are simultaneously experienced, and from which Minna and Wilfred return shaken and bewildered.

Thus, unlike other Balzacian figures of purity and innocence who are steered into corrupt worlds and materialistic ways, Séraphîta is a triumphant character who leads people up a spiritual path. His/her symbolic significance works positively with his/her didactic role to reorient Wilfred's and Minna's attention to the values of Divine love and the life of the soul. While s/he appears for Minna as the ideal man and for Wilfred as the ideal woman, his/her self-sufficiency and wholeness is resistant to their efforts to appropriate him or her for their personal dreams—whether hers of marriage or his of conquering the world. Séraphîta teaches them a new language and guides them to follow the path toward their own initiation into the world where "all was one."[54] "Wilfred and Minna thus understood some of the mysterious words of Him who on earth had appeared to each in the form that would make him comprehensible, to the one Séraphîtüs, to the other Séraphîta, when they saw that there, all was homogeneous" (*Sér,* 7:373).

At this point we can see how Séraphîta's social function begins to merge with an aesthetic function to project the poetic ideal of an immediate and transparent language. As his/her gaze "penetrates" right to the thoughts and soul of the other characters, so s/he penetrates the veils of the material world that separate man from divine truth (*Sér,* 7:351). Unlike Dr. Becker, whose attempts at narration and explication are not only dependant upon the availability and accuracy of his texts and documents but are colored by the skeptical point of view he gets from his reading, Séraphîta's omniscience seems to be inherently guaranteed; its source is neither books nor learning, but an unmediated understanding of essences. " 'How have you had the time to learn so many things? said the young girl'. 'I remember,' s/he answered" (*Sér,* 7:332).

Séraphîta claims to possess the gift of "specialism," which s/he explains in an analogy to the creation and reception of works of art, if not to Balzac's own goals as artist.

Specialism constitutes a kind of internal vision that penetrates everything, and you will only understand its range by a comparison.
In the large cities of Europe out of which come works where the
human hand tries to represent the effects of moral as well as of
physical nature, there are sublime men who express their ideas
with marble. The sculptor works on the marble, shapes it, puts in
it a world of thoughts. There are marbles that the human hand
has endowed with the power to represent a whole sublime side or
a whole bad side of humanity; the majority of men see only a human figure and nothing more; others, a bit higher placed on the
ladder of being, perceive a part of the thoughts translated by the
sculptor, they admire the form; but the initiates into the secrets of
art are of one intelligence with the sculptor: by seeing his marble,
they recognize the whole world of his thoughts. These are the
princes of art, they carry within themselves a mirror where nature
reflects itself in all its accidents. Well, I have inside me such a mirror where moral nature reflects itself with its causes and effects. I
can guess the future and the past by thus penetrating through consciousness. (*Ser,* 7:351)[58]

If we substitute the writer for the sculptor in this passage, we see
that Séraphîta is both an image of the ideal text and an ideal reader,
"creation and creature." Consequently, his/her aesthetic function is
to teach Wilfred and Minna how to read in him/her, the Word of
God. As s/he establishes a connection between the "book of nature"
and the work of art, furthermore, his/her role can also be seen as one
of initiating the reader into the correct reading of the Balzacian text.
Like Diotima's ladder, the ladder of love is also a ladder of aesthetic
education. The readers of *Séraphîta* will be instructed by the readers
of Séraphîtüs/a how to read, how to join his/her successive ap-
pearances and his/her varied discourses into a whole and how to see
that whole as part of a larger unity from which it is derived. Here is,
then, a Platonic and Hegelian project of reading, much like that Gilles
Deleuze describes in Proust. "To observe each thing as a whole, then
to discover its law as part of a whole, which is itself present by its
Ideal in each of its parts—is this not the universal logos, that totalizing impulse we variously recognize in the conversation of friends, in
the analytic and rational truth of philosophers, in the methods of
scientists and scholars, in the concerted work of art of 'littérateurs,'
in the conventional symbolism of words themselves?"[59] To learn to

read *Séraphîta* is, in fact, to learn to read the whole of the *Comédie humaine*. We must learn to "complete" Balzac's work—so he asks of us in *Séraphîta*'s dedication—by returning to the original creative principle that allowed it to be born.

Reading the Intertext

Seasoned readers of Balzac may feel uneasy with the depiction of the androgyne and his/her triumphant purity and innocence. It is rare for any character in the *Comédie humaine* to remain unscathed by the constant threat of corruption, except by means of a melodramatic death or disappearance. Balzac himself points out and indulges his aesthetic preference for the depiction of vice over virtue in the second Preface to *Père Goriot* published the same year as *Séraphîta*. "Virtue only affords the brush strokes of an excessive tenuousness. Virtue is absolute, it is one and indivisible, like the republic was; while vice is multiform, multicolored, undulating, capricious" (*PG*, 2:611). Characters projecting Platonic ideals of love and beauty are not themselves anomalies in Balzac's work, but their triumph is. Most often there is a flip side to such virtue, and the idyllic nature becomes the very mark of corruption. Such beauty, that is to say, is discovered too late to be only another of vice's many masks.

Thus we do not find the optimism of *Séraphîta* in *Sarrasine* (1830), which treats a similar theme, or in *La Fille aux yeux d'or*, which Balzac worked on simultaneously with *Séraphîta*. While love and beauty appear to be the very medium of divine communication in *Séraphîta*, in those stories they are forces that make truth simultaneously unknowable and undesirable as they also subvert the principle of (sexual) opposition or antithesis on which the meaning of *Séraphîta* relies. Initiating us into a very different reading process, they also direct us to a different reading of *Séraphîta*.

In *Sarrasine* and *La Fille aux yeux d'or*, the mystical correspondences of the northern setting of *Séraphîta* are replaced by the more mysterious correspondences between two worlds of Paris—one physical, one moral—and the seraphic figure of perfect oneness, beauty, and purity is shown his and her counterpart in the social world of the city. The hero/ines of these stories, Zambinella and Paquita, are initially seen, like Séraphîta, as glorifications of wholeness as well as of beauty. "He admired in that moment the ideal beauty for whose perfections he had up until then searched for here and there in nature. . . . La Zambinella united for him, pulsating and delicate, those exquisite proportions of feminine nature so ardently desired" (*Sarr*, 4:270). "Since I have studied women, my unknown is the only one whose virgin breast, ardent and voluptuous forms have realized for me the only woman I have dreamed of! . . . She is the total woman, an abyss of pleasures where one rolls without ever reaching bottom" (*Fille*, 4:113).[57]

Just as Séraphîta is said to surpass any representation of him/her—"no known person would be able to give an image of that figure, majestically male for Minna, but who, in the eyes of a man, would eclipse the most beautiful heads we owe Raphael by his/her feminine grace" (*Sér*, 7:331)—so the transcendent beauty of these creations can find no corollary in the art world. "All the revered marvels of Venus and rendered by the Greeks chisel" (*Sarr*, 4:270) cannot come close to the beauty of Zambinella, and Paquita is similarly described as a "saintly poetry, prostituted by those who have copied her for frescoes and mosaics" (*Fille*, 4:113). A Platonic rhetoric joins the three beauties, Séraphîta, Zambinella, and Paquita together, as it attributes to each the status of original and divine essence. Metaphors of whiteness and light are the most numerous: complexions of luminous marble, eyes that reflect the light of "superior" spheres, Séraphîta's and Paquita's eyes of brilliant gold. With one glance, these "celestial flowers" (*Sér*, 7:351) exert an irresistible and sublime power over their observers, who behold them with awe and reverence.

Described as ideal works of art, Séraphîta, the "work of the heavens" (*Sér*, 7:348), Zambinella, the incarnation of ideal beauty (*Sarr*, 4:270), and Paquita, a "masterpiece" (*Fille*, 4:122), each contain a mystery to be solved by their admiring observers as well as by the reader. Our reading follows the characters' paths of discovery, and in each text similar questions are posed. "Who is she?" asks Wilfred, "Did you see her when she was young? Was she ever born? Did she have parents?" (*Ser*, 7:339). Sarrasine sees that he must do research, "to scheme, to ask where Zambinella lived, to know whether she had a mother, an uncle, a tutor, a family" (*Sarr*, 4:271). So, too, Paul, beneath his blasé exterior, yearns for the answers to the question of Paquita's identity and for the code that will enable him to "read in that page of such brilliant effect, to divine the hidden meaning" (*Fille*, 4:125).

Yet, while this hermeneutic code impels us onward to discovery, the direction taken in the two "Etudes" appears to be diametrically opposed to the "pathway to heaven" represented in *Séraphîta*. The latter, at least on one level, is a lesson in love and in the reading of signs through the soul's initiation and elevation into the world of spirit. In *Sarrasine* and in *La Fille aux yeux d'or*, however, our initiation is not into light and the world of the spirit, but rather into the social world of "gold and pleasure," which constitutes a very different reading experience from the *Livre mystique*. "There exists a horrible book, dirty, frightening, corrupting, always open, that one will never close, the grand book of the world, without counting the other book a thousand times more dangerous, that is made of everything that is whispered between men or women beneath their fans, in the evening at the ball" (*Fille*, 4:125).

Reading is an activity we share with the characters in the stories, themselves initiates into a new world of signs that are not easily decoded. Not so much instructed as seduced by this world, we, like they, become victims of illusions. When Sarrasine discovers that the woman of his dreams is not a woman at all, all of his ideals are shattered. Here love and beauty are not proffered but defiled. "It's neither my blood nor my life that I regret, but the future and the fortune of my heart. Your feeble hand has undone my happiness. What hope can I take from you for all those you have blackened. You have reduced me to your level. 'To love; to be loved' are henceforth meaningless words for me, as for you. I will forever think of that imaginary woman when I see a real woman" (*Sarr*, 4:275).

Commenting on Sarrasine as a reader, Barbara Johnson diagnoses his mistake as a failure to "reread" the text of La Zambinella with the result that he discovers only too late the discrepancy between her "real" identity as a castrato and the fiction he has imposed upon him/her. "What he devours so eagerly in La Zambinella is actually located in himself: a collection of sculpturesque clichés about feminine beauty and his own narcissism. In thinking that he knows where difference is located—between the sexes—he is blind to a difference that cannot be situated between, but only within."[58] La Zambinella is not the incarnation of ideal feminine beauty, but instead reveals beauty and sexuality to be "empty," cultural signs determined by clothes and artifice. Thus s/he warns Sarrasine and the reader against any totalization—either of the subject/self, or of art. Zambinella's "otherness," which deprives Sarrasine's sculpture of the "essence" of femininity, contaminates any notions of truth and representation, which art (and Balzacian art is here implicated) has fashioned for itself. The "progress" of civilization toward its future is here defined by successive fictional avatars: that is, from Zambinella, to the portrait by Vien, to Girodet's *Endymion,* to the painting of Adonis, to Sarrasine's sculpture, and, finally, to the narrator's story, an illusion of totalized meaning by which the reader too has been duped. "Symbolic plenitude," writes Barthes, "is the last avatar of our culture."[59] The story of *Sarrasine* foreshadows the erotic intrigue of *La Fille aux yeux d'or* at the moment the sculptor implores Zambinella to tell him whether s/he might not have a sister. The existence of a twin could right the confusion and save the purity of his love.[60] But while Sarrasine's hope is not answered, in the story of 1835 the sudden appearance of the sister is no saving grace nor even the occasion for a happy reunion. The event only further inculpates an already defiled love with implications of incest. *La Fille aux yeux d'or* groups characters in a fashion similar to the pairings in *Séraphîta.* The male and female protagonists, Henri and Margarita, are brought together through their love/desire for the same "ideal" creature known as Paquita. In this case, however, her eventual death (or transcendence) reveals to them not only their desire for each other but also their blood relation as siblings. What is crucial in this story, as Christopher Prendergast points out, "is not difference, but similarity, not division . . . but connection." The resemblances between the two lovers pointed out very early on by Henri's friend, parallel the resemblances between the couples of Henri and Paquita, Paul and Margarita, Margarita and Paquita, Henri and Margarita, and so on.[61] But such identities do not amount to the ultimate unity suggested in *Séraphîta.* Rather, by association, androgyny appears incestuous; Paquita's "double-love" is identified as the infernal and parodic inversion of Séraphîta's purified world.

The shifting triads among the four characters can in no way allow for the elevation that is projected in *Séraphîta.* Social codes forbid the incestuous union of brother and sister, as they also impose moral taboos on the homosexual and master-slave relationship between Paquita and Margarita. Geneviève Delattre writes that, "ideally, Henri and Margarita should represent the masculine and feminine sides of the same being, a sort of human Séraphîtüs, not yet united to Séraphîta. In reality, they are the inverse of the androgyne, the symbol of the division and not yet the unity of being."[62] It is curious to note that in stressing opposing concepts, one of division and one of similarity, Delattre and Prendergast nevertheless come to a similar reading of the relationship between Henri and Margarita as an inversion of the primal androgyne: "a being in two people." What we find in the story is an endless interchange of difference and similarity, difference within similarity, and similarity within difference, which not only inverts but subverts the very notion of androgynous unity. This is most apparent on the level of sexuality and sexual definition. "Seen in conjunction with other elements of the text, the implications of the recognition scene point towards a radical transgression of the sexual divide, a confusion of masculine and feminine which seems to reproduce the intuition of an ambivalence at the heart of nature itself, the contradictoriness of primordial sexuality before the differentiations imposed and demanded by culture; each both 'masculine' and 'feminine,' taken together Henri and Margarita symbolically duplicate the figure of the Androgyne."[63] What is significant is neither the similarity nor the difference between Margarita and Henri, but, as we saw too in *Sarrasine*, the polymorphous couplings of masculine and feminine present in both characters—the repressed contradictions of primordial sexuality that surface in their resemblance. This unstable and dynamic interrelation of masculine and feminine, as well as of social classes, undermines any accepted opposition of sex or of class as coherent and necessary. "No longer pointing to opposed '*proper* places,' but to successive *roles* in a triangular, dynamic spatial figure, to respectively opposed but interchangeable positions in a structure which subverts propriety and literality, the polarity of masculine and feminine itself becomes dynamic and reversible. However, the substitutions of woman for man and of man for woman, the interchangeability and the reversibility of masculine and feminine manifests a discord which subverts the limits and compromises the coherence of each of the two principles."[64]

Shoshana Felman, like Barthes and Johnson, identifies the characters in the story as readers (and misreaders) or interpreters of masculine and feminine and thus addresses the curious link between sexuality and rhetoric.[65] Henri, she points out, sees Paquita as "the total woman" and is blind to the masculine in her, blind to a part of her that is not his sexual opposite and therefore not sexually desirable. Paquita, on the other hand, having known only women, blinds herself to the masculine in Henri by dressing him to suit her lesbian fantasy. The reading of sexuality and of sexual desire here, as in *Sarrasine,* seems to be determined by clothing as the true language of the body. Felman concludes that *La Fille aux yeux d'or* "could be viewed as a rhetorical dramatization and a philosophical reflection on the constitutive relationship between transvestism and sexuality, i.e., on the constitutive relationship between sex roles and clothing." As in *Sarrasine,* where the body acts as a cultural sign (in Zambinella's case, designating the institution of created sopranos) that functions in a shifting and arbitrary relation to sex, so in *La Fille aux yeux d'or* the relation of clothing to sex is purely conventional, having no recourse to a "true" sexual identity. "Transvestism, in Balzac's story, links sexuality to rhetoric, and rhetoric to sexuality: *'Tu travestis les mots'* ('You disguise—you travesty—your words'), says Henri to his friend Paul de Manerville, unwittingly suggesting that transvestitism as well as travesty are conditioned by the functioning of language, that sexes can be substituted, that masculine and feminine can be exchanged or travestied, because words can be."[66]

The link between androgyny and language described in *Sarrasine* and in *La Fille aux yeux d'or* subverts the possibility of sexual identity. The androgynous ideal of wholeness is superseded by an apparently perverse and hermaphroditic manifestation of the always other. Androgyny in these novellas thus appears to be the antithesis of androgyny in *Séraphîta.* But within them is also a subversive questioning of the notion of antithesis and its foundation in identity and opposition. How then can we describe the relation of these novellas to *Séraphîta?*

Fantasy Figures, from the Eternal to the Sometime Feminine

In *Sarrasine* and *La Fille aux yeux d'or,* what is posited as an ideal is revealed to be an illusion resulting from a blindness to or a repression of a difference that cannot be seen in terms of opposition from the self. Should we wish to see this discovery as a stage in a progressive movement toward enlightenment, we are warned that progress itself is no more than a structure of illusion begetting illusion. To read *Séraphîta* as antithetical to these two texts is also to disregard the explicit illusory nature of its own ideal and the repressive force at work within it. *Séraphîta* is a text of "fantasy," a "defensive, conservative, counterforce . . . still lives which resist change and hold contradiction and conflict in abeyance; a counterforce seductive enough to create a *phantasy reader* (a reader caught in phantasy)."[67] Wilfred and Minna are "readers caught in fantasy," they read Séraphîta's (sexual) identity according to the fictions created by their desire. "Minna's imagination was an accomplice of that constant hallucination under whose empire anyone would fall and that lent to Séraphîtüs the appearance of those figures dreamed of in a happy sleep" (*Sér*, 7:331).

Wilfred, too, from the day he meets Séraphîta and approaches her "hallucinating world," admits to having been "dragged" and "bound" by "a series of enchantments" (*Sér*, 7:338). And yet, unlike in the shorter novellas, these fantasies seem to have a purpose. Tempered with learning and philosophy, Wilfred and Minna's poetic fictions are directed to their dialectical correction and completion in the full meaning, the Ideal, that is projected beyond narrative and beyond sense experience: "there" (*là*), where "all is the same" (*Sér*, 7:373). This final resolution, as I mentioned before, is dependent upon the equilibrium of the dialectic's opposed parts, which is to say upon the antithesis of Séraphîtüs and Séraphîta. This equilibrium, however, is one that the narrative cannot maintain (and of which the ever-expanding middle is symptomatic). The ineluctable disequilibrium of narrative and of the narratable is what the myth of wholeness and "symbolic plenitude" convinces us—"ideal readers"—to suppress.[68]

From the first line of the novel, the narrator solicits the reader's complicity in this creation of a fantasy world. "Looking at a map of the Norwegian coastline, what imagination would not be filled with wonder at its fantastic, jagged outline, . . . who hasn't dreamed of the majestic spectacles offered by these shores without banks . . . ?" (*Sér*, 7:327). As the narrator only uses sexually unmarked terms like the "being" (*l'être*) or "creature" to describe Séraphîta/üs, his/her sexual duality results from the combination of Minna's masculine and Wilfred's feminine projections. As readers, we are asked to continue the metaphysical journey of Wilfred and Minna toward "dual unity" through our own totalizing of their successive references to Séraphîtüs and Séraphîta, "il" and "elle," as well as the varied discourses that s/he adopts. If there is a repressed "reality" here, it is only by resisting identification as the text's "ideal reader" that we can see through the "phantasmatic abolition of difference" and retrieve signs of its significance.[69] It is with this intention that I would like to reexamine the sexual division between male and female as represented in Minna and Wilfred and in their fusion in Séraphîtüs/Séraphîta.

It is no wonder that the representation of Séraphîta's masculine side has been criticized as unconvincing or flat. The "person whom Minna named Séraphîtüs" (*Sér*, 7:329) is described within the limitations of Minna's innocent and unworldly point of view. Androgyny, here, relates a look to an appearance, and girls like Minna have historically occupied the role of the spectacle, not the spectator.[70] Personifying *la jeune fille*, she also represents the feminine and, as such, is said to be candor itself. The metamorphosis of Séraphîtüs to Séraphîta introduces a new complexity and opacity into the figure of the feminine, due to the number of men who attempt to define her and to their amazement over her rhetorical and oratorical skills. For them she becomes the deceitful seductress. Wilfred cannot distinguish Séraphîta's "purity" from her coquetry; both seem to him to be tools of feminine wiles. " 'Tell me, don't I remind you of some coquette?'—'Oh, to be sure, I don't see that celestial young girl that I saw in you the first time in the church in Jarvis'—With these words Séraphîta passed her hands over her forehead and when she revealed her face, Wilfred was astonished by its religious and saintly expression" (*Sér*, 7:335).

Like Henri de Marsay, Wilfred sees Séraphîta as a mirror in which he can aggrandize his self-image. "You love me for yourself and not for me," explains Séraphîta. He sees in her "a prey" (*Sér*, 7:353) to be conquered and appropriated for his Napoleonic dreams. But it is this image of woman that the androgyne refuses to offer. "You're right, I'm forgetting to be crazy, to be that poor creature whose weakness pleases you. I torment you and you've come to this savage country to find rest" (*Sér*, 7:335). Attacking his passion at its most vulnerable point she asserts, "You see, my friend, that I am not a woman. You're wrong to love me" (*Sér*, 7:334). Such an assertion, like Séraphîta's love for Minna, is a threat to the (masculine) nature of his desire and self-identity. "Mademoiselle . . . don't play with me. You can only love Séraphîta like one girl loves another and not with the love she inspires in me. You don't know what danger you would be in if my jealousy were justly roused" (*Sér*, 7:365). Looking for the woman as "the female of the male," Wilfred finds the status of the "male" opened to question.[71] What is "masculine" in Séraphîta is a metaphor of a feminine difference that Wilfred cannot comprehend or will not see, what resists his attempts to appropriate her to his desires.

The project to gain mastery over Séraphîta's feminine identity is not Wilfred's alone. Minna's point of view is unacknowledged by the other characters, as the dominant force in the narrative responds to a masculine desire and need. Even the narrator relinquishes his "objective" point of view to sympathize with the male ego that Séraphîta threatens. "Men alone can know what rage a woman can excite in a man's soul, when, wanting to show that beloved woman his force or his power, his intelligence or his superiority, the capricious one inclines her head and says, "I know that!" (*Sér*, 7:367). His own "rage" excited, his jealousy piqued by her narrative skills, the narrator joins in the attempt to "reason away" Séraphîta's power and mystery. "Séraphîta appeared to them to be a more or less eloquent girl; one had to take into account her enchanting voice, her seductive beauty, her fascinating gesture, all those oratorical methods by means of which an actor puts a world of feelings in a sentence, while in reality, the sentence is often common" (*Sér*, 7:365).

The pastor, with his voluminous treatises concerning incantations, somnambulism, and Swedenborgian metaphysics, personifies the savant, the voice of rationality and science that can objectify and conquer Séraphîta's mystery. He is a major threat to her spirituality if only because of the number of pages allotted to his explanations of her "witchery" and his commonsensical reduction of her to a "capricious little girl, spoiled by her parents" (*Sér*, 7:349). To give in and fall victim to the charms of Séraphîta, he claims, can only be madness, "the mute fixity of intoxication" seen in the eyes of her crazed attendant, David, and heard in his language, which is "constantly figurative, often incomprehensible" (*Sér*, 7:352), the antithesis of reason.

Instead of being proven mad, however, Séraphîta undermines the grounds for the pastor's and Wilfred's claims to reason. The scientific methods these men use to demystify Séraphîta—the interviews, questions, and examinations—are precisely what prevent them from ever achieving their ends. Hoping to reason with what they have defined as being nonreasoning (or unreasonable), Wilfred and Becker are brought either to disclaim the opposition of woman (and, hence, the masculine status of their desire) or to accept an "otherness" that cannot be defined simply in relation to man, as Séraphîta ironically reminds them. "You are very pensive this evening, gentlemen. You're treating Minna and me like men to whom one speaks politics or economics, while we are girls to whom you should tell stories while having tea, as is the custom in our Norwegian evenings" (*Sér*, 7:363).

The men cannot accept Séraphîta's resistance to the narcissistic economy whereby the masculine defines and determines feminine as its specular opposite and whereby reason claims what it cannot understand to be madness. "What the narcissistic economy of the masculine universal equivalent tries to eliminate under the label 'madness,'" writes Shoshana Felman, "is nothing other than *feminine* difference."[72] In Séraphîta that difference is labeled rhetorically as masculine, the him in him/her that the men cannot acknowledge. The link between sexuality and textuality thus effectively undermines the androgyne's status as Platonic ideal and source of a paternal authority. Unlike the "eternal feminine" that Wilfred, the pastor, and the narrator would like her to be, Séraphîta/üs emerges as the partly or sometime feminine who, rather than reinforce and complete the image of paternal power, reflects its internal contradictions. The ending of the novel is itself double, and, here, I do not refer to the separation between Séraphîta's successful ascension to the World of Spirit and the projected spiritual synthesis of Minna and Wilfred, although this already entails a deferral and displacement of ends. I refer to the division between this illusion of closure and the final line, both a request and a question posed to the pastor, the narrative's one father figure. "We want to go to God, they said, come with us my father?" (*Sér*, 7:375).

As the narrator begins to lose his protective cover of sexual neutrality, the possibility is raised of a reading of *Séraphîta* that is not consonant with Minna's and Wilfred's, a reading that reopens to interpretation what, by its very nature, appeared to be complete and impervious. "Diamond out of the fire of sorrows," "spotless pearl," "fleshless desire" (*Sér*, 7:374), so many images of pristine and transparent light define Séraphîta, but like him/her, they are double. The figures of transparency reappear in the text, reified, exteriorized as decorative jewels or even as weapons, rhetorical arms defending against the discovery of a very different reality. Even as Séraphîta ascends to the celestial spheres of his/her origin, the figure of Charity "threw her oriental pearls, beautiful collection of tears" (ibid.). No longer an image of transcendence, the pearl comes back to haunt us in the following scene, where cloaks "covered in pearls" clothe and disguise man's fallen state and act as deceptive veils hiding "dried bodies, eaten by worms, corrupted, pulverized, wrought with disease" (*Sér*, 7:374–75). When enchantment or fantasy wears thin, the symbol of perfection and purity opens to violence, like the cries of "Violence, violence" that Séraphîta inspires in David, echo of the violence of desire ravaging him/her within. "The light of God protects her, but what if she gives in to the violence?" (*Sér*, 7:350).

Séraphîta opens under the sign of violence.[73] In this natural agon of land and sea, the water, "entering with violence," is "pushed back with an equal violence" (*Sér*, 7:327), exposing, in its movement, the "fissures" and "cracks" of the "dangerous gully" threatening both natural and symbolic coherence. The androgynous dream can only aggravate the fractures it hopes to repair, violating the purity of this pearl with a violent and sexual rhetoric. Plucked out of timelessness this "enigmatic, human flower" is compromised upon entering the text.[74] Writing, Balzac is only too aware, is a de-flowering, a compromising of the "sublime beauty" of the Norwegian landscape, which had been "virgin territory for poetry" (*Sér*, 7:327). Like the Norwegian waters rumbling beneath the placid but thinning ice, so many contradictory impulses are stirring beneath the pristine surface of this apocalyptic image of the androgyne rising at the dawn of the nineteenth century. As our only means of access to the ideal, such symbols remain bound by their own materiality and thus obstruct our vision of the ideal, like the "body" that Séraphîta leaves to Minna and Wilfred as their legacy. "Suddenly the two lovers found themselves kneeling before a body that the old-man David protected from every-body's curiosity and that he wanted to bury himself" (*Sér*, 7:375).

Whether hidden or buried, the body remains a reminder of the disunity between ideal beauty and the incarnate symbol. The divided and contradictory movement of the narrative becomes most apparent around this body and its relation to concepts of incorporation (in an image) or embodiment (of the idea in language) or even (Christian) incarnation. The configuration is best understood by analogy to what J. Hillis Miller describes as the doubleness of all allegory. Through reference to Walter Benjamin, Miller defines the allegorical work of art according to the "disjunction and necessary copresence" of two theories of its relation to time. In the first, the allegory, like nature and history, is part of a teleological and dialectical process toward spiritualization; in the second, art is inhabited by "no such teleologi-cal spiritual drive" and tends instead to decay, revealing, in its frag-mentation, the failure of art to transfigure and totalize. "Nature, history, the art-work become body merely body, without soul, a dead body so to speak . . . as if its ruination through time were to reveal what it has secretly been all along."[75]

As an allegorical figure Séraphîta/üs embodies the principle of incarnation but whereas s/he is also forced to explain that principle to his/her disciples—whether in terms of the Apocalypse, of The Revelation of the Word, or of the power to give a body to thought—*Séraphîta* can be considered an allegory of allegory and an infi-nite regress of his/her own doubleness. Exemplifying the dangers of Schlegel's "endless generation of little ironies," as we saw in chapter two, his/her exposition of what s/he aims to be is exasperating, a system of unclosed parentheses filled with anthropomorphic images and unjust comparisons that seem to take him/her further from the point. Even in him/her, the narrative faith in the spiritualizing of love and art is matched by the awareness of the need to defer that spiritual end and to hide (like David does) the unavoidable presence of a body (or of a language) ravaged by desire.

"The relation that ties two things," states Séraphîta, "leaves an impression,"—a mark (*une empreinte*) (*Sér*, 7:356). Séraphîta/üs—"new tie between earth and sky," tie also between the spheres of man and woman—and *Séraphîta*, the text that links author to the divine, author to public (Balzac to Mme. Hanska), also leave the mark of their mediation, elements in excess of their purpose. The narrator of *Sarrasine* similarly experiences this excess as he watches himself straddle the threshold of a window recess. As he physically mediates between two opposing worlds but remains outside both, so his narrative can only perform the mediation from outside, a position in language that circumscribes those opposed worlds but partakes of neither. The narrator and narration of *Séraphîta* bear the marks of excess, excess of language and languages: medical, philosophical, mathematical, religious, mystical, romantic; all of which constitute the opaque "veils" of truth, the pearls of rhetoric that accumulate around the "spotless pearl" they attempt to reveal.

It is thus within the rhetorical texture of *Séraphîta* that we find a fundamental questioning of the paternal discourse, whereby the artist, in a situation analogous to God, attempts to name what is or will be. The act of revelation, Séraphîta shows, is an act of translation and the attempt to represent truth involves a risk either of (self-)compromise or of incomprehensibility. Those like David and Louis Lambert, who have faith in the absolute revelatory powers of language, become victims of a self-defeating communication that no one, not even they themselves, can decipher. The "pure" language that they approximate and to which Séraphîta ascends is a solipsistic language doomed, as in *Louis Lambert,* to semantic isolation. "These last chants were expressed neither by word, nor by look, nor by gesture, nor by any of the signs men use to communicate their thoughts, but as the soul speaks to itself" (*Sér,* 7:371). The dream text of *Séraphîta* is also the product of a mystical impulse and such patriarchal self-reflexivity. "During these terrible winters . . . women knit and dye wool or cotton cloth to make clothes, while the majority of men read or open themselves to those prodigious meditations that have given birth to profound theories, to the mystic dreams of the north, its beliefs, its studies . . . semi-monastic habits that force the soul to react to itself, to feed on itself, and that makes the Norwegian peasant a singular being in the European population (*Sér,* 7:329).

But the Balzacian narrator is decidedly a European artist and not averse to a "feminine" activity of spinning yarns. He is even known to admit his attraction to such "clothes" themselves, to prefer the "indefinable grace" of the "folds" (*Sér,* 7:336) of Séraphîta's multiform wrap to what it covers. Indeed, the dream of Séraphîta is a dream at odds with the Balzacian temperament. The androgyne as an ideal is a contradiction to the novel and particularly to the novels of Balzac. Like the "hybrid flower," which, as Minna puts it "will produce no children," s/he is removed from the social and sexual history to which the narrator is irresistibly drawn. Aspiring to a realm beyond language and beyond desire, s/he attempts to remove him/herself from the system of difference by which life reflects upon itself and by which fiction is written and perpetuated. Such a one-to-one correspondence of work and idea can only be found in the pearl-gray silence of the frozen Norwegian landscape, where "one power alone, the unproductive force of the ice, reigned without contradiction" (*Sér*, 7:329). As the narrator explains, "such complete communication can only be had by absolute rest, the appeasement of all storms" (*Sér*, 7:370). The search for a language that is immune to irony can only end in silence and death.

To break the ice, to break the silence, is to subject and be subjected to the economic system by which all writing exists. In appearing to move toward the synthetic closure of the ideal text and the ideal sex, Séraphîta/üs and *Séraphîta* must displace that end whose unmarked and pure terms are beyond its capabilities. As it does so, it reveals in those displacements and in the layers of veils that the source of its authority derives, not from a transcendent Self, but from a self already divided between illusory dreams and subversive fictions.

5

An Obscure Object of Aesthetic Desire: Gautier's Androgyne/Hermaphrodite

ACCORDING TO typical literary mappings, the move from Balzac's *Séraphîta* to Gautier's *Mademoiselle de Maupin* might well be compared to a move from German to French romanticism, and hence, according to nineteenth-century cultural stereotypes, from the rational, analytic, and masculine mind to an intuitive, impassioned, and feminine sensibility. Whereas, for instance, in Lukács's *Theory of the Novel*, the *Comédie humaine* falls under the category of "abstract idealism" in which the human condition is objectivized, "translated into action," Gautier's *Mademoiselle de Maupin* would fall under the heading of "the romanticism of disillusionment." It is a novel of passivity, of brooding interior states, "of moods and reflections about moods."[1]

Inasmuch as we have already seen that the line separating objective from subjective is shifting and unstable, however, so we find that Balzac and Gautier have more in common than the ambiguous label of romantic. Like Balzac, Gautier's response to the romantic revolution of the thirties is ambivalent: he celebrates the movement, calling himself a barbaric romantic, and at the same time, he displays a reactionary conservatism. Where Balzac turns to mysticism to retain certain inalienable truths and values in a changing world, Gautier holds onto an almost religious faith in the eternal endurance of "ideal beauty." Thus the concerns for classical beauty and ideal form of the Gautier of Parnasse do not simply postdate the Gautier who was known to *épater le bourgeois* (shock the bourgeois) with his red vest or with his collection of essays on risqué authors entitled *Les Gro-*

tesques. Rather, his aspirations to an eternal, ideal beauty are in evidence from his earliest works, where those aspirations struggle against his awareness of beauty as subjective and historically contingent. His goal as artist and writer, consequently, must be seen as a fusion of what he regarded as classical and romantic.

Since Gautier was a prolific critic of the arts, his aesthetic vocabulary owes much to the polarization of classical and romantic schools in the academy and in the art criticism of the early nineteenth century.[2] His own use of that opposition, and the way he translates it into narrative forms, moreover, shows that its significance extends far beyond the decrees of contemporary fashion. Much as Hegel used the classical-romantic opposition to distinguish the stages whereby art as Spirit becomes conscious of itself, so Gautier constructs a dialectic in an effort to define art as a strange new organism connected to the life source that inspired it.[3] For him, the terms *classical* and *romantic* accrue masculine and feminine associations, such that their fusion is often figured as the union of male and female, or more specifically in an androgynous or hermaphroditic image.

Although Gautier's schooling in the plastic arts leads him to speak of a hermaphrodite rather than an "androgyne," I will retain both terms in order to distinguish two sets of values at work in his aesthetics. As I discuss in chapter one, the androgyne recalls Plato's myth and the harmonious oneness of the Platonic and classical ideal of art and beauty, while the hermaphrodite recalls the myth of Ovid's *Metamorphoses,* emphasizing the changing nature of beauty that Gautier identified with romanticism. The synthesis of classical and romantic is thus posited in terms of a union of masculine and feminine, and, at the same time, of Platonic androgyne and Ovidian hermaphrodite, not in the sense that these oppositions no longer exist, but that they do exist in reconciliation.

Gautier's critical writings, furthermore, illustrate that the aesthetic prescriptions of the academy are not sexually neutral. As Naomi Schor documents, "the normative aesthetics elaborated and disseminated by the Academy and its members . . . is an axiology carrying into the field of representation the sexual hierarchies of the phallocentric cultural order."[4] Each of the binary couples, classic/romantic and androgyne/hermaphrodite, describes a hierarchical relation between the two polar terms and a priority of the first term over the second. The traditional image of the androgyne as a reflection of original, eternal, and self-sustaining values, for example, is consistently given classical and masculine attributes, as opposed to beauty as mere appearance—subjective, ephemeral, effeminate. This hierarchy forms the basis of Gautier's aesthetic claims throughout his career as writer and critic. In its fictional context, however, the androgyne challenges the very foundation of that hierarchy as it confuses the boundary between the terms of opposition. Indeed, the interplay of androgyne/hermaphrodite prefigures the more recent chapters in the history of aesthetics where the "dominant paradigms of patriarchy" have been exposed, if not also, as Schor suggests, "eroded."[5]

Gautier's best-known novel, *Mademoiselle de Maupin,* reflects, at once, the priority of the classical ideal and the privileging of a romantic subjectivity and in so doing unmasks the commonality of these two theories as guardians of an "illusion of autonomy," whether with regard to beauty or to the creative self. "The objective and subjective fallacies are one and the same," René Girard writes, both depend upon the "lie of spontaneous desire" embodied in Gautier's hermaphroditic ideal. "Subjectivisms and objectivisms, romanticisms and realisms, individualisms and scientisms, idealisms and positivisms appear to be in opposition but are secretly in agreement to conceal the presence of the mediator. All these dogmas are the aesthetic or philosophic translation of world views peculiar to internal mediation. They all depend directly or indirectly on the lie of spontaneous desire. They all defend the same illusion of autonomy to which modern man is passionately devoted."[6]

Gautier's androgyne is a trope of the autonomy of artist and work of art, of the artist's self-sufficiency and of the oneness of the beauty he creates, separate from and unsullied by the masses of bourgeois society. A closer examination of that trope, however, reveals a different figure, pointing, not toward autonomy, but rather toward division, toward all that the androgyne must repress or silence to create the illusion of autonomy. An examination of how the "grammar" of this hermaphroditic figure operates in Gautier's criticism and fiction reveals not simply the "illusion of autonomy" but, more specifically, the equally cherished lie of art's or beauty's sexual indifference.[7]

Is Classical to Romantic as Masculine Is to Feminine?

Let us first examine the terms of opposition. Throughout his career as an art critic, Gautier reserved his highest praise for the ideals of ancient Greece. With the affiliates of the neoclassical school, for example, he shares an admiration for Ingres, whom he describes as having rekindled the venerable "ancient spark," that had lain dormant since the Renaissance. "That art which borrows nothing from the accidental, unconcerned with contemporary styles and passing obsessions, appears cold, we know, to worried minds and doesn't interest the masses [*la foule*], incapable of comprehending syntheses and generations. It is, nevertheless, great art, immortal art and the most noble effort of the human spirit; that is what the Greeks understood, divine masters whose legacy we must worship on bended knee. The honor of Mr. Ingres will be to have taken up again that torch that antiquity passed on to the Renaissance."[8] Gautier expresses his belief in a tradition of art that originated in classical Greece, was reaffirmed in the Renaissance by such painters as Leonardo and Raphael, and established eternal laws of beauty for all artists to pursue. Thus he writes that Da Vinci possesses "the purity, the grace and the perfection of antiquity." Pervasive in his writing is an image of Greece that is not tied to any place in the world but only to a mythological past in which once and for all the laws of art and beauty were established in models of absolute perfection. Even in his travelogues a fictional Greece has an overpowering presence as an artist's utopia: "'There, indeed, posed on the Acropolis as on a golden tripod, in the middle of the sculptural chorus of the Attic mountains, true, absolute, and perfect beauty shines immortally."[9]

With a sense of nostalgia and loss, Gautier praises "absolute beauty," defined, as Winckelmann defined it, in terms of unity and simplicity, and whose most pure manifestation he found in Greek statuary.[10] For Gautier as for Winckelmann, classical beauty is distinguished by a certain virility or masculine essence, as also by a certain nudity. Speaking of Michelangelo and Corneille he writes that, "Only the creature remains and even so Michelangelo rips off his costume as something useless, transitory, subject to fashion; to express his idea the untamed artist asks the universe only for naked man; that naked man in all his anatomical violence, will often be himself stripped of his skin as of an intrusive piece of clothing, as of a useless veil between the expression and the idea. Corneille's poetic approach is the same; his alexandrines have the severe nakedness . . . of a fresco."[11] Nakedness in this respect must be understood as an elementariness, an image of life stripped of the accidental veils of temporality, if not too of sexuality. The analogy to the Platonic androgyne is implicit both in the violent force of "naked man," similar to that with which the androgyne rivaled Zeus, and also in the reference to transparency of form and idea, in other words to a primal poetry. Gautier's use of the term *nakedness,* however, cannot always be taken as a reference to a Platonic form or ideal. More attractive than the abstract and metaphoric associations of nudity are its sensual and palpable manifestations. Gautier dreams long of Spartan youths parading before him, their oiled muscles bared to the sunlight. It is this aspect of the nude body that Gautier admires in Greek art as well and particularly in Greek statuary—beauty that is idealized but also present in its materiality, "poetic and real."[12] "Developed under an anthropomorphic religion where deified beauty was immortalized in marble and put on a pedestal, it attained a degree of perfection which can never be surpassed. Never has the hymn of the human body been sung in such noble verses; the superb strength of form shone with an incomparable brilliance during that period of Greek civilization that is like the youth and springtime of the human species."[13]

The reference to this period in Greece as the youth or springtime of human nature introduces a concept of temporality into Gautier's aesthetics that complicates the otherwise ahistorical "nakedness" of his ideal. That is to say, there exists a tension between attributing transcendent and divine origins to beauty and grounding it in time and geography. The same tension can be found in Winckelmann, since he accounts for the superiority of Greek art and its particular idealization of the human body by pointing to climate and way of life. Both recount in lavish detail how the warmth and light fostered a moral enthusiasm and a liberal mind and how it encouraged physical development and an appreciation for the nude body that had no need of cover. For these reasons Gautier admits that the Greek ideal appeared to be something of an anachronism. "Beauty must blush for herself and take a winding-sheet. Fine young men, with limbs rubbed with oil, wrestling in the lyceum or gymnasium, under the brilliant sky, in the full sun of Attica, before the marveling crowd; young Spartan girls who dance the bibase, and run naked to the summit of Taygetus, put on your tunics and your chlamys once again: your reign is past (*MM*, p. 189)."[14] Gautier offers a historical explanation for the disappearance of the "nude ideal" in the modern world. Like Diderot a century before, he blames this loss on the religious morality of his age and particularly on "that abominable Christianity" that degraded the ideals of Greece. Christianity, with its so-called virtue has destroyed the appreciation of the nude body and forced shame and clothing upon it. This idea, which Gautier returns to as late as 1866, is developed through the same rhetoric of nudity versus veils that he enlists to define the opposition of classicism and romanticism. "The romantic revolution as it prepared itself during the Restoration and broke out in full force in 1830 has had less impact on sculpture than on all the other arts. . . . Statuary, by virtue of its tradition and need of nudity, and borrowing almost all of its subjects from heroic life, mythology, or allegory, necessarily remains classical and pagan: Christianity, with its modesty and scorn for the flesh, has not been able to force it to clothe itself."[15]

Gautier's association of the romantic movement with costume and cover as opposed to classical nudity is part of a developing metaphor to which we shall return. What is especially significant for our purposes is the presence of two apparently opposed theories of representation—one that stresses art as an ideal, prescribed by fixed laws, and one that stresses its historicity; or in other terms, one that focuses upon the art object and one that stresses the importance of the subject or the creative mind. "Any man who hasn't his own interior world to translate," he writes, "is not an artist." It is thus that, in contrast to such emphatic praise for the art of Greece, Gautier also expresses his admiration for a very different sort of art. In the Preface to *Les Grotesques,* parts of which were first published in 1834 and whose title betrays the influence of Victor Hugo and hence of romanticism, he speaks of an art that does not look to antiquity for its models. "In this work it is true that imitation of Italy and Spain often takes the place of a more vibrant and contemporary imitation, one untouched by academics and the rules of the regents of rhetoric . . . these authors only make use of fashionable ideas, of present-day turns of phrase, and of elegant terms, and one can get a much more exact idea of the language of the time than from those master-pieces of the masters who seem to have lived nowhere but Athens or Rome."[16] Gautier attributes such attention to the changing aspects of the modern world and its many details of light, of color and exterior, to romantic artists like Delacroix or Balzac. Whereas he associates classical form with a singular, virile essence, he identifies romantic artists with the attraction to, and desire for, beauty that is diffused, varied, and indeed feminine. "At no time has the feminine theme furnished artists with such sparkling variations."[17]

The association of the feminine with romanticism and with the modern and vital is thematized in Gautier's fiction and is spelled out in almost mundane terms in his criticism. His review of the realist artist Meissonier provides one example. Gautier praises this painter despite his resistance to the charms of the romantic movement, but raises one slight objection, that "this . . . male and robust talent . . . has almost completely banished women from his work." What a pity, he explains, "never a blond servant who pours frothy beer for these drinkers, . . . never . . . a lovely lady in a white satin skirt; never a feminine model who poses in these studios so rich with art objects and curios. . . . We can't really explain the singular reserve of this artist who thus deprives himself of such an element of variety. The presence of women would add so much more charm to his work, which is already so interesting."[18] The need for art to incorporate a feminine element is indeed one of the themes that runs throughout *Mademoiselle de Maupin*. Beauty is conceived in the feminine, and this, the narrator explains, is a function of the modern, Christian world. "Since the time of Christ they have not made a single statue of a man in which adolescent beauty was idealized and rendered with the care which was characteristic of the ancient sculptors. Woman has become the symbol of moral and physical beauty" (*MM*, p. 196).

Despite the predominant visibility of the feminine in the modern art world, however, the prior status of the masculine/classical ideal is upheld within Gautier's critical writings, and, along with it, the priority of interior over exterior, beauty to his/her veils. Femininity, like romanticism, is associated with the many changing forms of beauty in the modern world. This proliferation of a disembodied and textualized femininity, similar to what Gautier sees as the brothel's "crowd of flesh and blood ideals . . . lively piquant beauties . . . precious beauties, indeed . . . beauties in every style" (*MM*, p. 79), manifests beauty as style, as exterior: a festive hairdo adorned with flowers and feathers; a satin dress enriched with brocade, "the brilliance, the softness and the variety of tones seem to invite the brush of a colorist and present him with a palette of seductive nuances."[19] According to critics like Georges Matoré, the obsession with fashion reflects the "feminine," if not the "effeminate," nature of romantic artists in general.[20]

Having identified the elementariness of classicism as masculine, it is not surprising to find Gautier associating the modern and feminine with what might best be called mere appearance. Indeed, throughout his work a Nietzschean play of veils reinforces this association; what Derrida said of Nietzsche can be said of Gautier as well: "It is impossible to dissociate the questions of art, style, and truth from the question of the woman. Nevertheless, the question 'What is woman' is itself suspended in the simple formulation of their common problematic."[21]

The role of the feminine in art and in its relation to the masculine classical ideal is displayed through the metaphor of the veil. On the one hand, femininity serves to enhance the attractiveness of the ideal by assuring its novelty and by inspiring a relation of passion or desire to the art object. Particularly through the related thematic of clothing as that which dates beauty and situates it within a historical present, Gautier adapts his classical ideal to the demands of modernity. His attention to details of fashion, whether in attire or in language, responds to even as it predates Baudelaire's desire to "extract from fashion what it can contain of the poetic in the historical, to discern the eternal in the transitory."[22]

But Gautier always seems to be caught somewhere between the past and the present, longing for the security of classical, ideal beauty and seduced by the freedom and variety of romantic color. It is no wonder that the androgyne or hermaphrodite should figure prominently in his work. Indeed, from the novel *Mademoiselle de Maupin* (1835) to the poem "Contralto" (1852), the hermaphrodite projects an image of classical sculpture suffused with romantic vitality, "Force united to Grace / The mistress embracing the lover."[23] The apparent opposition between the vibrant formlessness of the novel, a monstrous genre (*genre monstre*—MM, p. 39) as Gautier refers to it in the Preface to *Maupin,* and the well-wrought but lifeless structure of the later poem is already figured in Maupin. Gautier's hermaphrodite is indeed a clothed ideal whose infinite possibilities for appearance personify a Baudelarian "present beauty." Modernity, Baudelaire writes, is "the transitory, the fugitive, the contingent, that half of art of which the other half is the eternal and the immutable, . . . you have no right to scorn or pass up this transitory and fugitive element whose metamorphoses are so frequent. By suppressing it, you necessarily fall into the emptiness of abstract beauty like that of the unique woman before original sin."[24] While on the one hand the "fugitive" appearance seduces with the promise of the real and the present, it also protects the pristine nudity of the Platonic ideal. The decorative detail and the rhetorical frills by which the artist is seduced are the veils that protect the sight of true beauty from those who are unworthy of it and hence preserve its untainted freedom. In terms that recall the "princes de l'art" of Balzac's *Séraphîta,* Gautier explains: "beauty has more veils than Isis. She does not present herself all at once or in all her splendor, she has her hours of eclipse and weakness. . . . A discreet and persevering lover will not be discouraged by that, he knows to wait. . . . The cloud breaks, the ray bursts, the profile is outlined, the brow is lit up, beauty reveals herself, but only to the initiated, to the adept, the common man who may have been present suspected nothing."[25] Thus privileged in its manifestation as exterior veil, the feminine is emptied of a proper signification, since it bears little, if any, association with the woman. Its role is pure artifice, as Ross Chambers has demonstrated in a related context, "a means to make emptiness perceptible," and to do so for the artist/lover who will thereby be granted the status of "the initiated."[26]

If the modern world can only conceive of art or beauty in feminine terms, this is because the role of both is ultimately subservient to the artist-lover who is brought to his fullest potential, not in fusion with the woman, but in the absorption and mastery of the "feminine." Gautier often describes the artist as a "microcosm," one who bears within himself (I use the masculine deliberately) the image of beauty he will transfer to the page. Like others of the Petit Cénacle, Gautier lavished as much attention on details of clothes and ornament in himself as he did in his writing. A Baudelarian dandy *avant la lettre,* his self-conscious will to embellish reads not merely as the desire to create beauty everywhere but also as the desire to be, himself, an object of beauty. The figure of the hermaphrodite responds to this narcissistic desire to be both subject and object, lover and beloved, artist and work of art. As a microcosm, the artist is self-sufficient, dedicated to art and to beauty as feminine, mirror images of the masculine, artist self. The idealism of Gautier's critical writings is dependent upon this suppression of sexual and textual difference.

It is interesting, consequently, to compare Gautier's criticism with his prefaces, particularly those that proclaim and defend a theory of art for art's sake. There, in the spaces between fiction and nonfiction, a willingness to play and just to play with art reinforces the relation of textuality and sexuality, but only as it also makes more "apparent" the "emptiness" beneath its veils. Idealism quickly turns to its own ironization as the "woman" reveals herself as that which "will not be pinned down."[27]

Ironic Foreplay and the Self-Critical Preface

In his concise and provocative study of Gautier, P. E. Tennant points to the presence in his writing of "two irreconcilable yet fundamental artistic needs—necessity of order and freeplay of fancy."[28] These two needs are expressed in the generic transgressions of much of his early work—the contradictory impulses toward poetry (as ordered form) and prose (as free form), or the combination of the novel (as the realm of verisimilitude or the mimetic) and theater (as the realm of the fantastic) into one "monstrous class of writing" (*MM,* p. 33). They are also expressed in terms of gender, the boring monotony of the bourgeois male and his fascination with and need for an exotic, "feminine" unknown. Particularly in Gautier's early works one can detect an attempt to extend the already hazy generic boundaries and to fuse genres in the same way in which he transgresses and combines categories of gender in a search for that ideal poetic form. His early poetry approaches narrative in its length and temporal structure; his novels adopt aspects of the theater and seem to reduce chronology to the timelessness or circular time associated with poetry.[29] If, as Tennant suggests, it is true that these needs exist in relation to each other, we can assume that the predominance of "sensual play" in the works of his youth is a reflection of a yet prevailing sense of order from which that "play" is distinguished. Even in the earliest works, however, and particularly where the most idealizing claims for art take place, the "deep irony" that Tennant rightly alludes to as permeating Gautier's writing is in evidence, as if the distinction between play and order were not that clear-cut. As Tennant states, "Gautier presents the same curious dichotomy as Byron and Hoffmann, in whom skepticism and mockery are constant correctives of the lyrical, asserting the dignity of man by affirming his self-control. In Gautier the self-parody, the deliberate dissociation, the affective of impassivity constitute a defense mechanism against deception and vulnerability, a recognition too of the ambivalence of reality."[30] What we find in Gautier's strident formulation of art for art's sake in the Preface to *Maupin* and in the novel itself, is this double movement of the lyrical and its corrective in the skeptical, a double movement that expresses the ideals of both classicism and romanticism even as it parodies the idealism they share in their claims for art and the artist.

The relationship of the figure of the hermaphrodite to the theory of art for art is more complex than the fusion of genres and aesthetic modes evident in his work. Both that theory and the figure involve a certain scandalousness that excited Gautier. A figure with the impact to shock the bourgeois, it is also one that reflects a notion of art above and beyond petty questions of morality and sexuality that preoccupied Gautier's critics. At the same time, his cult of art is intimately bound to a cult of love, or more accurately of desire, that is integral to his representation of the androgyne/hermaphrodite. As Gautier breaks with his contemporaries' reliance on morality and utility as aesthetic criteria, so does he break with idealist aesthetics and particularly with Hegel, who writes that the "relation of desire is not that in which man stands to the work of art." Whereas Hegel considers desire to be only a base and "savage" instinct that has no place in aesthetics, for Gautier desire is a synthetic force like art itself, reconciling past models with future aspirations, reality with imagination. It is also, however, a disruptive force, not because it "occupies the whole man," as Hegel fears, but because it (like irony) divides him, leading the subject to an ever-increasing multiplicity of beautiful objects that challenge the dream of singular beauty. Driven in various and often conflicting directions, the subject loses its presumed stability to a fictional and thereby irretrievable past.[31]

The double movement by which Tennant describes Gautier's irony repeats the tension I have discussed between Aristophanes' androgyne and Ovid's hermaphrodite, especially as that tension is expressed in the rhetoric of veils and in the relation between the nude ideal and its artificial representation in a clothed figure. As a corrective of desire and a means of distancing oneself from faith in absolutes, irony can only salvage self-dignity at the expense of self-definition. What we find in the prefaces is that the play of veils does not result in a reassertion of a Platonic Idea or ideal that asserts itself beneath their appearance, but rather in a confusion of the boundaries between veils and nudity, artifice and origin, or other and self, and, consequently, in a subversion of the hierarchy that defines the terms and their relationship to each other.

Gautier's concept of art for art, however ambiguous its meaning, participates in the French reception of Kantian metaphysics, where art and beauty act both as a separate sphere and as a bridge between the realms of science (pure reason) and ethics or moral freedom. Lecturing on Kantian aesthetics in his 1818 *Leçons,* Victor Cousin was the first to formulate the equivalent of art for art in France, writing, "we need religion for religion, morality for morality, art for art."[32] Cousin's interpretation of Kant, moreover, shows less concern with the relation of art to other realms of thought and more interest in its self-enclosure. For Gautier this niche grows even smaller, consecrating art's separateness or privileged status as the precious other world (*au-delà*), untouched by an ever-expanding bourgeois culture.[33] Not so much a question of metaphysics, although it takes on that aura, Gautier's art for art's sake has more to do with nostalgia for that singular and pure ideal of ancient Greece and, simultaneously, with a romantic rejection of bourgeois insistence on utility and morality as aesthetic standards; a rejection of the masses (*la foule*) upon which the artist was becoming increasingly dependent. "With regard to utilitarians, utopians, economists, Saint-Simonians, and others who will ask him [the author] . . . What is the purpose of that?—[he will answer:] Its purpose is to be beautiful. Isn't that enough? like flowers, perfume, birds, like all that man has not been able to divert and deprave to his use."[34]

Gautier's declarations about the role of art in society often take the form of declamation against the whole business of criticism, which he found to be wholly distasteful, even while he practiced it himself. Like Diderot, he believed that the only purpose of criticism was to point out beauty to others. The prefaces to *Mademoiselle de Maupin* and to his earlier prose pieces deal in witty and mocking tones with what he saw as the critic's infraction of the aesthetic experience. It is in these prefaces, where artist and critic meet in an ironic self-critical act, that the formulations of art for art's sake and art for beauty's sake first take place. The tension between the artistic and the critical impulse is significant. Prefaces, for Gautier—like criticism and like art—must only serve the beautiful, but his prefaces are also unmistakably self-serving: a response to the exaggerated attacks on his work and on his person as immoral and indecent. Had he himself only been a beautiful work of art, the contradictory impulses between self and art in the prefaces would have posed no problem; indeed, the desire to be beautiful is dramatized by the narrator of *Mademoiselle de Maupin*. But the tension is present in both Preface and novel and is played with and played out in the same rhetorical terms we have been looking at, the rhetoric of sex and the rhetoric of veils or clothing, particularly as both "the sex" and the veils are seen to manifest a feminine other.

"What is the purpose of a preface?" Gautier asks outright in the Preface to *Les Jeunes France*. His ironic response reveals his dislike for the way the question itself reflects a practical and purposive attitude toward art, as toward reading and writing. For some, he writes, the preface is a useless appendage to a book and not worth reading. For others, it is said to contain the kernel of the author's thought and thus can be read instead of the book that follows. "O readers of this century . . . who live on the run and barely take the time to die, pity such prefaces which contain a volume in a few pages, and which spare you the burden of skimming through a string of chapters to get to the author's idea. The author's preface is the postscriptum of a woman's letter, her most cherished thought: you don't need to read the rest."[35] But don't suspect that there is a point to this Preface he warns: art is not made of points or ideas. "I swear to you on my soul, in which I hardly believe, on my mother, in whom I have a bit more faith, that there is really no more idea in my preface than in any book of M. Ballanche; that there is neither myth, nor allegory, that I am not founding a new religion like M. G. Drouineau, that there is no poetics nor anything that is going somewhere, I don't even make an apology for my work" (*JF*, p. 25).

In either case Gautier demonstrates the pointlessness of the point. Making an analogy between books and women, he denounces the nineteenth-century reader's utilitarian attitude toward art that is only concerned with the idea and disregards what for Gautier is its essential quality—its form or style. Contemporary readers treat books like women, as consumable objects intended only to be sapped of their value and then discarded. "There are books like women: some have prefaces, others don't, some give in right away, others have a long period of resistance; but all finish in the same way . . . by the end" (*JF*, p. 24). The preface, for the modern reader, is merely another discardable device, a useless garment intended to pace the reading process so as to postpone sexual consummation. But while such devices as prefaces or corsets with intricate lacings may delay the reading subject in his endeavors, they cannot deter him (again, I use the masculine intentionally) from focusing on that moment of conquest nor prevent him from ripping through pages, carelessly tearing off layers of clothing to arrive at that end. "[The book] is yours, you can use and abuse it; you won't even grant its virginity a quarter hour of grace, you touch it, handle it, you drag it from your table to your bed, you break through its innocent cover, tear its pages, poor book" (*JF*, p. 24). Such haste and abuse Gautier sees as symptomatic of a society for which reading and loving are strictly functional or purposive activities.

His attack on this attitude is sharpened in the Preface to *Mademoiselle de Maupin,* where his primary victim is the newspaper critic. A metaphoric treatment similar to that above exposes the degraded status of the critic, whose role among artists is merely to "check coats." As he is only concerned with what is useful, the job is suitable; the functionality of clothing is placed in opposition to poetry and "style," which is essentially nonutilitarian. "You don't make yourself a cotton cap out of a metonymy, you don't put on a comparison instead of a slipper; you can't use an antithesis as an umbrella. . . . I have a deep conviction that an ode is too light an apparel for the winter, and that one wouldn't be better dressed with a strophe, an antistrophe and epode, than the cynic's wife who contented herself with her virtue alone for [a] shift and went about stark naked, so the story goes" (*MM*, pp. 36–37). True, it is not in the nature of clothing itself to be merely functional, and the relation of apparel to wearer is not one of a necessary correspondence—a fact of which Gautier's own dress is proof. But this is what critics and their like do not understand. If the critic is restricted to the position of poet's valet, it is because he is doomed to confuse art with its extraneous elements; he cannot see Isis for her veils. He will judge art only for its semblance to reality, but then he will turn that fictional world against the real life of the author and accuse him of the errancy of his characters: "It is one of the manias of these little scribblers with tiny minds, always to substitute the author for the work and to turn to the personality to give some poor scandalous interest to their wretched rhapsodies" (*MM*, pp. 34–35). For Gautier, on the other hand, the relation between artist and work of art is not one of necessity, but one of artifice and "play." As the arena of costume and make-believe, theater becomes an important metaphor, particularly as it reinforces a distinction between who/what you are and who/what you act or create. That is the distinction the critics refuse to acknowledge. "It is the character who speaks and not the author. His hero is an atheist, that doesn't mean that he himself is an atheist" (*MM*, p. 34).

Blind to true beauty, the critics are blind also to the fraudulence of their critical stance. "To think one thing and to write another happens every day, especially to virtuous people" (*MM*, p. 19). As in the novel it precedes, a metaphor of disguise is employed to expose the hypocrisy of a moral standard of social and literary criticism. Both Madeleine's adoption of a masculine cover in the novel and the display of various rhetorical covers in the Preface combat the image of "La Vertu" as a chaste and fragile woman whose needs must be served by the censors.[36] Morality itself, Gautier suggests, is a hyperbolic posture masking the critic's true envy toward the poet. "It is envy which goes crawling and winding through all these hypocritical homilies. However it tries to hide itself, from time to time, above the metaphors and the rhetorical figures, one sees the glint of its little viper's head; one catches it licking its lips all blue with venom, with its forked tongue, one hears it whistling softly, and very low, in the shadow of an insidious adjective" (*MM*, p. 28).

What emerges from Gautier's protestations against the critics, the journalists, and the reading public in general is an aesthetic doctrine that upholds, on the one hand, a classical and formal ideal of art as beauty, separate from historical reality, and on the other hand, an art that responds to the changeable nature of artistic creativity and thus sanctions the belief in originality. The plea of art for art's sake is a plea in defense of that exclusive realm of theater or "play" where language, like clothing, is not functional but ornamental.[37] "Nothing is really beautiful unless it is useless" (*MM*, p. 39). It is against the false idols of utility and morality that Gautier upholds an ideal of purposeless beauty, object only of a "play impulse," and embodies it in an image of the "living statue," which, for him, is the hermaphrodite.[38] As image of this ideal, the hermaphrodite answers to the sexual rhetoric of Gautier's attack, for its self-serving beauty is seen to thwart its prostitution to any service. Its self-sufficiency, moreover, provides an image of a text, safeguarded against the rapacious pens of journalists and hostile critics, reserving itself only for the "initiated."

Much later, in his more studied treatise "Du Beau dans l'art" (1856), Gautier declares that to consider art for art's sake alone is "the most philosophical manner in which to envisage art," and he calls upon a learned tradition of aesthetic philosophers to consider the nature of beauty.[39] Already in the 1834 Preface to *Mademoiselle de Maupin*, however, the plea of art for art attempts to deal with the problem of beauty as a historical notion and points toward a dialectical relationship between the eternal ideal and the individual consciousness within history. The idealism of the age of Kant and Schiller is absent here though, and the play impulse described seems to bid defiance in the face of its loss. The concept of the autonomy of art proffered in the 1834 Preface registers the ambivalence associated with the aestheticism of the latter part of the century. Peter Bürger presents the paradoxical dilemma of "the autonomy of art" in bourgeois society in terms that have relevance even for this preaestheticist document. "The 'autonomy of art' is a category of bourgeois society. It permits the description of art's detachment from the context of practical life as a historical development—that among the members of those classes which, at least at times, are free from the pressures of the need for survival, a sensuousness could evolve that was not part of any means-end relationships. . . . What this category cannot lay hold of is that this detachment of art from practical contexts is a 'historical process,' i.e., that it is socially conditioned."[40] The impetus behind the claim that art exists only for art's sake is the need to transcend an unresponsive historical and social reality; but the result, as Gautier was only too aware, was to entangle the idea of art ever more deeply with that reality. The more he attempted to define art only in terms of itself, the more that other world became necessary to art's distinction.[41]

This dilemma is also expressed in the sexual rhetoric of the prefaces, which equates the ultimate aesthetic experience with *jouissance* or sexual pleasure and, at the same time, with a kind of virginity whose contact with society remains pure. On the one hand, then, the notion of play as a creative act carries with it a sexual connotation. Indeed, what distinguishes the poet from the critic is the latter's lack of sexual vigor, his inability to consummate his affair with the muse. "You only become a critic when it is well proved in your own eyes that you cannot be a poet. Before you degrade yourself to the wretched task of looking after the coats and noting the moves like a billiard-boy or a ball-boy, you have long courted the Muse, you have tried to possess her [*de la dévirginer* (p. 35)]; but you lack the strength for it. Breath has failed you and you have fallen weak and pale at the foot of the holy mountain" (*MM*, p. 29). So too, for the observer, the aesthetic experience must be sexual. Unlike for Winckelmann, who would have the observer "suspend, as it were, his sexual impulses," for Gautier love of beauty is highly erotic.[42] Similarly, where Winckelmann equates the eunuch and the hermaphrodite as images of purposeless beauty, Gautier will oppose the two.[43] The eunuch is his image for the impotence of critics, envious of the artistic or poetic role they can never fulfill. "From the depths of my heart I sympathize with the unfortunate eunuch obliged to watch the sport of the Grand Signor . . . the most secret beauties appear unveiled before him. People are not troubled by him. He is a eunuch. The Sultan caresses his favorite in his presence and kisses her on her pomegranate mouth. . . . It is the same for the critic who sees the poet strolling in the garden of poetry with his nine lovely odalisks" (*MM*, p. 29). In contrast to the eunuch, Gautier's hermaphrodite does not imply a negation of sexuality. It is the very image of eternal sexual desire that it is meant to inspire in its observer—desire whose pur-pose is not appropriation but an endless self-gratification. "The pur-pose of art . . . is not the exact reproduction of nature, but rather, by means of the forms and colors that she offers, the creation of a microcosm where the dreams and sensations and ideas that the sight of the world inspires can live and produce themselves."[44]

What desire or the creative impulse must avoid or defer, on the other hand, is the moment of consummation, regarded also as the moment of self-consumption. For this reason the preoccupation with sexuality goes hand in hand with an insistence on virginity. The 1834 Preface is critical, on the one hand, of a false notion of virginity cherished by hypocritical censors in the name of "virtue" and in whose cause the charge of immorality is brought against the artist. For Gautier, a true sense of virginity, not opposed to sensuality, must be understood, not through Christianity and the image of the Virgin Mary, but rather as it is immortalized in the Greek Temple of the Virgin and in an image of creation within the male imagination, untouched by women who participate in history. "Pallas Athena was the most pure creation of pagan mythology; having emerged fully armed and fully grown from Jupiter's brain, she never knew any stain, not even that of original sin."[45]

The claim that the true aesthetic experience is "virginal" upholds not simply the romantic illusion that "our desires are really our own, that they are truly original and spontaneous," but that the experience is men's own, that women have no part in it.[46] It is this autonomous and unmediated experience that the practice of criticism "sullies" and destroys, according to Gautier. "We don't know what pleasures the papers deprive us of. They take the virginity of everything; they ensure that we have nothing of our own, and that we cannot possess a book just for ourselves" (*MM*, p. 52).

The declarations of the autonomy of art and of the artist, for which Gautier is most often remembered, can only constitute a self-undermining practice similar to that which Geoffrey Hartman traces among modern poets. To describe the aesthetic experience as virginal is to claim for the artist/poet the task of "understanding experience in its immediacy. He has neglected the armature of the priest—the precautionary wisdom of tradition—and often, the inculcated re-spect for literary models." The price of autonomy, however, is solipsism and a contradiction. "Personal experience becomes the sole authority and source of conviction, and the poet a new intermediary."[47] In Gautier the act that brings together critic and artist as well as virginity and sexuality results in an analogous form of autoeroticism. In his own criticism, for example, he is reluctant to judge a work of art and prefers to recreate it through a more subtle appropriation of its inscribed passion for beauty. Delacroix has described his noncritical criticism in such terms. "He [Gautier] takes a painting, describes it in his own manner, makes a painting himself which is charming, but he hasn't performed an act of true criticism; as long as he manages to put on sparkling display those macro-expressions that he finds with a pleasure that sometimes wins you over, and cites Spain and Turkey, Ahambra and Atmandam of Constantinople, he is happy." Gautier's own criticism, that is to say, is not referential, but self-referential, taking pleasure in its own poetic status or, in Ross Chambers's terms, "loaded with the secret sensual delights of auto-eroticism [*la jouissance de soi*],"[48] a means of asserting the primacy of his own experience and his own creative desire. As Castex has pointed out, his criticism often becomes a mere pretext for "lyrical effusions" that carry him to ecstasy with the sound of his own language.[49]

Like Barthes, Gautier derives an endless pleasure from the text or artwork. His prefaces as well as his fiction are defenses of such textual pleasure as a writer's duty and right. "For enjoyment [*la jouissance* (p. 46)] seems to me to be the end of life, and the only useful thing in the world" (*MM*, p. 40).[50] Equated with *la jouissance*, the true aesthetic experience is both critical and artistic, virginal and sexual, heroic and narcissistic: each term apparently contradicted by its other half. Irreconcilable with itself, such an experience leads to the predicament of the modern poet who, according to Hartman, "having committed himself to unmediation, comes to know the need of mediation only the more strongly."[51]

I have already suggested that as clothed ideal the figure of the hermaphrodite mediates as an integral part of the aesthetic experience it projects. In the Preface to *Maupin*, the author directly declares his preference for textual veils or cover to the so-called nudity of the work of art—the controversial points that critics are so quick to jump upon. "If there is any nudity in a picture or a book, they go straight to it like a pig to filth, and they pay no heed to the flowers in bloom, or the luscious golden fruit that is hanging from every bough" (*MM*, p. 20). That preference, however, is not a matter of choice. "For myself," Gautier emphatically writes, "I am among those to whom the superfluous is necessary" (*MM*, p. 39). Indeed, the displacement of desire or pleasure to an endless proliferation of veils is a means of endlessly deferring its consummation and of guarding against its potential consequences—the discovery of impotence, loss of self, sexual difference.

The mediation of experience is not only external and nameable. Gautier's treatment of the "veiled" rhetoric of the critics reveals the metaphoric or veiled nature of all language, which prevents the very experience that language also makes possible. In mediating, art separates the subject from its object as from itself. As the necessary is diffused in the manifold appearance of beauty, we find that art for art denies the singular and all-encompassing experience it attempts to assert. More crucially, such mediation, as Geoffrey Hartman suggests, is often a necessary response to a fear of "unmediation." The fear of direct sense intuition that Hartman argues is one cause of the need for mediation, can be seen to be associated with the obsessive fear of death that critics are quick to point out in Gautier's fiction. Death offers the only possibility for the total unmediated experience. The threat of mortality is linked both to the threat of impotence or death of creativity and to the fear of woman as creator/mother, a reminder of our flesh-and-blood mortality.

Similar to his treatment of the veil, Gautier's "romantic irony" only exacerbates the deceptions and illusions it is intended to protect. Posing is what Gautier was known for, whether in terms of his scandalous red vest or his explosive language. But posing appears to preclude a stable and autonomous self-image. "After having tried to tear off Nessus's vest, which seemed to have encrusted itself to our skin, we bravely accepted it before the imagination of the bourgeois, whose hallucinating eye never sees us clothed in another color."[52] His voyages too, whether real or imaginary, manifest a "written" or clothed self that prefigures the indigenous: "As soon as I put my foot in a country, I become a native, I put on the costume."[53]

The inevitable fact of mediation, which is not only external but also constitutive (and thus deconstructive) of the self, negates the possibility for autonomous desire and for the aesthetic experience as a self-affirming *jouissance*. The nude ideal of the androgyne, in which desire and its object have the same, spontaneous origin, in which image is transparent to reality, is precluded by the appearance of the hermaphrodite, a clothed figure that emphasizes, in the end, the mediation of desire. As we turn to *Mademoiselle de Maupin,* we shall see how the hermaphroditic character upsets any stable relation between self and costume and, coterminously, masculine and feminine. Indeed, what the reader is presented with in the fictional figuration of the hermaphrodite is, not the legibility or transparency of attire, but its opacity and determining role with relation to the signified. Any clear definition of sex and self is lost in this novel's play of disguises.

In Quest of True Difference

Following the July Revolution, considerable controversy arose over the nature of the novel as a literary form. The year 1833, during which Gautier signed a contract for his first novel, *Mademoiselle de Maupin,* marked a high point of this genre's popularity in France; it was also the year in which hack novelists flooded the market.[54] The need to discriminate among writers and to better define the genre became a pressing problem.

It is around this time that the critical vocabulary applied to the plastic arts or to the established genres of poetry and drama is introduced into discussions of the novel and that the novel entered the ongoing classical-romantic polemic.[55] While there seemed to be "classics" among novels of the past, there were no classical models per se and no accepted means to say just what the novel was. Most often the novel was defined in relation to other genres—poetry, drama, or history—a practice that resulted in the novel's acknowledged status as a hybrid or bastard genre.

The illegitimacy of the novel as a genre and its relation to a deviant sexuality or gender find concrete expression in *Mademoiselle de Maupin.* At the same time, the difficulty of distinguishing what is deviant (outside nature) and what is ideal (superior to nature) is central to that novel and to the hermaphrodite who emerges as a figure for the text. The identification of hermaphrodite and novel, moreover, is not a completely new one. That connection had already been made by de Latouche, whose novel *Fragoletta* (1829) instituted a certain ambiguity over gender as well as genre.[56] "*Fragoletta*, at once history and novel, is the work of a patriot and a poet," stated *Le Constitutionnel* at the time of the novel's publication.[57] History and fiction, politics and art, were brought together in this novel of the hermaphrodite, which critics considered to be a triumph of romanticism. Similar expectations were raised with the announcement of the projected publication of *Maupin* in 1833. Gautier's novel was not, however, the adventure novel expected. Although the source of the novel is a documented subject of history—the escapades of Madeleine de Maupin, née d'Aubigny—it could not be called a historical novel, and one cannot but remark the unimportance of historical authenticity to its plot. Indeed, Gautier's novel rejects mimesis on two counts—the imitation of classical models and the reproduction of history or "reality." His novel thus appears to forge its own place in the classical-romantic debate.

The fact that there were no legitimate models for the genre had both advantages and disadvantages for romantic authors. On the one hand, it meant that writers could claim self-sufficiency and assure their originality in the creation of their work. On the other hand, this freedom from imitation had its price. Such novelties grow old quickly in a materialist society quick to appropriate and quicker still to discard one novelty in favor of another. The fear of such degeneration is apparent from the opening of Gautier's novel. Gautier, like his narrator, d'Albert, is guilty (if only cerebrally) of the very consumer mentality he hopes to combat. Author and hero confront the same question: how to imagine (create) a work of art that can resist the ravages of time and bourgeois caprice, how to reinvent a classical model worthy of endless imitation. This is the role given to the hermaphrodite as the ideal object of desire and the inscribed figure of the text.

"It is indeed among the most subtle creations of the pagan genius, this son of Hermes and Aphrodite. You can't imagine anything more ravishing in the world than these two bodies, both of them perfect, harmoniously fused together" (*MM*, p. 196). The dual ideal responds to the double needs of the chevalier d'Albert, who is both the narrator of the story writing the letters that comprise this epistolary novel and the object of its narration. As the writer/narrator, d'Albert finds himself an incurable romantic, unable to control and contain his own words, which take on an unruly life of their own. "Phew! that was an interminable tirade, and rather unepistolary in style. What a rig-marole! I have waxed lyrical with a vengeance, my very dear friend, and I've already Pindarized rather stupidly for a long time. It's all a very long way from our subject, which is, if I remember rightly, the glorious and triumphant story of the Chevalier d'Albert in pursuit of Daraide, the most beautiful princess in the world, as the old romances say" (*MM*, p. 78). The lack of closure in his writing, moreover, replicates a sense of incompletion in himself that complicates his role as a worthy object for this "glorious" narrative. Something, he feels, is missing, lacking in him. "Is it an opportunity for love, an adventure, a woman, an idea or a fortune, something which I lack and am seeking? . . . Is it my life which needs to be complete?" (*MM*, p. 58). For d'Albert, love and narrative are structured by the same motivating force, the desire for a harmonious completion that is both known and ideal. "In that respect I am rather like those people who take the novel by the tail, read the ending first, and go back to the first page. This way of reading and loving has its charm. You savour the details better when you are happy about the ending" (*MM*, p. 64).

D'Albert's quest as artist/lover is one long associated with the romantic mind and identified with the romantic narrator, a quest to overcome a subject/object split, to be simultaneously self and other and thereby to arrive at the transcendent and total consciousness associated with the classical ideal. He expresses that need to see himself as Other in sexual terms, as the desire to observe himself as a woman. "I began by wanting to be another man. Then I reflected that I could, by analogy, pretty much foresee what I should feel, and I shouldn't know the changes and surprises which I expected. I should therefore have preferred to be a woman . . . for it is very tiresome not to be conscious of the effect that one is producing and not to judge the pleasure of others except by one's own" (*MM*, p. 102). The desire for a whole, androgynous union of male and female thus responds to a demand for formal completion that is both erotic and aesthetic. D'Albert would like to be simultaneously man and woman in one body in order to combine the love and awareness of beauty by which he defines himself with the state of being beautiful by which he defines women: "I have loved . . . women, so that I might at least possess in someone else the beauty which was lacking in myself" (*MM*, p. 142).[58]

D'Albert's erotic drive can also be likened to his ironic impulse as narrator. D'Albert constitutes (and loves) self and other by highly and self-consciously illusory means: he first fantasizes, then critiques both the form and the content of his fantasies, and finally criticizes that self-reflective act itself, which, he admits, is dangerously narcissistic and solipsistic. D'Albert is among those ironizing artists and philosophers who, in Baudelaire's *De l'Essence du rire* (On the essence of laughter)," would define and differentiate themselves from nature through language, a practice that inevitably results in a splitting of empirical and ironic self.[59] Here, that splitting is formally reflected in the alternation between first- and third-person narrators and narration and theatrical dialogue. The sexual dimension further exacerbates the Schlegelian parabasis. The "language-determined man" reflects an increasingly unexpected and womanly nature that, in itself, produces something like that "new generation of little ironies" of which Schlegel warns.[60] "But a word brings a sentence, and parentheses grow fat with other little parentheses which, in turn, have others in their wombs about to be born. There is no reason why it should end" (*MM*, p. 243). The ironic consciousness can offer no reassurance to the self. By displacing otherness from a secure, objectifiable outside to an unknown realm within the self, the boundaries between self and other, male and female, are destabilized and an endless movement of self-differentiation is propelled. In seeking the total consciousness of the ideal romantic narrator, d'Albert's ironic self- and sex-consciousness undermines his desire for androgynous completion, lending support to Schlegel's claim that "true irony . . . is irony of love."[61]

From d'Albert's first letters, what is most obviously missing is the presence of the woman of his dreams, one who would exteriorize his "other half." This lack creates the ungainly detours in his plot and hinders his attempts at self-definition—how can he substantiate his claims to be artist, lover, or man without the object who can fulfill and reflect his talents? This is the role projected upon Madeleine de Maupin from the moment she appears. When d'Albert first sets eyes on her, he is sure that he has found his ideal beauty "realized at last, before my eyes" (*MM*, p. 146). Now he can be the hero of his own romantic love story. There is only one obstacle (but then the genre calls for such hurdles): Madeleine appears to be and calls herself a man, Théodore de Serannes. The conquest thus entails proving that Théodore is really a woman. "She has appeared to me in this disguise to test me, to see if I should recognize her, if my loving glance would penetrate the veils which enveloped her, as they do in those fairy-tales" (*MM*, p. 198). As we shall see, however, Madeleine/Théodore will challenge the conventions of gender as of genre. Designated as his "other half," s/he will prove to be other to d'Albert's openness, mirror to the sexual ambivalence he must recognize in himself.

In order to establish Théodore's true, feminine self, d'Albert must first establish that his/her exterior clothing is a deceptive mask of his/her true self. This quest is metaphorically expressed in the desire to undress Théodore-Maupin and uncover the "travestissement" (*MM*, p. 163). Not unlike the bourgeois reader criticized in the Preface to *Les Jeunes France* for "abusing" books as he does women, d'Albert has admittedly "used and "abused" the women he has known thus far (*MM*, p. 121). But Théodore/Madeleine as figure for the ideal work of art is not so easily undressed and appropriated by the observer/reader, nor by the lover. Neither dress nor language function for him/her according to the bourgeois code of transparency or super-fluity. If the adoption of breeches and a sword in lieu of skirts and petticoats is first thought to be a mask, in a short time that mask becomes the defining element, "My disguise seemed to be my ordinary dress," s/he admits (*MM*, p. 273). Clothes and appearance shape his/her own language and determine the relationship between self and other; "for, indeed, it is difficult to speak love to someone who has the same clothes as you." Unsettling the boundaries between masculine and feminine, Théodore/Madeleine undermines d'Albert's designs to "assimilate that perfection," to make him/her his own (*MM*, p. 178). Instead, it is his own masculine, heroic role that comes into question: "You pitied me for not loving. Pity me, now, for loving whom I love. What misfortune, what an axe-blow on my life, which was already cut in so many pieces! What senseless, guilty, hateful passion has taken hold of me! It is a disgrace, and I shall never cease to blush for it. It is the most deplorable of all my aberrations, I can't begin to understand it, I don't comprehend it in the least, everything in me is upside-down and in confusion; I no longer know who I am, or what others are, I wonder if I'm a man or a woman, I have a horror of myself" (*MM*, p. 181). Sexuality and sexual difference are thus displaced from essentializing notions of gender to enact a concept of pure difference that disallows stable identity.

The idea that there may be no essential or naked self under a veiled appearance is put into play in the staging of Shakespeare's *As You Like It* within the novel. The themes of appearance versus reality and costume versus true identity are there interwoven with gender distinctions that identify "true" gender with the naked self. The central character, Rosalinde, dresses as a man to test her lover's (Orlando's) insight and devotion. When in Gautier's novel Théodore/ Madeleine plays Rosalinde, the distinction between costume and true garment presents an even greater difficulty. Théodore's sexual ambivalence makes him/her seem properly costumed as both Rosalinde and Ganymede. His/her clothes may signal a sexual identity, but only as they also prepare for an inversion and subversion of that identity—a "masculine attire" with a "feminine lining" (*MM*, p. 249).

For d'Albert, the result is no less than dramatic. The sexual confusion of the play's "hermaphrodite words" (*MM*, p. 252) reflects and exacerbates the confusion of fictional inside and real outside. "Orlando was myself at least as much as I was Orlando" (p. 248). Indeed, d'Albert/Orlando's uncertainty over the true identity of Théodore/Rosalinde is doubly his; neither as actor nor as director, neither onstage nor offstage, can he know whether his leading lady is in or out of costume. Even as he projects upon their love a vision of holistic and androgynous fusion of self and other, he also admits to a frightening loss of self and to the discovery of his own otherness. "The meaning of my existence completely escapes me. The sound of my voice surprises me to an unimaginable degree, and I should sometimes be tempted to take it for someone else's voice" (*MM*, p. 234).

If d'Albert has expected to represent his own experience in this play and thereby to accelerate the conclusion of his affair with Madeleine/Théodore by enacting Shakespeare's conclusion, it is clear that he has not fully understood the function of art or representation. The attempt to create and direct "real theater" (*MM*, p. 237; un théatre véritable [p. 255]) only repeats and confuses the issues already posed by the attempt to create and direct a "real French novel" (*MM*, p. 98; "un véritable roman français" [p. 102]). The question d'Albert as artist and art critic has not asked and that his use of *véritable* seems in effect to answer is the question of truth in art, whether truth can be named or unveiled. Playing her role to the limit, Théodore goes beyond the unmasking of Ganymede who, in Shakespeare's version, unveils the unmasculine and most positively feminine Rosalinde. Image of the veiled text, his/her apparent mediation precludes the function of art as a mirror that reveals some objective ideal or reflects the unique nature of a unified subject. True, s/he can play the mimetic role and thereby substantiate d'Albert's/Orlando's dreams, reflect his Pygmalion's touch: "Rosalinde was endlessly obliging, and did not resist—and she tried to return his caresses as faithfully as possible" (*MM*, p. 341). But s/he also calls attention to the motivation behind that role, whose "truth" lies either in the "fallacies" of the male subject or in the essential untruth and difference of what he objectifies.[62] If, as a woman, Madeleine or Rosalinde has a talent for acting and playing roles, she does not devote herself to any one—no "uniform" defines her. As Luce Irigaray writes, "if women are such good mimics, it is because they are not simply resorbed in this function. *They also remain elsewhere.*"[63]

Determined as woman/object/art, Théodore/Rosalinde is also freed by the habits of subjecthood s/he adopts as writer, lover, and actor, calling attention to the fact that art not only represents, it also produces meaning. S/he unveils the ideologies (and particularly the male ideologies) that determine and are determined by such acts of representation—the fact that "since time immemorial, fathers, husbands and lovers have had the privilege of seeing nothing" (*MM*, p. 168). Leaving d'Albert's room on the night of the consummation of their love, s/he subverts both narrative and social expectations and enters the room of his former lover, Rosette. S/he enters a realm that marks the limits of d'Albert's foresight, the limits of narrative truth, and, more importantly, the limits of representation in its acceptable, masculine form: "What she said there, what she did there, I have never been able to discover, although I have done the most diligent research. . . . I've made a thousand conjectures about it, each more preposterous than the other, and so far-fetched that I really don't dare to write them down, even in the most suitable periphrased style" (*MM*, p. 345).

Shattering d'Albert's faith in the classical unity of the beautiful, the good, and the true, frustrating his romantic desire to claim his ideal, s/he also deprives him of the closure and (self-)knowledge he and an androgynous tradition have associated with love. Indeed, s/he duplicates his "ironic consciousness." His/her final letter to d'Albert acknowledges his/her (Rosalinde's) absence from that which represents him/her (whether it be the letter itself or his/her name or the fantasy s/he has embodied); it acknowledges that s/he is indeed always elsewhere: "Don't try to follow me or find me again: you won't succeed" (*MM*, p. 345).

Madeleine/Theodore thus inscribes both self and sex, not in terms of the either/or that d'Albert and the reader have expected, but outside the binary logic of polarities as a both/and, "a third sex, a sex apart which has as yet no name." Protesting the repressive nature of desire, aesthetic or erotic, that satisfies only "one side of [her] nature," s/he envisions love as a process of endless self-fragmentation and creation. "My dream would be to have each sex in turn, and to satisfy my dual nature: man today, woman tomorrow. . . . My nature would then be completely fulfilled, and I should be perfectly happy, for true happiness is to be able to develop freely in all directions and to be everything that you can be." S/he thus introduces d'Albert and the reader to a new and modernist relationship with art and beauty and to a new type of critical reading, one that emphasizes a Nietzschean idea of process without totalization or conclusion. "In love as in poetry, staying still means falling back" (*MM*, pp. 330, 348).

Whereas, for Gautier, the feminine can be seen to embody an idealized other whom the writer/hero creates as his symmetrical opposite, this image of the feminine must also be seen to reflect only one side of his particular poetics of desire in which artist and art are created simultaneously and where the boundary between masculine and feminine shifts between fiction and reality. A more appropriate figure of art and of Gautier's text (perhaps in its impropriety) is that of the hermaphrodite, whose veiled appearance and constant transformations dramatize an endless process of signification and aesthetic creativity and hence the desperate need for play. In this staging of sexual difference, what is at stake is the play of identity, whether of self, sex, or text.

In the preceding pages we have seen how the image of the androgyne is linked to a conservative, if not a reactionary, ideal in the early nineteenth century, both in its aesthetic precepts and in its social and psychological claims. In response to the postrevolutionary sense of a loss of shared ideals, and loss of a common language to represent those ideals, writers turned to this image, and to related paradigms of division in totality, to make sense of the changing social world around them. The difference between male and female was, it appeared, the most obvious and the most perdurable of binarisms and hence could compensate for, if not correct, the increasing loss of distinctions in bourgeois society. By establishing an original difference (between sexes as between self and other), and simultaneously transcending that difference, the androgyne served as a transcendental signified that restored meaning to classical notions of truth, beauty, and knowledge. An image of origins, it also functioned as an image of ends and of a historical process that gave reason to the present state of social confusion. In the image of the androgyne, authors stated, "I know the difference and how to transcend it"; "I know how to speak to and for my other."

And yet as we found in Schlegel, so in the narratives of Balzac and Gautier, the certainty of such knowledge of sexual difference is immediately undercut by a concomitant statement of "I know better, but . . . ," in other words, "I know that this difference I claim is of my own making, a fantasy I have created, but I prefer my dreams to the world around me." This voice that knows better is the ironic voice that pervades their writing, an authorial presence that understands that the difference it seeks to know and define (and in these narratives such difference is above all a feminine difference) is never where he thinks it is. The ironic voice is one who knows, not androgynous totality, but hermaphroditic fragmentation, and the endless play of (sexual) "différance."

Play is a term I have used in this chapter to describe a modernist aesthetic and a new relationship to both text and sex that become evident in the figuration of the androgyne/hermaphrodite. Play and irony and the Derridean concept of *différance* demand this relation because they work to undo the structure of oppositions that define identity and because they expose the fraudulent boundaries that are used to distinguish object from subject, other from self, woman from man. These concepts, furthermore, have been important in my analyses because they signal a connection between the identity of genre and the identity of gender, allowing me to stage the figure of the androgyne/hermaphrodite at that intersection. This figure can also be seen to stand at a crossroad of poststructuralist and feminist theories. However, *play*, like Schlegel's irony, cannot always be assimilated to a feminist practice. Such play in Gautier, and to a lesser extent in Balzac, can itself be a defensive strategy, a means of retextualizing feminine desire so as to establish at least some form of intellectual mastery over its unknown power. If, consequently, Gautier's text, with its willingness to learn to play with difference, looks ahead to the moment when feminist and poststructuralist theories will come together to challenge the patriarchal and often misogynist foundation of the androgynous ideal, it also illustrates some of the less apparent dangers to be encountered by feminists in such a collaboration.

Part III

The normal and comfortable state of being is that when the two live in harmony together, spiritually cooperating. If one is a man, still the woman part of the brain must have effect; and a woman also must have intercourse with the man in her. Coleridge perhaps meant this when he said that a great mind is androgynous. It is when this fusion takes place that the mind is fully fertilized and uses all its faculties.

—Virginia Woolf, *A Room of One's Own*

There are words I cannot choose again: humanism, androgyny.

—Adrienne Rich, "Natural Resources"

Androgyny in a new key? Why not? Or better still, androgynandry, gynandrogyny. The possibility of such multiple blurrings (which are not an attempt to deny difference . . . but rather an attempt to redraw and mix up the lines of differences in new, energizing ways) is the "dream" my own essay ends with. . . . It is, I think, a dream worth pursuing.

—Susan Suleiman, Introduction to *The Female Body in Western Culture*

6

Androgyny, Feminism, and the Critical Difference

HOW HAS androgyny figured in feminist theories and criticism within the American academic institution? What is the relation of androgyny to feminism in the United States? These are questions I would like to address in this final chapter by reviewing academic feminist reactions to the concept of androgyny over the past century and more particularly over the past thirty years. The epigraphs above outline three phases of the history of this reception. A first phase, particularly apparent during the sixties, called upon Virginia Woolf to authorize its campaign for a necessary cooperation and co-presence of male and female within the individual as within the institution. Thus, the concept of androgyny was integrated into a fight for psychological and sociopolitical equality between the sexes. A second phase, more explicitly separatist in its goals, reacted against this notion of androgyny, rejecting it along with equality and even humanism as viable ideals for women. Such words were understood to be deceptive covers of male privilege and standards. At the same time, however, particularly under the influence of so-called French feminism, a conceptual redefinition of sexual difference and consequently of androgyny was initiated within the academy. With its emphasis on the body and on the ever-changing boundaries between sexes and sexualities, a new ideal was constructed that could be called (for reasons we shall see below), a dream of hermaphroditism. Lest I appear to be positioning that dream as the third stage of a dialectic and claiming its advance over the other two, let me say now, as I shall discuss more fully, that I recognize that this position too, is a problematic one for feminists, and that any sublation of the former two categories could have dangerous consequences for women.

While, in the order that I have placed these phases they appear to chart a historical development in feminist theory, they are neither necessarily chronological nor successive. I see them corresponding rather to Julia Kristeva's three "generations" of women, each one implying "less a chronology than a 'signifying space,' a both corporeal and desiring mental space. So it can be argued that as of now a third attitude is possible, thus a third generation, which does not exclude—quite to the contrary—the 'parallel' existence of all three in the same historical time, or even that they be interwoven one with the other."[1] My intention is not simply to reconstruct these fragile categories, but to identify significant moments and problems in the feminist construction and reception of a notion of androgyny, particularly as I see that these problems persist in the ongoing feminist effort to come to grips with sexual difference and devise a politics around it. I shall be referring to the work of Virginia Woolf throughout this chapter, in part, because she has been the catalyst for much of the feminist critical attention to androgyny. Her writing exhibits clear continuities with the androgynous tradition examined in this book. But it also makes apparent the difficulties that arise when this tradition and its rhetoric are appropriated for feminist purposes.

Recognizing Woolf's Androgyny

In the last chapters of *A Room of One's Own,* published in 1929, Virginia Woolf discusses the effect of sex on novel writing and on the novelist. "It is fatal," she writes, "for anyone who writes to think of their sex. It is fatal to be a man or woman pure and simple; one must be womanly-manly or man-womanly." To be conscious of one's sex, she suggests, is a form of repression; it interferes with what she refers to as "the unity of the mind" and consequently with the "fullness" of the work. "Some marriage of opposites must be consummated. The whole of the mind must lie wide open if we are to get the sense that the writer is communicating his experience with perfect fullness." Such statements, with their emphasis on "wholeness" and "fullness," draw heavily from the classical tradition. Woolf's link between writing and the androgynous mind recalls an idealist faith in language as a transparent representation of the idea. "The androgynous mind is resonant and porous, it transmits emotion without impediment."[2] In even more explicit terms than in Balzac and Gautier, Woolf advocates androgyny as a psychological and poetic ideal, a transcendence of sex, self, and language.

Writing in homage to Virginia Woolf and the entire Bloomsbury group—described, "not as the apotheosis of the androgynous spirit, but as the first actual example of such a way of life in practice"— Carolyn Heilbrun was also one of the first women within the academy to claim "the recognition of androgyny" as a forward step and positive goal for women.[3] Defining androgyny as "a movement away from sexual polarization and the prison of gender toward a world in which individual roles and the modes of personal behavior can be freely chosen" (*TRA*, p. ix), her discussion moves between literary criticism—the uncovering of an androgynous tradition in literature from classical Greece through Shakespeare to Woolf—and a social plea. It is in androgyny, she says, that our "future salvation lies" (*TRA*, p. 115).

A highly acclaimed book that was based on articles first published from 1964 to 1973 and that appeared in 1982, *Toward a Recognition of Androgyny* presents a plea to break free of strict gender definition and promotes a social ideal of equality between the sexes within the established social and symbolic order. What Heilbrun calls "the recognition of androgyny," refers to the uncovering of the necessary and positive role that women have played within the social order, even as they have so often remained hidden. Equating literary androgyny with "the re-entry of the 'feminine principle' as a civilizing force" (*TRA*, p. 21), she traces that force through an impressive list of works from the *Iliad* through Shakespeare and Spenser and up to Thomas Mann, demonstrating throughout a continuity of support for an ideal of "wholeness" defined as the union of masculine and feminine.

Since Heilbrun, however, feminists have questioned to what extent such an ideal is adequate or workable for those wishing to assert a different set of aesthetic assumptions as well as a different subjectivity, one that does not risk appropriation by or effacement within the "whole" of a classical and patriarchal order. The concept of wholeness, like that of recognition, is problematic for this goal. Both imply the presence of an essential and knowable, universal femininity (or for that matter, masculinity), lying in wait to be uncovered. To recognize androgyny in literature neglects the ways in which such texts produce the very feminine principle projected as so necessary for its ideal. More importantly, it neglects how the feminine is produced for the purpose of "civilizing" or perfecting a male subject whose implicit supremacy is never challenged. Heilbrun appears unaware of this prioritizing of the masculine, particularly in part two of her book, where the "androgynous force" in the modern period is discussed in terms of the "woman as hero," who becomes "the embodiment of the male writer's artistic vision" (*TRA,* p. 49). Equally idealistic is her admiration for the hippie generation of the sixties, whose long hair and unisex clothing she views as an homage to androgyny and a sign of the widespread acceptance and valorization of a feminine principle. (Undoubtedly she would not make the same claim for the corporate gray suit as the eighties or nineties version of gender-free dressing.) The sixties, however, were not unlike other periods of war during which the apparent reversal of gender hierarchies and promotion of a feminine/pacifist principle had little, if any, positive effect on the image and lives of real women. Indeed, as has frequently been discussed, women of the hippie generation did not share in the same expansion of gender boundaries. If men became more 'feminine' in their attachment to nonaggressive or nonviolent behavior, women were more strictly tied to their conventional identification with nature and sensuality. Earth mothers, they were regarded as naturally destined to nurture and love the men around them. Such exaltation of the feminine, like the choice of "the woman as hero," often goes hand in hand with an effacement of women or a misogynistic attitude. Flaubert's "Madame Bovary, c'est moi" is an androgynous statement only if we accept that androgyny is a masculine ideal that says that men can be women too and that, therefore, women are superfluous. Heilbrun goes so far as to point out the paradoxical situation whereby the ideal of androgyny in the novel arose during a period of intensified sexual polarization, but she does not consider the ways in which a cultivated, literary androgyny might compensate for and thus contribute to sexual polarization or vice versa.

I do not mean by this to discount the motives of Heilbrun's book nor the insights of her readings, which retain a great deal of validity. Hers is a brave work, written in the face of obvious resistance. Heilbrun fears a readership to whom the mere idea of androgyny might be "viscerally unbearable" (*TRA*, p. x). Wishing to promote an ideal that is equally valid for men and women alike, she insists that androgyny is distinct from feminism—a statement that says more about Heilbrun's apprehension about feminism as a separatist movement than it does about the nature of androgyny.[4] She also wishes to make clear that androgyny is not the same as the "physical anomaly" of "hermaphroditism" (*TRA*, p. xii), and should not be confused with homosexuality or bisexuality even while these physical states seem to occur frequently amongst producers of androgynous works (*TRA*, pp. xiii, 118). *For* women, but against feminism, against sexual polarization but exclusively for heterosexuality—such is the problematic platform on which androgyny is hailed in Heilbrun's book, as indeed in much of the literature I have examined in this book. For her, androgyny is a spiritual or intellectual ideal that denies the importance of the body, of sexual desires, or for that matter, of any material markings of sexual difference.

The Flight from Androgyny

In 1977, Elaine Showalter published *A Literature of Their Own*, a book wherein she rejects both androgyny as an ideal and Virginia Woolf as a positive model for women authors. In a chapter entitled, "Virginia Woolf and the Flight into Androgyny," she refutes the vision of Bloomsbury as a gender-relaxed utopia, arguing instead that androgyny is an evasive fantasy that allowed Woolf to ignore her needs and self-expression as a woman writer. "Androgyny was the myth that helped her evade confrontation with her own painful femaleness and enabled her to choke and repress her anger and ambition."[5]

Unlike Heilbrun's, Showalter's book was part of a new generation of scholarship and of women scholars who emphasized the importance of calling themselves feminists. Her book represented a new phase of what has come to be known as gyno-criticism, focusing on literature by women and concerned with establishing a different female tradition. For this reason, however, Woolf's writing frustrated

Showalter because she could find in it neither "an articulation of women's experience" nor the "autonomous self-expression" that she claims in her Introduction is what defines a "female literature." Identifying "female experience" primarily with experiences of the body—menstruation, passion, menopause—Showalter says that Woolf "avoided describing her own experience" in her essays and was "unable to express . . . the claims of female experience" in her novels (*LTO,* p. 294). She blames this avoidance, in part, on the link between Bloomsbury's aesthetics and its "sexual ethic of androgyny," which demanded and "provided an escape from confrontation with the body" (*LTO,* p. 34), above all the female body. Quoting what appears as the first epigraph to this chapter Showalter argues that androgyny is for Woolf, not an ideal, but a form of sexual sublimation. If one reads further, she points out, one can see that Woolf, without looking, "made the writer male" (*LTO,* p. 288). "Some marriage of opposites has to be consummated. The whole of the mind must lie wide open if we are to get the sense that the writer is communicating his experience with perfect fullness. There must be freedom and there must be peace . . . the curtains must be close drawn. The writer, I thought, once *his* experience is over, must lie back and let *his* mind celebrate its nuptials in darkness. He must not look or question what is being done."[6] Assuming Woolf's identification with "the writer," Showalter thus makes her point—androgyny is a myth that distanced Woolf from herself and from the claims of her woman's body, a myth that allowed her to dream of sexual equality all the while that it reconfirmed the dominance of the masculine. A strong accusation, to be sure. Yet it is not clear that Woolf does identify with "the writer," a profession that *A Room of One's Own* deliberately defines in masculine terms. In that essay, Woolf critiques the self-conscious virility of men's writing and the sterility of their self-confident and dominating "I," so as to distance herself and her own "I" from a "masculine" mode of writing, even as she dislodges both male and female pronouns from their secure ground in a unified, controlling subject. This recasting of identity and sexuality, as I shall discuss below, is not assimilable to the understanding of feminism laid out in Showalter's book.

Showalter's book followed a special forum on androgyny at the 1973 annual meeting of the Modern Language Association and the eventual publication of the papers presented there under the title *The Androgyny Papers* as the second volume of *Women's Studies*. In this collection of essays including one by Carolyn Heilbrun, the term *androgyny* is reexamined from a "literary, cultural, and political perspective."[7] Consisting mostly of rereadings of the major myths of androgyny in Greece, in hermetic philosophy, even in Jungian psychology, the majority of these essays conclude that androgyny is essentially a masculine ideal and one inappropriate for women wishing to advance themselves or to promote the new discipline of women's studies in the academy. The articles by Barbara Gelpi and Cynthia Secor, for example, state that androgynes are always feminized males, never masculine women.[8] Referring to the representations of the seventeenth-century female mystic Antoinette Bourignon, Gelpi emphasizes that within the androgynous tradition, even women are brought to see their most glorified image as that of a man. Secor furthers the argument by pointing out that the myth is not only sexist but heterosexist, focusing on the complementarity of genital differences and promoting the oppressive institution of marriage. Daniel Harris and Catherine Stimpson confirm this last point by showing how the myth of androgyny has been used to deride homosexuals, suggesting that they and women are the feared targets and victims of this so-called ideal.[9] Harris's warning is urgent: "Although the myth is a purely imaginative construct, unusually malleable because it corresponds to nothing we commonly observe in our experience, it has a history; and it is dangerously naive, as well as peculiarly American, to think that we can cauterize from our cultural consciousness the values and connotations which a word acquires in its evolution."[10] Hence Adrienne Rich's elimination of *androgyny* from the words she could ever again choose to write.

For the most part, then, the contributors to the *Women's Studies* volume agree that the concept of androgyny belongs solely to a patriarchal order and can have no place as an ideal for women. Only the essays by Heilbrun and by Nancy Topping Bazin and Alma Freeman attempt to hold on to the concept, exhibiting faith that we *can* move beyond history if not beyond language itself.[11] "Our concept of androgyny must be new; it must not be limited by what A. J. L. Busst or Samuel Coleridge or Virginia Woolf or even Simone de Beauvoir seemed to mean by it." Heilbrun's essay restates the

Introduction to her book, claiming again that despite what her readers think and say, she is not talking about homosexuality or bisexuality or hermaphroditism, but about Coleridge's androgyny of the mind. Bazin and Freeman similarly stress that they are using the term "in a cultural rather than in a physical sense."[12] Thus these essays salvage the ideal only be reinstating the mind/body dualism and the concept of wholeness that have constituted the underpinnings of patriarchal ideology. In the tradition of classical aesthetics, as well as in psychoanalytic theory, wholeness has been the privilege of the masculine—woman being defined alternatively as immanence, and hence too close to nature, or as lacking (castrated), a hole instead of a whole.[13]

This last point is forcefully made by Mary Daly, who, having promoted androgyny as a state of "psychic wholeness" and "transcendence" in her first book, *Beyond God the Father* (1973), turns radically against the concept in *Gyn/Ecology* (1978), stating that "feminist theorists have gone through frustrating attempts to describe our integrity by such terms as *androgyny*. Experience proved that this word, which we now recognize as expressing pseudowholeness in its combination of distorted gender descriptions, failed and betrayed our thought. . . . When we heard the word echoed back by those who misinterpreted our thought we realized that combining the 'halves' offered to consciousness by patriarchal language usually results in portraying something more like a hole than a whole."[14]

This much is true of the textual body as well. The demand for wholeness is fundamental to classical aesthetics and to a humanist tradition that, if it sees women at all, sees them as always representative of the part or the "hole" of Man. Nor is it only those feminists who support androgyny, whose aesthetic prescriptions, like their understanding of subjectivity, are shaped by the ideology of wholeness. As Toril Moi writes, it is "by their more or less unwitting subscription to the humanist aesthetic categories of the traditional male academic hierarchy" that feminists have failed to challenge the institution, and failed "to read Virginia Woolf as the progressive, feminist writer of genius she undoubtedly was."[15] Seeing herself as having moved beyond humanist aesthetic categories, Toril Moi envisions a third generation, based on a rereading of Woolf.

The Third Generation, Where *Orlando* Comes of Age

Whereas the rejection of the "ideology of wholeness" led Mary Daly more deeply into radical feminism and a female-centered world, for Toril Moi it leads, and must lead, to a view that the categories of male and female are themselves false. In *Sexual/Textual Politics*, Toril Moi borrows Kristeva's three-tiered scheme to define three stages of feminist criticism—much as I have been doing here—placing herself, along with Kristeva, in the third position. From this vantage point she launches her critique not only against the first stage's fight for equality in the institution but even more so against the promotion of a "real" difference that she associates with the second generation. Indeed, she quickly effaces the differences between the first and second generations, taking Elaine Showalter as representative of an "essentialism" that defines both and that, henceforth, becomes the focus of her critique.

According to Moi, Showalter's reading of *A Room of One's Own*, is "not reading it at all" (*S/T*, p. 3). Rather it is exemplary of a whole tradition of criticism whose preconceptions of what literature is—and consequently how to read it—are at odds with any feminist practice. Showalter seeks an "effective feminist writing . . . which would present truthful images of strong women with which the reader may identify" (*S/T*, p. 7). Her search thus privileges a certain kind of writing known as "bourgeois realism," and assumes that a feminist would necessarily write realist fiction (*S/T*, p. 6). It should not be surprising then, that Showalter links Woolf's self-compromising androgyny to her move away from realism.[16] Moi contends that the very way Showalter reads precludes "any recognition of Virginia Woolf's modernism" (*S/T*, p. 4). Indeed, Woolf undermines the very concepts of writing and of self on which Showalter's feminism, like male humanism, depends. What "feminists such as Showalter . . . fail to grasp," Moi states,

> is that the traditional humanism they represent is in effect part
> of patriarchal ideology. At its center is the seamlessly unified self
> either individual or collective—which is commonly called
> "Man." . . . In this humanist ideology the self is the "sole author"
> of history and of the literary text: the humanist creator is potent,

phallic and male—God in relation to his world, the author in relation to his text. History of the text becomes nothing but the "expression" of this unique individual: all art becomes autobiog-
raphy, a mere window on to the self and the world, with no reality
of its own. The text is reduced to a passive, "feminine" reflection
of an unproblematically "given," "masculine" world or self. (*S/T,*
p. 8)

For Moi, on the contrary, Woolf's problematizing of the notion
of identity—whether of self or of text—makes her into the strongest
of feminist forbears because her writing deconstructs the philosophical logic that sets the first two stages in opposition to each other. As
Julia Kristeva explains, in the third stage or "attitude," "the very
dichotomy man/woman as an opposition between two rival entities
may be understood as belonging to 'metaphysics.' What can 'identity,' even 'sexual identity,' mean in a new theoretical and scientific
space where the very notion of identity is challenged?"[17] Articulating
the third stage through the theories of Jacques Derrida and Jacques
Lacan, both Moi and Kristeva describe it as one that refutes the
basis of Western metaphysics, and understands identity as forever
split by the forces of desire and language. Sexual difference in this
stage is "*différance,*" emphasizing that identity is only constituted
in language by what it is not, by what is absent or excluded from
it.[18] The boundaries of identity, or those between identities, are not
(god-)given.

Even though she "cannot . . . be considered a purely *feminist*
theorist," Kristeva is, for Moi, the most challenging thinker for
feminists because of her "uncompromising anti-essentialism," which
is to say, her steering clear of the first two stages and what Moi calls
the "minefield of femininity and femaleness" (*S/T,* pp. 149, 148).
Thus, Kristeva will speak of "a certain bisexuality" in all subjects, but
refuse to *name* woman. "A woman," she writes "cannot be," her role
can only be negative, to say no to the names or definitions that have
been imposed upon her.[19] Moi's praise for Kristeva and her own
antiessentialist stance seem motivated, in part, by Moi's discomfort
with issues of the body (as if any mention of the body necessarily
"slips" into biologism, hence essentialism, hence is bad), and especially with any theorist who would dare attribute a positive difference
to a woman's body—hence Moi's attack on Showalter.[20] It is for this

reason that Moi is leery of Hélène Cixous and Luce Irigaray, both of whom describe a similar bisexuality or deconstructed androgyny, but do so with reference to woman's "different" sexuality.

In "The Laugh of the Medusa," Cixous speaks of an "other bisexuality," one that is not asexual, nor necessarily heterosexual, and whose multiple and constantly changing sexuality is opposed to the masculine "fantasy of a 'total being.'" "Bisexuality: that is, each one's location in self (repérage en soi) of the presence—variously manifest and insistent according to each person, male or female—of both sexes, non-exclusion either of the difference or of one sex, and, from this 'self-permission,' multiplication of the effects of the inscription of desire, over all parts of my body and the other body."[21] Here, sexuality is a set of effects, not causes, and its inscriptions on the body are multiple, not dual.

The title of Irigaray's *This Sex Which Is Not One* reflects a similar rejection of unity and oneness even as it figures this difference in female anatomy. Wholeness, like oneness, she makes clear, has always collapsed difference, fused it into a masculine sameness. Thus, instead of oneness, she promotes "an odd sort of two. And yet not one. Especially not one."[22] Instead of a nondifferentiated oneness, Irigaray describes a two whose "indifference"—which is to say whose detachment from the patriarchal one and whose infinite difference within its selves—denies any possibility either for simple opposition or for completed union. Thus, there is an apparent contradiction in Irigaray's text between a theory of sexual difference that dislodges sexual identity from any stable, unifiable meaning, and, at the same time, the attribution of a positivity to female sexuality. As Moi might explain it, Irigaray joins the third generation in her rejection of metaphysics, but lapses into the essentialism of the second generation, "falls for the temptation to produce her own positive theory of femininity. But as we have seen to define 'woman' is necessarily to essentialize her" (*S/T*, p. 139).

Is this necessarily true? Is there no way to name woman without essentializing her, and if so, is this necessarily the evil that Moi claims it to be. I do not wish to reopen the question of the possible "strategies" behind Irigaray's essentialism here, but I would like to address it by taking Moi's suggestion and rereading sexual difference as it is figured in Virginia Woolf.[23] I turn to *Orlando* (1928), a novel Woolf worked on at the same time as *A Room of One's Own* and where she redefines androgyny by reconceptualizing both sexual and textual identity in what appear to be antiessentialist terms. If androgyny is projected in the essay as a "marriage of opposites," a fusion of male and female resulting in an ideal of wholeness and unity, in the novel there is no such fusion.[24] Instead, the opposition of male and female, and hence the patriarchal construction of woman as different from man, is called into question, challenging the androgynous ideals of psychological equilibrium and aesthetic harmony and fullness, which are defined by means of that opposition.[25] And yet *Orlando* never loses sight of the importance of naming woman.

Orlando is the make-believe biography of a person freed from the restraints of time and gender.[26] A would-be poet born in the Elizabethan age, Orlando's story takes "him" through three centuries until, during the reign of Queen Victoria, he becomes both a writer and, lo and behold, a woman—though one whose sex is only fully ascertained in the twentieth century. The very first line of this novel/biography simultaneously asserts and problematizes sexual identity: "He—for there could be no doubt of his sex, though the fashion of the time did something to disguise it."[27] Establishing the thematic link between sex and dress, this opening also makes use of a sexual opposition in order to structure and engender a system of analogous relationships implicated in this work—biography versus novel or poetry, objective truth versus subjective fiction. "Happy the mother who bears, happier still the biographer who records the life of such a one! Never need she vex herself, nor he invoke the help of novelist or poet" (*O,* pp. 14–15).

In *Orlando* Woolf plays both with the idea that biography necessitates an objective—hence male—viewpoint and with the idea that the subjects of biography are stable identities that can be objectified and thoroughly judged. The developing indeterminacy of Orlando's sex unseats the biographer from his/her position of control. Thus, so long as Orlando is a boy with masculine (even though adolescent) desires, the moral quality of his relationships appears unproblematic; as, for example, in his early attraction to the Russian prince, revealed later to be a princess. "When the boy, for alas a boy it must be—no woman could skate with such speed and vigor—swept on tiptoe past him, Orlando was ready to tear his hair out with vexation that the person was of his own sex, and thus all embraces were out of the question" (*O,* p. 38)*.* As it becomes increasingly difficult to distinguish between same and different sex, however, sexual identity loses its claim as a "given," appearing, rather, as an effect of the cultural codes of desire and of changing relations to "others." Terms such as *man* and *woman* lose any necessary relation to identity, functioning instead as conventional masks that conceal the multiple divisions of man and woman within the self—as Orlando's transformation makes apparent. "And as all Orlando's loves had been women, now through the culpable laggardy of the human frame to adapt itself to convention, though she herself was a woman, it was still a woman she loved; and if the consciousness of being of the same sex had any effect at all, it was to quicken and deepen those feelings which she had had as a man" (*O,* p. 161). Here sameness is no more than a repression of difference within—of man within woman, woman within man. Sex, Woolf seems to be saying, can be taken on and off like clothing since "there is much to support the view that it is clothes that wear us and not we them; . . . they mold our hearts, our brains, our tongues to their liking" (*O,* p. 188). Sexuality, like writing a biography, is a continuing process of construction and destruction that never reaches a unified end—like Orlando's poem, which, we are told, looked as if "in the process of writing it would be completely unwritten" (*O,* p. 18). Rather than veil "otherness," Woolf's text deliberately voices this form of "*différance*" for a new understanding of its generative function within identity: "Everything was partly something else, and each gained an odd moving power from this union of itself and something not itself so that with this mixture of truth and falsehood her mind became like a forest in which things moved; lights and shadows changed, and one thing became another." As this work challenges the very concepts of self and identity on which realist fiction, like biography, relies, Woolf also exposes the flaw in Showalter's opposition between the experience of the body and the "aestheticism" of her androgyny. For here the body is experienced in its clothes, as in the language and writing through which it presents itself. To challenge forms of experience, one must thus change the forms of writing, not promote faith in its own bodilessness or immediacy.

"Androgyny in a new key?" asks Susan Suleiman of similar

dreams of "sexual minglings" that "mix up the lines of differences in new, energizing ways;" dreams, she explains, whose object "is to get beyond not only the number one—the number that determines unity, of body or of self—but also beyond the number *two,* which determines difference, antagonism, and exchange conceived of as merely the coming together of opposites."[28] Let me pause here for a moment, before we become comforted by the apparent progress implied in this third generation. One must approach the three "generations" as themselves conventional or critical constructs, and we would be wrong only to see in Woolf an example of a poststructuralist poetics, challenging the metaphysics of identity and celebrating a Nietzschean play of difference. Indeed, her undermining of identity does not preclude her recognition of real, material difference. The relationship between sex, economic class, and writing is, of course, central to *A Room of One's Own. Orlando,* too, in more whimsical fashion, points to the way in which men and women's experiences are shaped differently by the social and cultural contexts in which they occur. Thus, if clothes make the person, it is nevertheless important to realize that there are many more moral restrictions on women's attire and, consequently, on the kinds of experience her habits allow. Similarly, the effect of legal restrictions defining women's person is such that, with respect to rights and property, being a woman amounts to the same thing as being dead (*O,* p. 168). In such instances Woolf brings her satire to bear on the physical and social inequities of growing up as male or female.

Orlando also affirms the recognition of the differences it makes to be a woman writer, and to be a woman writer writing on women. Even though the sex of Orlando's biographer is never divulged, as soon as Orlando changes to a woman, the "sexual indifference"[29] that would distance biographer and subject gives way to a far more complex psychological closeness between them, causing him or her to question the presumed "immunity of all biographers and historians from any sex whatever" (*O,* p. 220). What becomes apparent is the desire to dispel the endlessly repeated myths about women—that they have "nothing to say to each other," and that they hold other women "in the greatest aversion" (*O,* pp. 219–20)—and indeed to defend Orlando as a woman and as a woman who likes other women, just as in *A Room of One's Own,* Chloe liked Olivia. Woolf's novel-biography thus foresees the poststructuralist dilemma of the feminist who wishes to affirm the female subject without reifying the woman. Through her fantastic ability to change selves with a change of wardrobe, Orlando discovers that being a woman need not mean not being a man, or not being a number of selves yet to be discovered. "For she had a great variety of selves to call upon, far more than we have been able to find room for, since a biography is considered complete if it merely accounts for six or seven" (*O*, p. 309). And yet the biographer "state[s] the simple fact" that at the age of thirty "he [Orlando] became a woman and has remained so ever since" (*O*, p. 139).

A utopian ending, perhaps. As a feminist who is wary of essentialism, but wishes to speak as a woman, I am left with a contradiction. Must I choose between the essentialist and antiessentialist camps? What are the consequences for an image of androgyny and/or sexual difference of choosing one side or the other, or of not choosing at all?

In the Garden of Cyborgs: The Ethics of Sexual Difference

Recently, feminist critics have claimed that contradiction itself can form the basis of a feminist theory and practice. Such contradiction stems from a dual need to hold onto a concept of woman that names real, embodied subjects and to deconstruct essentializing definitions of women's nature that have determined and limited her becoming in the world. Teresa de Lauretis, for example, describes an emerging notion of subjectivity in feminist writings that is based on "the concept of a multiple, shifting, and often self-contradictory identity, . . . an identity that one decides to reclaim from a history of multiple associations and that one insists on as a strategy." Nancy Miller links the enactment of contradiction to a rhetorical strategy, writing that "the possibility of future feminist intervention requires an *ironic* manipulation of the semiotics of performance and production" (my emphasis). Miller's understanding of irony and performance is analogous to the strategy that Luce Irigaray calls "mimicry" or "playing with mimesis." "There is, in an initial phase, perhaps only one 'path,' the one historically assigned to the feminine: that of *mimicry*. One must assume the feminine role deliberately," so as to "convert a form of subordination into an affirmation."[30] This duplicitous stance is not a new tactic, to be sure, having long been an instrument of the oppressed,[31] but Irigaray is particularly interested in its usefulness for women to "recover," if not to construct, the place of their desire. Through mimicry women take control of the role they must play by a deliberate act, and thereby enact and affirm the disjunction between that role and themselves. This is the strategy that Irigaray adopts in *Speculum of the Other Woman,* where, for instance, by repeating Freud's pronouncements on female sexuality she shores up the distance between his theory and her subjectivity. "If women are such good mimics," she writes, "it is because they are not simply resorbed in this function. *They also remain elsewhere:* another case of the persistence of 'matter,' but also of 'sexual pleasure.' "[32] The value of this ironic role-playing is that it points to a space of feminine desire that exists outside of patriarchal logic, but it does not name or describe that place or desire.

The case for irony as a feminist strategy, if not *the* feminist strategy for our times, is most strongly presented by Donna Haraway in her essay "A Manifesto for Cyborgs: Science, Technology, and Socialist Feminism in the 1980's."[33] The manifesto, she explains in the first sentence, "is an effort to build an ironic political myth faithful to feminism, socialism, and materialism." "Irony," Haraway explains, "is about contradictions that do not resolve into larger wholes, even dialectically, about the tension of holding incompatible things together because both or all are necessary and true. Irony is about humor and serious play" (*MC,* p. 173). Clearly, we are dealing with irony, not as a trope, but as a philosophical and political attitude much like Schlegel defined it. Indeed, in Haraway's explicitly nondialectical understanding of irony, she comes very close to Barthes's paradoxism and Schlegel's second level or "irony of irony"—irony that cannot be defined in terms of opposition, but only in terms of an unstable difference.[34] While, furthermore, for Barthes and Schlegel such irony is linked to a body image, to what I would call a disfigured androgyne or hermaphrodite that disrupts stable oppositions (between self/other, male/female, culture/nature, etc.), Haraway articulates her ironic manifesto with reference to the equally lawless and paradoxical figure of the cyborg. Like the hermaphrodite, the cyborg is about "transgressed boundaries," (*MC,* p. 178) not only those between male and female, but also between human and animal, and between animal and machine. Amalgam of natural and artificial organs, it is a creature of a "post-gender" (*MC*, p. 175) and postmodern world in which technology has eliminated nature in any pure sense. Like the carnivalesque or grotesque body of the Renaissance discussed by Bakhtin, the cyborg is a figure of perversion, hybridity, and disproportion.[35] Cyborgs show disrespect for the closure and symmetry of the "classical body" as well as for classical narrative. Cyborgs have no "origin story in the Western sense," Haraway explains, no relation to "the myth of original unity, fullness"—the very myth behind the ideal of the androgyne. They represent the West's "telos," but one that has no singular shape, nor unity, "a 'final' irony" adds Haraway. "Illegitimate" creatures, "wary of holism," "committed to partiality," cyborgs are disruptive of the notions of plenitude upon which the androgynous ideal is founded (*MC*, p. 175).

In her ironic essay Haraway seeks to promote a kind of perverse play, a pleasure in our "monstrous selves" (*MC*, p. 197) that will enable us to learn from technological "pollution" (*MC*, p. 199). "There are . . . great riches for feminists in explicitly embracing the possibilities inherent in the breakdown of clean distinctions between organism and machine and similar distinctions structuring the Western self" (*MC*, p. 197). Such pleasure may begin to structure a politics that can embrace contradictions, that will shore up differences rather than attempting to resolve—read efface—them in some totalizing concept of Man. Haraway's manifesto is, in fact, a theory about the pitfalls of theory. The "major mistake" of the "production of universal, totalizing theory," is one of two arguments that cyborg imagery can help put forth, Haraway claims. Teaching us to be wary of theory, cyborg imagery also persuades us not to reject the study of techne, of artifice, in favor of a naturalistic paradigm. We must refuse an antiscience, antitechnological "metaphysics" (*MC*, p. 204). We are all cyborgs, whether we like it or not. To retain faith in a concept of nature or wholeness as well as in the dualisms such faith depends upon, is to perpetuate a false and "imperialist" myth (*MC*, p. 197). Indeed, the ultimate irony that guides Haraway's manifesto is that it is only by taking pleasure in the "confusion of boundaries" that we may take up the tools of technology and take "*responsibility* in [the] construction" of such boundaries (*MC*, p. 174).

Here, one may pause to consider the contradictions of this ironic coupling of irony and responsibility, or of what is implicit, irony and the political, irony and the ethical, irony and feminism. What is there to prevent irony from dominating this couple, from running rampant as we saw in Schlegel, from infecting and undoing all systems of meaning as we saw in Barthes, from ultimately glossing over all notions of difference? How can we be ironic and responsible at the same time? On what grounds do we judge or know our responsibilities? Are irony and politics compatible? Hayden White says no, irony can have no political effectiveness—"as a world view, irony tends to dissolve all belief in the possibility of positive political actions."[36] Nancy Miller considers irony to have similar risks but concludes that, as a feminist strategy, its time has come nevertheless. "To the extent that the ethos (character, disposition) of feminism historically has refused the doubleness of 'saying one thing while it tries to do another' (the mark of classical femininity, one might argue), it may be that an ironic feminist discourse finds itself at odds both with itself (its identity to itself) and with the expectations its audience has of its position. If that is true, then irony, in the final analysis, may be a figure of limited effectiveness. On the other hand, since nonironic, single, sincere, hortatory feminism is becoming ineffectual, it may be worth the risk of trying out this kind of duplicity on the road."[37] If the time for irony and duplicity has come, is this a sign that feminism (like Romanticism in the 1830s in France)—and I should say white, middle-class feminism—has appeared to move from the margins to the center of the academic community? And that it now has the time and luxury for the self-reflection that irony entails (if also aggravates to the point of no return)?[38] If this is the case, then are feminists clear on who determines the rules of this game?

With regard to the question of gender, one might say that it is irony toward the classical, heterosexual aesthetics of stardom that creates new hero/heroines like Divine in John Waters many movies. Divine's female impersonation, as Judith Butler writes, "implicitly suggests that gender is a kind of persistent impersonation that passes as the real. Her/his performance destabilizes the very distinctions between the natural and the artificial, depth and surface, inner and outer through which discourse about genders almost always operates."[39] In rhetorical terms, Divine is a contemporary Zambinella, a figure of Barthes's "paradoxism," whose mimetic performance of the feminine subverts all links between gender and the real and destabilizes the grounds upon which all representations of gender are constituted. Surely this is a liberating act when one considers the kinds of narrative and historical roles to which women have traditionally been tied. But, as Butler also asks, What happens to politics when the grounds for representation have been undone? Hasn't the absence of representation by and for women also been at the source of their political subservience?[40]

Butler, is careful to point out that "parody," such as that involved in Divine's performance, is not "by itself subversive. . . . [It] depends on a context and a reception in which subversive confusions can be fostered."[41] This is a critical point. For while the context of much feminist theory—those who produce and receive it—may be post-gender, the context of the *real* that it must address is not. In an age of reproductive and body technologies in which the exchange of clothes may be followed by an exchange of organs, irony may not always be the best strategy and may indeed be a dangerous one for feminists. Such biotechnologies have seemed to make it possible to transcend sexual difference, if not to manufacture a third sex. But if Michael Jackson is an example of this third sex or of a cyborg, we cannot ignore the aesthetic and sexual as well as the racial hierarchies reinscribed in his performance of the beautiful object—patriarchy's object: feminine, white, and with a little nose—and how his desire is thus written for him. Nor, on the other hand, can we ignore the issue of privilege—economic privilege in Jackson's case; for others, privileges of race, ethnicity, education . . . —that affords him a more user-friendly relationship to such technologies than others might experience. Technologies can be invasive: unannounced HIV testing, testing and monitoring of pregnant women deemed unfit to take care of their fetuses, surveillance that puts control over bodies in the hands of the medical profession.[42] While Haraway reminds us that our bodies exist as so many codes, it cannot be denied that there is not equal opportunity to redesignate those codes. "'In theory,'" Lisa Nash has argued, "medicine cannot contain all readings of the female body, but 'in practice,' medicine as an institution has authority; its readings are the 'authoritative' ones and its constructions have hegemonic power."[43] The irony of cyborgs is that they too can gloss over the different relationships that different bodies have to technology and to its control.

In this context, what is equally imperative as Haraway's "yes" to all kinds of perverse pleasures and connections is the ability and judgment to say no. Is no something a cyborg knows how to say, wonders Christina Crosby in her commentary on Haraway's essay. "I want a politics of exclusion as well as inclusion," she writes, "I want to be a cyborg that knows how to make the right connections and block the wrong ones." Indeed, as Nash explains, "while [Haraway's] theory speaks eloquently for the deconstruction of boundaries, it seems to afford few epistemological or political resources for the construction of bodily boundaries."[44]

Similar fears about control over the construction of bodily boundaries are expressed with greater urgency by Rosi Braidotti when she questions what the postmodern discourse on gender has to do with "real-life women. . . . the question that is crucial to feminist practice." There is little irony in Braidotti's tone, no promotion of duplicity in her argument as she points out how the recent "discursive inflation about 'the feminine'" has allowed the body, and particularly the female body, to disappear. "Just like the body, the 'feminine' is re-presented as an absence in that it signifies a set of interrelated issues but is not one notion per se. Not one corpus." For her, Michael Jackson is one example of "the triumph of the image over the represented object" and the reduction of the body to "pure surface" destined for scopic consumption.[45] More importantly, she argues, such blurring of sexual difference arrests generational time and any consideration of the body's relation to death. Thus, rather than bringing us any closer to an understanding of what embodied subjectivity is, such gender-benders paradoxically reinscribe Cartesian dualisms of mind/body, along with their insidious associations of masculine and feminine.

For Braidotti, the greatest dangers of recent biotechnologies lie in the false symmetries they create. Having become, as the title of her article suggests, "organs without bodies," we have lost all bodily unity, all unity of the subject. And this idea has "taken a perverse turn" (a perversion in which she locates only danger, not pleasure) by promoting "a very dangerous idea: the interchangeability of the organs."[46] A new market thus opens up in which one woman's womb or uterus is worth another's, in which a mother can carry her daughter's child. The Baby M case has already demonstrated that while such fragmentation of women's bodies and division of motherhood into egg donor, womb donor, nurturer, disrupts paradigms of the heterosexual, nuclear family, it has also resulted in the loss of women's rights over their children. But the organic symmetry also extends across lines of sex. Movies like *Three Men and a Baby* suggest that women as mothers may not really be necessary at all.[47] A uterus can be exchanged for an abdomen, a sperm donor for an ovum/uterus donor, "as if the two sexes were perfectly comparable; as if sexual difference did not mean that the sexes are asymmetrical. . . . From the interchangeability of organs to the symmetry—and therefore complementarity—of the sexes, we witness the rehabilitation of one of patriarchy's most persistent fantasies," writes Braidotti. "The fantasy of a 'third' sex—or of being 'beyond sex,' that is to say outside time—is one of the most pernicious illusions of our era." This fantasy (a remake of the old dream of androgyny) is especially pernicious, Braidotti explains, in a cultural order governed by a "male homosocial bond," in which men govern the use of technology and where it can only lead to a denial of difference—the assimilation of woman as "the feminine" to a male model.[48]

The overriding question for Braidotti is not so different from Crosby's: Will we know how to say no. "How can one judge as 'perverse' the myth of the interchangeability of organs, without referring to a naturalistic paradigm?" she asks.[49] It is not that Braidotti would disagree with Haraway's claims that we are all cyborgs, or that she would wish to replace the image of cyborgs with a nontechnological or organistic being. What she implies, it seems to me, is that all cyborgs are not one.[50] Technology is about knowing this difference within difference and finding ways to do something about it. What we need is cyborg ethics, an ethics of difference, an ethics of sexual difference.

"The Ethics of Sexual Difference" is also how the title of a collection of essays published by Irigaray in 1984 would be translated. "For the work of sexual difference to take place, a revolution in thought and ethics is needed. We must reinterpret the whole relationship between the subject and discourse, the subject and the world, the subject and the cosmic, the microcosmic and the macrocosmic."[51] It is such a revolution in thought that Irigaray begins to undertake in the essays of that volume, as in later essays, on the relationship of women to the divine and the sacred. Here, above all, she seeks to envision a new time in which a "meeting between the sexes" would be possible, where each could confront the other in a manner that protects their fundamental difference rather than attempting to dominate it or to appropriate it to a "sameness."[52]

It is significant that in these later texts, Irigaray abandons the ironic and more playful modes of her earlier writings. Which is not to say that she has abandoned her practice of citation and "paleonymy"—repeating old terms and old words out of context so as to open up a new concept.[53] But whereas mimicry provided a strategy for women to maintain a positive difference while participating in a patriarchal world, Irigaray here envisions a nonpatriarchal or prepatriarchal world where the duplicity of mimicry is replaced with the innocence of a new/old concept from Descartes, that of "wonder." "To arrive at the constitution of an ethics of sexual difference, we must at least return to what is for Descartes the first passion: *wonder.*" "Wonder" is an explicitly nonironic and nonmimetic concept because it is the first passion. It can have no opposite and can engage in no conflict or duplicity. "This passion is not opposed to, or in conflict with, anything else, and exists always as though for the first time."[54] Thus, wonder is prior to or outside the violence of deconstructive strategies that work to overturn conflictual hierarchies.[55] Yet for Irigaray, *wonder* defines an ethical relationship between the sexes because it arises from the recognition of the irreducible difference between man and woman and of that "residue" of the unknown and unidentified that must lie between them. "This feeling of wonder, surprise, and astonishment in the face of the unknowable ought to be returned to its proper place. . . . Man and woman, woman and man, are therefore always meeting as though for the first time, since they cannot stand in for one another. I shall never take the place of a man, never will a man take mine."[56]

Unlike for Descartes, for Irigaray the ethical subject is an embodied subject, demanding a carnal ethics. To this first passion of wonder, consequently, there corresponds a first gesture. In a reading of the philosopher Levinas she describes the "touch of the caress"— an always "preliminary gesture" performed "with respect for the boundaries of the other," and that "searches and affirms alterity while protecting it." The caress is a physical gesture of love that is to be set against both the master-slave dialectic and the fantasy of an androgynous union of self and other. "He approaches me and speaks to me with his hands . . . those palms with which he approaches me without traversing me, giving me back the boundaries of my body."[57] Not unity, but separation—not identity, but difference—defines the starting point from which the two sexes must approach each other, touch each other.

What emerges in this utopian ethics is a new/old dream of symmetry between the sexes: new, because it is articulated through the positivity of difference, rather than through the complementarity of sameness. It proceeds from an absolute duality and a "double desire." Unlike in the Platonic symmetry where man alone occupies the position of the positive element while woman reflects what he is not, in this new symmetry there is positive and negative on both sides. "If there is no double desire, the positive and negative poles divide themselves among the two sexes instead of creating a chiasmus or double loop in which each can move out toward the other and back to itself. If these positive and negative elements are not present in both, the same pole will always attract, while the other remains in motion but possesses no proper place."[58]

In the place of the figure of the androgyne, we thus have that of the chiasmus, of the double loop signifying two different desires, not two halves of a shared love. While the old symmetry was governed by one male standard (of aesthetics, psychology, morality, sexuality, etc.) this symmetry requires two. In an essay entitled "Equal to Whom?" Irigaray writes that "what I see as a manifestation of sexual liberation is God made a couple: man and woman and not simply God made man." This is not the same as the androgynous God of the Saint-Simonians, for instance, not a one-made-two, but again an absolute duality structuring two separate relations to the divine.

> In other words, can a claim to equality be acceptable without a fundamental respect for the subjective rights of both sexes, including the right to a divine identity? This would imply nothing more nor less than the remodeling of our culture so as to reconcile the reigns of women with patriarchal history. Only this historical synthesis (often defined as both prehistoric and historic) can reforge

sexist hierarchies so as to bring about a cultural marriage between the sexes. All the rest can be tolerated in the interim only as a wish for the equal "redemption" of women and men. But equal means different and, once again not along the lines of the mother-son relation.[59]

In her carnal ethics, Irigaray deconstructs the opposition between first- and second-generation feminists, revitalizing the importance of equality, but only by redefining it so that it does "mean different," not equal to the same standard. She resists the essentialist pitfalls of both generations, moreover, by posing both equality and difference as goals to be worked for and constructed, rather than accepting either of the terms as they are defined within patriarchal dualisms of body and soul, physics and metaphysics. "A sexual or carnal ethics would demand that both angel and body be found together. This is a world that must be constructed or reconstructed. A genesis of love between the sexes has yet to come about, in either the smallest or the largest sense, or in the most intimate or political guise. It is a world to be created or recreated so that man and woman may once more finally live together, meet and sometimes inhabit the same place." This is the "old dream of symmetry" thought from the "other" side, doubling its single measure so as to "confound the mirror-symmetry that annihilates the difference of identity."[60] It is a return to that dream through a complete reworking and redefining of the terms *man, woman, love.*

It is a troubling dream, nevertheless. There is in this essay a tone unfamiliar to those used to the irony of her book *Speculum,* or to the lyrical metaphoricity of essays like "When Our Lips Speak Together." Here Irigaray seems to be speaking the "nonironic, single, sincere, hortatory feminism" that Nancy Miller said didn't work, even while she rejects separatist goals or reversals of hierarchies.[61] Irigaray distinguishes her project from that of feminists like Mary Daly, whose attempts to define a relationship of woman to the divine risk falling back into a "narcissistic and imperialistic inflation of sameness."[62] But in rejecting both the ironic and the separatist positions of female subjects within patriarchy, Irigaray also appears to reject her desire *not* to "speak universal," or at least to speak for all women.[63] One must question not only the validity of using the relationship between two individuals as "the model for a whole culture or society," as Margaret Whitford suggests, but, more specifically, the ideology behind Irigaray's use of the relation between a man and a woman as that model.[64] Even if we can assume that this relationship does not presume to contain sexual difference within a rhetorical act of *Aufhebung,* and that there will always be an excessive outside to each individual, can we accept this model as representative of all relations of difference?[65] Such prioritizing of the heterosexual couple as the paradigm of the ethical relationship subordinates—indeed, elides—discussion of race, ethnicity, sexuality that cannot simply be separated from the discussion of sex and that at times must take precedence over it. This carnal ethics is paradoxically blind to different forms of subjective embodiment in the world that are not simply symmetrical.

Irigaray's ethics restores the ground for representation of both male and female difference that irony takes away. It also removes the dream of androgyny from its circumscription by the patriarchal fantasy of one, undifferentiated sex, replacing it with a vision of a meeting (not a joining) of two, positively different sexes, governed by (at least) two different standards and value systems. It is a welcome end to the trajectory of androgyny we have been following in these pages. But it must be seen as an incomplete and unself-critical vision of how to correct the pernicious denial of difference at work in our culture.

Notes

Introduction

1. John Leo, "The Eleventh Megatrend," *Time*, 23 July 1984, p. 104; Mary Cantwell, "The Sexual Masquerade Is Conveying a New Kind of Message," *New York Times*, Sunday, 16 January 1983, sec. 2, p. 1; Carolyn G. Heilbrun, "Androgyny and the Psychology of Sex Differences," p. 265.

2. Thus Paul de Man sees the figure of the *schöne Seele* as the embodiment of the romantic myth of the "unity of appearance (sign) and idea (meaning)" ("Criticism and Crisis," in his *Blindness and Insight,* pp. 12–13).

3. This is also the function of the "transcendental hero" as defined by Ralph Freedman in *The Lyrical Novel,* chap. 2.

4. See, for instance, Francette Pacteau's discussion of this point in "The Impossible Referent," pp. 68–71.

5. Samuel Weber, *The Legend of Freud,* p. 148; Sigmund Freud, *The Three Essays on the Theory of Sexuality,* p. 2 (the editor, James Strachey, notes that "this is no doubt an allusion to the *theory* expounded by Aristophanes in Plato's *Symposium"* [my emphasis]).

6. Sigmund Freud, *Beyond the Pleasure Principle,* pp. 35, 52.

7. See, for instance, Freud, *Three Essays,* chap. 2.

8. Ibid., p. 51. Freud, in other words, exhibits the "amnesia" toward infantile sexuality of which he accused other writers who, in their attempt to explain the origins of the sexual instinct, "devoted much more attention to the primeval period which is comprised in the life of the individual's ancestors—have, that is, ascribed much more influence to heredity—than to the other primeval period, which falls within the lifetime of the individual himself—that is, to childhood" (ibid., p. 39).

9. Ibid., p. 53.

10. Luce Irigaray, "The Blind Spot in an Old Dream of Symmetry," in her *Speculum of the Other Woman,* pp. 27, 21.

11. Jacques Lacan, *The Four Fundamental Concepts of Psycho-Analysis,* p. 205.

12. Kaja Silverman, *The Subject of Semiotics,* p. 152.

13. Lacan, *Four Fundamental Concepts,* pp. 197, 205.

14. Ibid., p. 197, 196, 197.

15. Plato, *Symposium,* p. 147. Page references will hereafter be cited in the text to *Sym.* Unless otherwise indicated, all such quotations are from the Jowett translation.

16. On this point see Silverman, *Subject,* p. 176.

17. Lemoine-Luccione elaborates on this point, explaining that "if the penis was the phallus, men would have no need of feathers or ties or medals. . . .

Display [*parade*], just like the masquerade, thus betrays a flaw: no one has the phallus" (E. Lemoine-Luccione, *La Robe* [Paris: Seuil, 1983], p. 34, (quoted in Stephen Heath, "Joan Rivière and the Masquerade," p. 56). In "The Meaning of the Phallus" (in his *Feminine Sexuality*), Lacan defines femininity as "masquerade" in order to show that woman is alienated from her desire, that, as Heath says, "alienation quickly becomes a *structural* condition of being a woman (overlying the alienation which for Lacan is a structural condition of subjectivity in general, the subject's division in the symbolic)" (p. 54).

18. Lacan, "The Meaning of the Phallus," in his *Feminine Sexuality*, p. 85.

19. Freud, *Beyond the Pleasure Principle*, pp. 53–54.

20. Luce Irigaray, *This Sex Which Is Not One*, p. 87; Lacan, "The Meaning of the Phallus," p. 76.

21. Sarah Kofman, *The Enigma of Woman*, pp. 14–15.

22. The *O.E.D.* and *Webster's Third International Dictionary* both list "hermaphrodite" as the first definition of *androgyne*. See also how A. J. L. Busst collapses the two into one definition in "The Image of the Androgyne in the Nineteenth Century," p. 1.

23. Francette Pacteau calls attention to the different psychical processes at work in representations of the androgyne and the hermaphrodite, which must be distinguished ("The Impossible Referent," pp. 73–74).

The current opposition between the two terms seems to have been the product of German romanticism, according to J. Halley Des Fontaines, who, in *La Notion d'androgynie dans quelques mythes et quelques rites*, explains that in romantic discourse the term *androgyne* was used to indicate an asexual union of sexes, and *hermaphrodite* was used to indicate its physical and erotic manifestations.

24. See Marie Delcourt, *Hermaphrodite, mythes et rites de la bisexualité dans l'antiquité classique*, p. 65.

25. Elizabeth Abel, Introduction to *Writing and Sexual Difference*, ed. Abel, p. 1.

26. Jacques Derrida, "Différance," in his *Speech and Phenomenon*, p. 129.

27. In the words of Terry Eagleton, expounding Derrida's views, Western philosophy "has yearned for the sign which will give meaning to all others—the 'transcendental signifier'—and for the anchoring, unquestionable meaning to which all our signs can be seen to point (the 'transcendental signified'). . . . Since each of these concepts hopes to 'found' our whole system of thought and language, it must itself be beyond that system, untainted by its play of linguistic differences" (*Literary Theory*, p. 131).

28. Ibid., pp. 132, 149.

29. Kofman, *Enigma*, pp. 38–39.

30. Irigaray, *This Sex*, pp. 72, 75.

31. Donna Haraway, "A Manifesto for Cyborgs," p. 174.

Chapter 1: "Androgyny and the Origins of Love"

1. Plato, *Symposium*, p. 144. Unless otherwise noted, this and further page references in this chapter are to the Jowett translation and are cited in the text to *Sym*.

According to Jean Libis, the importance of the spherical shape of these dual beings is its "closure," indicating a "certain plenitude" that should be seen in opposition to the idea of indeterminate, open, and "imperfect space" (*Mythe de l'androgyne,* p. 111).

2. Marie Delcourt suggests that Plato may have had the second chapter of Genesis in mind (*Hermphroditea,* p. 9).

3. Ovid, *The Metamorphoses,* pp. 102–4.

4. Kofman, *Enigma of Woman,* p. 59.

5. Expounding on Luce Irigaray's "The Blind Spot of an Old Dream of Symmetry," Jane Gallop defines: " 'Symmetry' from the Greek summetros—'of like measure'; from "sun"—'like, same,' and "metron"—measure.' Symmetry is appropriating two things to like measure, measure by the same standard: for example the feminine judged by masculine standards. Judged by masculine measures, woman is inadequate, castrated" (*The Daughter's Seduction,* pp. 57–58).

6. Luce Irigaray, "The Power of Discourse and the Subordination of the Feminine" in *This Sex,* p. 74 (original emphasis).

7. On *paradoxism,* a word I borrow from Barthes, see chapter 2.

8. Roland Barthes, *S/Z,* p. 213.

9. Irigaray's writing of *hom(m)osexual* suggests that the representation of desire has always been representation of male desire (*de l'homme*) and that male desire is none other than man's desire for himself, for *l'homme* (see especially, "Any Theory of the 'Subject' Has Always Been Appropriated by the 'Masculine,' " in her *Speculum of the Other Woman*).

10. Martha Nussbaum points out the importance of Diotima's fictional status in "The Speech of Alcibiades," p. 144. David Halperin, however, takes issue with Diotima'a fictional status, despite what many "authorities" hold to be true. Halperin's excellent study, which I read after writing this chapter, is historically grounded in a way that mine is not, but his understanding of Diotima's role within the ideology of Plato's text has many points of convergence with mine. (See "Why Is Diotima a Woman?" in his *One Hundred Years of Homosexuality,* pp. 113–51).

11. " 'Love,' " writes Jane Gallop, "is entangled with the question of woman's complicity; it may be the bribe which has persuaded her to agree to her own exclusion" (*The Daughter's Seduction,* p. 79).

12. John Brenkman, "The Other and the One: Psychoanalysis, Reading, *The Symposium,*" pp. 448–49.

13. Samuel Weber comments that, because they are retold in a mixture of direct and indirect discourse, all the speeches of the *Symposium* are of the form of mimetic discourse condemned in the *Republic,* whereby one delivers a speech "as though he were someone else" and thus refuses to take responsibility for his words (*The Legend of Freud,* pp. 150, 170 n. 10). Socrates' speech is, however, the only one that itself is structured by this form of mimesis.

14. On this point see also Martha Nussbaum, "The Speech of Alcibiades," p. 152. I have found Nussbaum's article extremely inciteful and helpful for my own argument.

Building on Nussbaum, what I am insisting on in this will to "self-sufficiency," is the role of the feminine within that will—the way in which desire for the Other as personification of Truth is expressed as the desire to speak for her while masking "her" otherness. Socrates is like Lacan in his appropriation of woman as other in order to speak her truth. As Diana Fuss writes, "Derrida's attempts to speak (as) woman have provoked considerable controversy, but little has been said of Lacan's perhaps more veiled attempts to do the same. Desire for the other often manifests itself as desire to speak as Other, from the place of the Other (some would even say, instead of the Other). I read Lacan's difficult and equivocal style not just as a strategic evocation of the laws of the Unconscious (which is how it is usually understood) but also, since woman is presumed to be closer to the Unconscious, as an attempt to approximate the speech-less, the not all, the elusive figure of Woman who personifies Truth" (Diana Fuss, *Essentially Speaking*, p. 12).

15. Irigaray, "Cosi Fan Tutti," in *This Sex*, p. 103.

16. Lacan, "The Subversion of the Subject and the Dialectic of Desire in the Freudian Unconscious," in *Ecrits*, pp. 322–23.

17. Nussbaum is particularly suggestive on this point (see "The Speech of Alcibiades," p. 157).

18. Walter Hamilton's translation is more suggestive, writing of a man who "penetrates within and sees the content of Socrates' talk exposed" (*The Symposium*, p. 111). Nussbaum comments on the "central use of the image of 'opening up the other' which is both sexual and epistemic" (ibid.).

19. This is the reciprocality of love, which according to John Brenkman, "defines for Lacan the essentially narcissistic character of love." Brenkman's reading of the *Symposium* concentrates on this equivalence of lover and beloved to show how Alcibiades' speech deconstructs the conceptual oppositions that structure the idealist theory of love ("The Other and the One," p. 431).

20. I am indebted to Nussbaum ("The Speech of "Alcibiades," pp. 162–63) for the significance of Alcibiades' crown.

21. Ibid., p. 157.

22. Jacques Lacan, "God and the Jouissance of the Woman," in his *Feminine Sexuality*, p. 144; Irigaray, "Cosi Fan Tutti," p. 88.

23. Nussbaum, "The Speech of Alcibiades," p. 167.

24. Gallop, *The Daughter's Seduction*, p. 20.

25. Elaine Marks, "Breaking the Bread: Gestures toward Other Structures, Other Discourses," *Bulletin of the Midwest Modern Language Association* 13 (Spring 1980): 55, cited in Jane Gallop, *Reading Lacan*, p. 16.

Chapter 2: "The Rhetoric of Androgyny"

1. Barthes, *S/Z*, pp. 26–27. Future page references to this edition will be cited in the text to *S/Z*. References to *Sarrasine* cited in the text in this chapter will be to the version reprinted in *S/Z*.

2. Francette Pacteau makes a similar remark, writing that, "any attempt to 'define' androgyny reveals an ever evasive concept which takes us to the limits of language . . . confronted with the ubiquitous representations of the figure of the androgyne disseminated across visual and literary texts, such definitions ask for their own surpassing ("dépassement'") (see "The Impossible Referent," p. 62).

3. Erich Auerbach, *Mimesis*, pp. 195–97.
4. John Vignaux Smyth, *A Question of Eros*, p. 271.
5. Roland Barthes, *Roland Barthes by Roland Barthes*, pp. 51–52. Future page references to this edition will be cited in the text to *RB*.
6. Roland Barthes, *The Pleasure of the Text*, p. 4. Future page references to this edition will be cited in the text to *PT*.
7. Barbara Johnson, *The Critical Difference*, pp. x–xi.
8. According to the *Grand Larousse* and *Robert* dictionaries, the term *paradoxism* dates from 1803 in France and refers to a rhetorical figure that consists in uniting two irreconcilable ideas. The *O.E.D*s definition is even more suggestive of the connotations I believe that Barthes attaches to this term. Defining it as "the utterance or practice of paradox," it emphasizes the inseparability of the speaking (and hence, bodily) subject from the production of meaning.
9. See Delcourt, *Hermaphrodite, mythes et rites*, p. 65.
10. Michel Foucault, *Herculine Barbin*, pp. vii–xvii. On this point, see also, Pacteau, "The Impossible Referent," p. 74.
11. Ovid, *Metamorphoses*, book 4, p. 104.
12. The most thorough discussions of the topic are Sara Friedrichsmeyer, *The Androgyne in Early German Romanticism*, and Fritz Giese, *Der Romantische Charakter*. Also see discussions in Hans Eichner, *Friedrich Schlegel*, and in Libis, *Le Mythe de l'androgyne*.
13. Smyth, *A Question of Eros*, p. 271.
14. Friedrich Schlegel, "Uber die Diotima," p. 71. Future page references to this edition will be cited in the text to OD. Translations are my own.
15. Friedrich Schlegel, "Uber die Philosophie, an Dorothea," p. 42. Future page references to this edition will be cited in the text to OP. Translations are my own.

For the influence of Dorothea on this letter and of his earlier relationship to Caroline Böhmer on "Uber die Diotima," see Friedrichsmeyer, *The Androgyne*, esp. pp. 123–42. Friedrichsmeyer attributes the change in Schlegel's attitude toward women in this essay partly to his having his first successful sexual relationship with Dorothea.

16. See, for example, Kant on "The Ideal of Beauty" in *The Critique of Judgement*, pp. 68–73.
17. Friedrich Schlegel, "Critical Fragment 42," in *Friedrich Schlegel's Lucinde and the Fragments*, p. 148. Further page references to this edition will be cited in the text to CF (*Critical Fragments*), AF (*Athenaeum Fragments*), I (*Ideas*), or L (*Lucinde*).
18. Friedrich Schlegel, "Fragment 668," in *Kritische Ausgabe*, Band 18, *Philosophische Lehrjahre*, (1796–1806), ed. Ernst Behler (Paderhorn: Ferdinand Schöningh, 1962), p. 85, cited in Paul de Man, "The Rhetoric of Temporality," in his *Blindness and Insight*, p. 218.
19. René Bourgeois, *L'Ironie romantique*, pp. 16, 18.
20. Peter Szondi, "Friedrich Schlegel and Romantic Irony, with Some Remarks on Tieck's Comedies" in his *Textual Understanding and Other Essays*, p. 68.

21. De Man, "The Rhetoric of Temporality," p. 219.

22. *Encyclopédie ou dictionnaire raisonné des Sciences, des Arts et des Métiers, par une Société de Gens de Lettres* (Geneva: Pellet, 1765), 19: 86, quoted in Ernst Behler, *Irony and the Discourse of Modernity*, p. 76. Behler comments that the encyclopedia's definition "contains the essence of the definitions of irony found in numerous handbooks of various European literatures as they had developed from older manuals of rhetoric."

23. Lilian Furst, *Fictions of Romantic Irony*, p. 12 (original emphasis).

24. I use *himself* and *his* intentionally, since, as I shall comment on below, the ironist for Schlegel, is necessarily masculine.

25. De Man, "The Rhetoric of Temporality," p. 214.

26. Schlegel, "On Incomprehensibility," in *Lucinde and the Fragments* (pp. 259–71). Future page references to this essay will be cited in the text to OI.

27. Friedrich Schlegel, "Letter about the Novel," in *Dialogue on Poetry and Literary Aphorisms*, pp. 102–3. Future page references to this edition will be cited in the text to LN.

28. Fichte, whose influence is evident throughout *Lucinde*, writes in the *Grundlage der Gesammten Wissenschaftslehre* (ed. Fritz Mendicus [1794; Hamburg: Felix Meiner Verlag, 1979], and translated as *Science of Knowledge with First and Second Introductions*, trans. Peter Heath and John Lachs [Cambridge: Cambridge University Press, 1982]) that "Every entity which is like another is its opposite, unlike it, in one property: *unterschieden* [different]" (quoted in Paul de Man, "The Concept of Irony," p. 22 n.22).

29. De Man writes that, "Irony clearly is the same distance within a self, duplications of a self, specular structures within the self, within which the self looks at itself from a distance. It sets up reflexive structures, and irony can be described as a moment in a dialectic of the self" ("The Concept of Irony," pp. 13–14).

30. In "On Diotima" (p. 93), Schlegel includes *Bestimmtheit* (determination or definition) as one of the two characteristics of masculinity, the other being *Umfang* (volume).

31. Jean Libis makes a similar remark when he writes that "it seems that physical love—under the condition, of course, that it is founded on the 'divine' game of passion—offers the occasion to experience the time of the future Androgyne in advance" (*Le Mythe de l'androgyne*, p. 151; my translation).

32. De Man, "The Concept of Irony," p. 12.

33. Friedrich Schlegel, *Lucinde*, in *Dichtungen*, p. 13.

34. See J. Hillis Miller, "The Two Allegories."

35. G. W. F. Hegel, *The Phenomenology of Mind*, p. 676.

36. Philippe Lacoue-Labarthe and Jean-Luc Nancy, *The Literary Absolute*, p. 78.

37. Jeffrey S. Librett gave a very interesting reading of this passage in "Writing (as) Perverse Body in Schlegel's *Lucinde*," a paper delivered at the IAPL Conference, University of California at Irvine, April 1990.

38. For a somewhat more positive, but still critical, reading of Schlegel's move to the feminine as the "unrepresentable," see Margaret R. Higonnet, "Writing from the Feminine: *Lucinde* and *Adolphe*."

39. Naomi Schor, "Dreaming Dissymmetry: Barthes, Foucault, and Sexual Difference," p. 100; Jane Gallop, *Thinking through the Body*, pp. 19–20.

40. Jacques Lacan, "God and the Jouissance of the Woman," in *Feminine Sexuality*, p. 144.

41. On Hegel's theory of human nature as what distinguishes Western man from the rest of the world, see Rey Chow's essay " 'It's You, and Not Me': Domination and 'Othering' in Theorizing the 'Third World,' " in *Coming To Terms*, ed. Elizabeth Weed, esp. p. 158.

42. On the ironist as eroticist, see Smyth, *A Question of Eros*.

43. On the gendering of representational modes in the nineteenth century and the consequent demise and decanonization of the idealist novel, see Naomi Schor, "Idealism in the Novel: Recanonizing Sand."

Chapter 3: "The Aesthetics of Romantic Androgyny"

1. Libis, *Le Mythe de l'androgyne*, p. 222.

2. For further discussion on these versions, see especially the chapter on "Divided and Reunited Man" in M. H. Abrams, *Natural Supernaturalism*, pp. 154–69.

3. Cited from the *Bereshit rabba* in Mircea Eliade, "Mephistopheles and the Androgyne," in *The Two and the One*, p. 104.

4. June Singer, *Androgyny*, p. 97. Her book is an excellent source for various versions of androgynous myths and rituals.

5. On Adam's fall from the "Mysterium Magnum," see Abrams, *Natural Supernaturalism*, pp. 158–59.

6. Libis, *Le Mythe de l'androgyne*, p. 228.

7. In Janice Raymond's opinion, similar statements about Eve separating from Adam in the Kabbala "giv(e) the impression that the female part of the original androgyne was more fragmented and less perfect than the male" and that "the male portion of androgyny remains steady and constant, while the female is the wayward, unsteady half" (*The Transexual Empire*, p. 157).

8. Ronald Gray, *Goethe the Alchemist*, p. 222.

9. Balzac, *Séraphîta* and Preface to the *Livre Mystique*, vol. 7 of *La Comédie humaine*, pp. 346, 606 (my translation).

10. Balzac and Saint Martin quoted in Jacques Borel, *Séraphîta et le mysticisme Balzacien*, pp. 166, 179.

11. On Schiller and universal history, see Abrams, *Natural Supernaturalism*, chap. 4.

12. On the androgyne in Novalis, see Friedrichsmeyer, *The Androgyne in Early German Romanticism*. For a broader examination of the "problem of the androgyne" in German romanticism, see Fritz Giese, *Die Entwicklung der androgynen-problems in der Frühromantik*.

13. J. J. Winckelmann, *History of Ancient Art*, p. 208.

14. Ibid., p. 206.

15. Busst, "The Image of the Androgyne in the Nineteenth Century," p. 19.

16. Ballanche, *La Vision D'Hébal*, p. 138. Translations of this and future quotations from Ballanche are my own.

17. Ibid.

18. Eliade, "Mephistopheles and the Androgyne," p. 94.

19. On this point, see Ludmilla Jordanova, "Natural Facts." She documents the identification of women and nature in the eighteenth and nineteenth centuries in France, a concept that made "woman" into an attractive specimen for the scientific discourse to investigate, explain, and conquer.

20. Jean Molino, "Le Mythe de l'androgyne," p. 405.

21. Roland Barthes, *Michelet*, p. 187.

22. The term *coincidentia oppositorum* (coincidence of opposites) was first used by the fifteenth-century German theosophist Nicholas of Cusa to describe the union of contraries and the mystery of totality that, he believed, was the "least imperfect" definition of God. See Eliade, "Mephistopheles and the Androgyne," pp. 80–81.

23. On the role of woman and the feminine in Saint-Simonian discourse, see my "Femino-centric Utopia and Male Desire." For an excellent overview of Saint-Simonian feminism and the role women played, see Claire Goldberg Moses, *French Feminism in the Nineteenth Century*.

24. Jordanova explores the analogous opposition of man to woman and of culture to nature. See "Natural Facts."

25. For the changing role of women in bourgeois society and their identification with aristocratic values, see Priscilla Clark, *The Battle of the Bourgeois*. Ronnie Butler also gives insight into writers' ambivalence toward social change at this time in *Balzac and the French Revolution*.

26. Ballanche, *Vision*, pp. 142–43. Language was also the problem for Michelet: "I was born of the people. I have the people in my heart. . . . But the people's language, its language was inaccessible to me. I have not been able to make the people speak" (quoted in Barthes, *Michelet*, p. 188).

27. Ballanche, *Vision*, p. 238.

28. A. J. L. Busst, Introduction to Ballanche, *Vision*, p. 85 (my translation).

29. Frank Bowman refers to the poet in Ballanche as an "initiateur du progrès" in *Le Christ romantique*, p. 228.

30. A concise account of Cousin's transmission of German idealist aesthetics in France can be found in Frederic Will, *Flumen Historicum: Victor Cousin's Aesthetic and Its Sources*.

31. F. W. J. von Schelling, *The Ages of the World*, trans. Frederick de Wolfe Bolman, Jr. (New York, 1942), pp. 84, 90–91, and quoted in Abrams, *Natural Supernaturalism*, p. 31.

32. "And it was not until the last day of the last century that the Child of man reappeared as on Thabor. And no longer a word of irony, but a word of truth said: 'Here is man'" (Ballanche, *Vision*, p. 238).

33. When I refer to the artist as "he," as I do quite often in this study, it is specifically to emphasize that in nineteenth-century France, the artist-creator was regarded as essentially male (though often with feminine attributes), while the work of art was associated with the female as a passive object of beauty.

34. This is Jean Rousset's definition of the ideal text in *Forme et signification*, p. xx (my translation).

35. On this point, see Edward Said, *The World, the Text, and the Critic*, pp. 273–74.

36. Hans Aarsleff, *From Locke to Saussure*, pp. 32–33.

37. Philippe Perrot, "Le Jardin des modes," p. 101. My translation. Perrot comments that this dimorphism took place despite an official liberalization of dress codes. Nevertheless, that liberalization did not extend to transvestism.

38. Ibid., pp. 102, 112.

39. Susan Brownmiller, *Femininity*, p. 82.

40. See Foucault's introduction to *Herculine Barbin* and his *History of Sexuality*, 1:7.

41. Foucault, *History of Sexuality*, 1:55.

42. Irigaray, *This Sex*, p. 88. Italics in the original.

Chapter 4: "Balzac's Androgyne: Ideal Sex, Ideal Text"

1. Honoré de Balzac, Avant Propos, to *La Comédie humaine*, 1:51. Subsequent references to the *Comédie humaine* will be to this edition, and page and volume numbers will be cited in the text with appropriate abbreviations: AP = Avant Propos; Fille = *La Fille aux yeux d'or*; LL = *Louis Lambert*; LM = *Livre mystique*; PG = *Père Goriot*; Sarr = *Sarrasine*; Sér = *Séraphîta*. All translations, except as otherwise indicated, are my own.

2. Honoré de Balzac, *Lettres à Madame Hanska* (24 November 1833), pp. 127–28. All translations of the letters are my own.

3. Théophile Gautier and Hippolyte Taine, *Honoré de Balzac*, p. 102 (my translation).

4. Maurice Bardèche, for example, sees *Séraphîta* as "completely separate" from the rest of the *Comédie humaine*. "She [*sic*] is not a novel of Balzac but a sort of poem without its place in the evolution we've described" (*Balzac*, p. 271). Since *novel* is masculine in French, Bardèche's comment stresses the link between ambiguous gender and ambiguous genre.

5. Balzac to the Marquise de Castries, 10 March 1835, in Balzac, *Correspondance*, 2:655.

6. I draw my understanding of Taine's theory of the ideal in art from Naomi Schor, "Idealism in the Novel," pp. 63–65.

7. Ibid., p. 71; Balzac quoted from George Sand, *My Life*, trans. Dan Hofstadter (New York: Harper, 1980), p. 218, cited ibid., p. 65.

8. Leyla Ezdinli has argued this point from the other side, that Sand actively sought a double gender identity to promote public interest in her work. See "George Sand's Literary Transvestism."

9. Honoré de Balzac, "Des Artistes," in Balzac, *Oeuvres diverses*, 2:224, 226. This and subsequent translations of Balzac's letters and articles are my own.

10. The description of Séraphîta seems also a somewhat cynical response to a statement in the first preface to Sand's *Indiana*, where she, feeling the need to choose between heaven and earth, shows her allegiance to realism: "The current fashion is to depict a fictional hero so ideal, so superior to the common run that he only yawns where others enjoy themselves. . . . These heroes bore you, I'm sure, because they are not like you, and that in the long run lifting your head up

to watch them float above you makes you dizzy. I place mine firmly on the ground and living the same life as you do" (cited in Schor, "Idealism in the Novel," pp. 71–72). The statement, Schor says, was deleted from the 1833 edition in conjunction with Sand's move toward idealism.

11. This is according to Spoelberch de Louvenjoul's reconstruction of that letter, which was lost (cited in Balzac, *Lettres à Madame Hanska,* p. 6).

12. My understanding of this figure in Baudelaire is indebted to the reading by Paul de Man in "The Rhetoric of Temporality," in his *Blindness and Insight,* pp. 187–228.

13. Charles Baudelaire, "De l'essence du rire," in *Curiosités esthétiques: L'Art romantique et autres oeuvres critiques,* ed. H. Lemaître (Paris: Garnier, 1962), p. 251, cited ibid., p. 223 (my translation); ibid., p. 223.

14. Balzac to the Marquise de Castries, in Balzac, *Correspondance,* 2:654.

15. See, for instance, the remarks by Suzanne Nash in "Story-telling and the Loss of Innocence in Balzac's *Comédie humaine.*"

16. Balzac, "Lettre à Charles Nodier sur son article intitulé: De La Palingénésie humaine et de la résurrection," in Balzac, *Oeuvres diverses,* 3:168.

17. Balzac, "Lettre aux écrivains français," in *Oeuvres diverses,* 3:226.

18. Balzac, "Lettre à Charles Nodier," 3:167. Frederic Jameson argues this point, writing that, "In Balzac . . . it has for whatever historical reason become necessary to secure the reader's consent, and to validate or accredit the object as desirable, before the narrative process can function properly. The priorities are therefore here reversed, and this narrative apparatus depends on the 'desirability' of an object whose narrative function would have been a relatively automatic and unproblematical secondary effect of a more traditional narrative structure" (see Jameson, *The Political Unconscious,* p. 156).

19. For Hegel, recognizing and asking for forgiveness for one's particularity is prerequisite to the reconciliation of finite and infinite.

20. Janet L. Beizer, *Family Plots,* p. 10.

21. Balzac, *Lettres à Madame Hanska* (January 1834), p. 153.

22. Balzac, "Lettre à Nodier," 3:171, 177.

23. Ibid., 3:167–68.

24. For related discussions of Balzac's use of an "affective discourse . . . which is not designed to convince the reader . . . but to strike his imagination," see J. L. Tritier, *Le Langage philosophique dans les oeuvres de Balzac,* esp. chap. 6, "Le Rôle du mot dans le discours." Referring to the didacticism of *Séraphîta,* Tritier describes how Balzac discusses other philosophers without questioning them, but so that a "quasi-mystical revelation" takes place before the reader's eyes.

25. Balzac, "Lettre à Nodier," 3:178.

26. Martin Kanes, *Balzac's Comedy of Words,* p. 166.

27. Balzac, *Lettres à Madame Hanska,* (23 November 1833) p. 128.

28. Ibid., (March 1833) p. 38.

29. Ibid., (January 1834) p. 152.

30. One can detect a narrative contract—if not a narrative seduction—in the correspondence between Balzac and Eva that is not unlike that to which critics have called attention in his fiction. Drawing on Barthes's discussion in *S/Z*

of the "contract narrative," Ross Chambers explains how narrative authority "derives from an act of authorization on the part of the other . . . the narratee. . . . Unless one posits absolute identity between the interests (needs, desires, etc.) of the narrator and those of the narratee, it follows from this that in the narrative situation there is always a degree of duplicity." At that point the narrative itself becomes an act of seduction, "a technique of recruiting the desires of the other in the interest of the needs of a narrative self" ("Narrative as Oppositional Practice," pp. 55–56). See also Chambers's *Story and Situation,* where he describes how, in a number of short fiction works, a contextual act of "seduction" is inscribed within the texts themselves. In this case both the aesthetic needs of the narrator and the passionate needs of the author are dependent upon the "textual seduction" of the other, Eva, who will proclaim, as he states in his dedication to her, either his success or his "impuissance."

31. This, again, is according to Louvenjoul's reconstruction of the letter in *Lettres à Madame Hanska,* pp. 5–6.

32. Ibid., (11 March 1835) p. 309.

33. Ibid., (January 1834) p. 152, (15 February 1834) pp. 178, 180.

34. Proust commented also on the similar constructions of Balzac's correspondence and his novels, explaining that "in the letters to his sister where he speaks about the chances of marriage with Mme. Hanska, not only is everything constructed like a novel, but all the characters are posed, analyzed, described as they are in his books, as elements that clarify the action" (*Contre Sainte Beuve,* p. 232; my translation).

35. Balzac, *Lettres à Madame Hanska,* (March 1833) p. 38, (9 September 1833) pp. 69–70, (21 February 1834) p. 186, (end of March 1833) p. 38, (January 1834) pp. 155, 157.

36. Alice Jardine, *Gynesis,* p. 115.

37. Albert Béguin, *Balzac Visionnaire,* p. 87 (my translation).

38. Balzac, *Lettres à Madame Hanska,* (January 1834) pp. 152–53.

39. Ronald Gray remarks that the term *sublimation* was one used by alchemists as well: "That is the so-called lower impulses were to be refined and brought to a higher level, just as, according to Freud, the anti-social, sexual libido can be sublimated into a socially useful urge" (*Goethe the Alchemist,* p. 25).

40. On Irigaray's spelling of "ho(m)mosexual," see chap. 1 note 9, above.

41. Luce Irigaray, "Cosi Fan Tutti," *This Sex,* p. 103.

42. The editor's note beside that comment states, "that virtuous declaration is completely incompatible with the confidences made to his sister on the preceding October 12 where Balzac, after having alluded to the maternal promise of Maria Du Fresnay, cites a mysterious mistress, 'voluptuous like a thousand cats,' who wants her daily ration of love" (*Lettres à Madame Hanska,* p. 152 n. 2).

43. Hippolyte Taine, "Analyse critique de la *Comédie humaine,*" in *Honoré de Balzac,* by Gautier and Taine, p. 93 (my translation).

44. Albert Béguin, *Balzac lu et relu,* pp. 76–77. (my translation).

45. Luce Irigaray, "The Blind Spot in an Old Dream of Symmetry" in *Speculum.* See my discussion in chap. 1.

46. Gérard Genette, "Vraisemblance et Motivation," in *Figures II,* p. 85.

My translation. Genette makes specific reference to the "chatty" Balzacian narrator, whose "explanatory and moralistic discourse" is held in equilibrium by an author "just as attached to dramatic movement."

47. Ibid., p. 86.

48. Perhaps this is the reason the narrator suggests that such stories should be told by one of the precious stones present throughout history, which "transmitted from heritage to heritage . . . would make the most faithful stories about humanity if they took their turn to speak" (*Sér*, 7:354).

49. Honoré de Balzac, *Le Chef d'oeuvre inconnu* (Paris: Editions du Seuil, 1966).

50. Gaëton Picon is one of the first to discuss the "mythe de la paternité" in *Balzac par lui-même*. Citing Picon, Christopher Prendergast demonstrates how Balzac's work questions the very ideologies to which he was committed, such as the "authoritarian father," in *Balzac: Fiction and Melodrama*, p. 178. For a similar stand on the way Balzac both "displays the father" and undermines him, see Janet Beizer's elegant readings in *Family Plots*.

51. Prendergast, *Balzac*, p. 181.

52. Beizer, *Family Plots*, p. 4.

53. Translation of these passages is especially difficult since, unlike English, the gender of the possessive pronoun in French always agrees with the object, not the subject. There is thus an ambiguity in the original I can only suggest by translating the pronouns as "his/her."

54. In many of these passages, Balzac's language comes very close to that of Ballanche.

55. In a letter of January 1833 to Madame Hanska, Balzac compares his imagination that can "conceive of all and remain virginal," to a mirror in his brain that "is not dirtied by any of its reflections" (*Lettres*, p. 26).

56. Gilles Deleuze, *Proust and Signs,* pp. 93–94. The Hegelian process of reading that Deleuze describes in Proust is, to my mind, one that Balzac's narrator alternately demands, implores, or seductively elicits from his readers.

57. Balzac, of course, also referred to Mme. Hanska as "L'Inconnue" and described her as the complete woman. Thus, there is some of her in Paquita as well as in Séraphîta.

58. Johnson, *The Critical Difference*, p. 10.

59. Barthes, *S/Z*, p. 201.

60. The theme of boy-girl twins is especially popular in German romanticism and is related to the theme of the androgyne. See, for example, Carolyn Heilbrun's discussion of the theme in *Toward a Recognition of Androgyny*.

61. Prendergast, *Balzac*, p. 64.

62. Geneviève Delattre, "De *Séraphîta* à *La Fille aux yeux d'or*," pp. 201–2 (my translation). With particular attention to events in Balzac's personal life, Delattre examines the curious emergence of these two antithetical texts at the same time. She points out that De Marsay "contaminates" 'Wilfred (p. 215), even while she maintains, I think, too strong an emphasis on a fundamental opposition between the texts.

63. Prendergast, *Balzac,* p. 65.

64. Shoshana Felman, "Rereading Femininity," p. 31.

65. Ibid., pp. 27–29. Ross Chambers also discusses Sarrasine's role as a "narratee," indeed, as one completely captivated by Zambinella's story in contrast to Mme. de Rochefide's more distanced reception (see his *Story and Situation*, chap. 4). What Chambers doesn't mention is the relation between seduction and sexual difference in Balzac where the feminine occupies the privileged position both for practicing the art of seduction and for resisting it.

66. Felman, "Rereading Femininity," p. 29.

67. Peter Lock, "Melancholia, Mourning, and the Question of Symbolization," p. 1. Using the terms of psychoanalysis, Lock addresses the question of "loss" in Balzac's *L'Enfant maudit* ("loss of origin, of the ideal, perhaps of the subject itself"), and distinguishes between two contradictory reactions to loss in that narrative: awareness resulting in the symbolization of the lost object, or lapse into the imaginary and the idealization of the object. I have found Lock's terms fruitful for distinguishing narrative voices in *Séraphîta* as well.

68. I take the term *narratable* from D. A. Miller, *Narrative and Its Discontents*, where it is defined as the "instances of disequilibrium, suspense, and general insufficiency from which a given narrative appears to arise." I find the term useful for emphasizing what Miller sees as narrative's "inherent lack of finality," which is to say, of closure, and, thus, of its disjunction with the "utopic" state of wholeness for which narratives like *Séraphîta* appear to strive.

69. Lock comments that the reader of *L'Enfant maudit* is placed in a position of identification with the idealized maternal figure in the text and must break out of this fantasy "for the re-enactment of the text's unconscious." Similarly, the readers of *Séraphîta* must break free of the fantasies projected onto Séraphîta/us by Wilfred and Minna ("Melancholia, p. 4).

70. On androgyny as the "relation between a look and an appearance, in other words *psyche* and *image*," see Francette Pacteau, "The Impossible Referent," p. 62.

71. Even though Balzac admits in his Avant Propos of 1842 that there is a difficulty in defining the female of the human species in relation to the male, he nevertheless does just that by restricting her social role to one of *femme* as wife: "in society woman is not always found to be the female of the male. There can be two perfectly dissimilar beings in a household. The woman/wife of a merchant is sometimes worthy of being a prince's, and often a prince's is not worthy of being an artist's (AP, 1:51).

72. Shoshana Felman, "Woman and Madness: The Critical Phallacy," p. 8.

73. Nature in this valley of the Falberg is analogous to that which Saint Preux describes in *La Nouvelle Heloise* and where as Paul de Man quotes, "nature still seemed to take pleasure in opposing itself." Both are what de Man refers to as "transitional landscapes," spaces of violent contradictions between the forbidding mountains and the socialized lowlands. Séraphîta and Saint Preux attempt to escape from these realms, and their emotional ascension to purer spheres appeases the violence of nature's turmoil and their own. (See de Man, "The Intentional Structure of the Romantic Image," in his *Rhetoric of Romanticism*, pp. 13–14.)

74. For a more detailed discussion of how this flower and the surrounding environment in general represent the "problematic" identity of Séraphîta, see

Dorothy Kelly, *Fictional Genders*, pp. 158–61. Her chapter on *Séraphîta* also focuses on the problematics of representing gender identity whose nature is essentially "symbolic" and exists only in language.

75. J. Hillis Miller, "The Two Allegories," p. 363. Miller cites a line from *Louis Lambert* to explain this doubleness in its metaphysical relation to the Incarnation: "So, maybe, one day the inverse meaning of Et Verbum caro factum est, will be the resume of a new evangelist who will say, 'And the flesh will be made Word, it will become the Word of God'" (*LL*, 7:323, quoted pp. 360–61— my translation). Commenting on this citation Miller writes, "In one case the Word precedes its incarnation in the concrete pictures of allegory. Word becomes flesh in allegory. In the other case the embodiment generates the spiritual meaning" (p. 361). Séraphîta seems to fulfill this evangelical role even as s/he herself/himself breaks the bonds of the *voile de chair* (veil of flesh) and rises to *La Parole* (The Word). As s/he does, however, s/he illustrates further the difference between becoming and generating, since his/her flesh does not become *la Parole*, but merely refers to it in an allegorical fashion. His/her body is left behind as what cannot be spiritualized and, at the same time, as what generates the desire/need for spiritualization.

Chapter 5: "An Obscure Object of Aesthetic Desire: Gautier's Androgyne/Hermaphrodite"

1. Georg Lukács, *The Theory of the Novel*, part 2, chaps. 2–3, and p. 113.

2. For a concise discussion of the two schools of art criticism in the nineteenth century, see P. G. Castex, *La Critique d'art en France au XIXe siècle*.

3. Although Hegel's *Aesthetics* were not published in France until 1835, they formed the basis of Victor Cousin's 1818 "Leçons" and thus were in the air. For discussions of Cousin's transmission of Hegel, see Bernhard Knoop, *Victor Cousin's Aesthetics and Its Sources*, and Paul Stapfer, *Questions esthétiques et religieuses*. While Stapfer sees the concept of Art for Art as inspired by Hegelian aesthetics, he also claims that Hegel himself would entirely disapprove of it, since it bears more relation to the German school of play or irony. This is, indeed, my sentiment, although I do not, as Stapfer does, find Gautier's theories of lesser importance for that reason.

4. Naomi Schor, *Reading in Detail*, p. 4.

5. Ibid.

6. René Girard, *Deceit, Desire, and the Novel*, p. 16.

7. I referring to Irigaray's call for "an examination of the *operation of the 'grammar'* of each figure of discourse" (*This Sex*, p. 75). See also the text that contains the reference to note 30 in the Introduction, above.

8. Théophile Gautier, "Ingres," in *Critique artistique et littéraire*, p. 72. Except where otherwise noted, this and all subsequent translations of Gautier's critical writings are my own.

Gautier's first article, "Un Buste de Victor Hugo," had already appeared in *Le Mercure* in 1831, while his career as an art critic actually began in 1836, when he joined the staff of *La Presse*. By 1856 he was an editor of *L'Artiste*, a journal devoted to art criticism.

9. Gautier, "Leonardo da Vinci," in *Critique artistique*, p. 19; Gautier, "En Grèce," in *Loin de Paris*, in *Oeuvres complètes*, 11:230.

10. For a discussion of "Winckelmann's part in Gautier's perception of classical beauty," see the article of that title by Raymond Giraud in *Yale French Studies*.

11. Gautier, in *La Presse*, 25 October 1852, cited in Helen E. Patch, *The Dramatic Criticism of Théophile Gautier*, p. 13.

12. Théophile Gautier, *Mademoiselle de Maupin*, trans. Joanna Richardson, p. 66. All future page references to this edition are cited in the text to *MM*. Page numbers following quotations in French are to the original text in the Garnier Flammarion edition.

The terms *naked* and *nude*, which may both translate the French *nu*, appear themselves to be locked into a gendered opposition. A *nude* is understood to be a nude woman, and, like the Spartan youths, one whose body is presented to the male gaze. *Naked*, on the other hand, suggests the impropriety of such bodily presentation.

13. Théophile Gautier, "Suite du Petit Cénacle" in *Histoire du romantisme*, p. 29.

14. A similar sentiment can be found almost a century earlier in the writings of Diderot. Like Gautier, he deplored the proscription of all nudity in his society and the discouragement of sensual indulgence, and he longed for a renewed appreciation of the human body like that which was inspired by the Greek games. If only life and art were like they were then, Diderot dreams, "You would see what would become of our painters, our poets, and our sculptors, . . . with what eye we would look upon beauty to whom we owe the birth, the incarnation of our savior and the grace of our redemption" ("Essai sur la Peinture," in *Oeuvres*, p. 1174).

15. Gautier, "Bayre," in *Histoire du romantisme*, p. 245.

16. Théophile Gautier, "Du Beau dans l'art" in *L'Art moderne*, p. 136; Théophile Gautier, Preface to *Les Grotesques*, p. x.

17. Gautier, quoted in Emile Bergerat, *Théophile Gautier: Entretiens, Souvenirs, Correspondances*, p. 97.

18. Gautier, "Meissonier," *Gazette des Beaux Arts* 12 (1862): 426.

19. Théophile Gautier, "Gavarni," from *L'Artiste* (1855), reprinted in *Ecrivains et artistes romantiques*, p. 248.

20. "The 'artist' and the 'dandy' of 1830 . . . are eminently feminine and impressionable beings; like that of women, their emotions easily attain a level of paroxysm" (Georges Matoré, *Le Vocabulaire et la société sous Louis-Philippe*, p. 49).

21. Jacques Derrida, *Spurs/Eperons, les styles de Nietzsche*, p. 71.

22. Charles Baudelaire, "Le Peintre de la vie moderne," p. 694. In a number of articles published in the fifties and sixties in which Gautier discusses contemporary artists and writers, he comes back repeatedly to a notion of "modernity" and praises the likes of Balzac and Baudelaire for their ability to "be of their time." More interestingly, Gautier relates this fact of being 'modern' to their ability to understand and love the modern woman. Only when we understand that "woman seems to have frightened our artists . . . and very few have con-

cerned themselves with modern beauty," can we understand why, for Gautier, "Gavarni's greatest glory is not to have understood the Parisian. . . . he has understood the Parisienne! he not only understood her, he loved her" ("Gavarni," in *Ecrivains et artistes romantiques*, pp. 245–61). Of Baudelaire and of Balzac too he will cite "modernity" by claiming, in the case of Balzac, "He loved the woman of today as she is and not a pale statue" ("Honoré de Balzac", ibid., p. 123). My point is that what Gautier will thus theorize twenty years later, he will prefigure in his own fashion-conscious statue of Maupin.

23. Théophile Gautier, "Contralto," in *Emaux et Camées, Poésies complètes*, 3:31–34.

24. Charles Baudelaire, "Le Peintre de la vie moderne," p. 694.

25. Théophile Gautier, "De La Composition dans la peinture," from *La Presse*, 22 November 1836, quoted in Louise B. Dillingham, *The Creative Imagination of Théophile Gautier*, p. 31.

26. Chambers, "Pour Une Poétique du vêtement."

27. Derrida, *Spurs/Eperons*, p. 55.

28. P. E. Tennant, *Théophile Gautier*, p. 110.

29. Theater, for Gautier, should not be confused with *le drame* (drama or melodrama) or the idea of a presentation of "a slice of life" that was so important for Balzac and whose place in the novel was much discussed around 1830 (see Marguerite Iknayan, *The Idea of the Novel in France*, pp. 127–28). In Gautier's work, the idea of theater derives instead from the tradition of the commedia dell'arte, from Shakespeare, and from a tradition of masquerade.

30. Tennant, *Théophile Gautier*, p. 102.

31. G. W. F. Hegel, "On Art," in his *On Art, Religion, Philosophy*, pp. 64, 78.

32. Victor Cousin, *Leçons*, quoted by Jacques Gaucheron in "Ombres et lueurs de l'art pour l'art," p. 76. The particular reception of Kant in France has attracted much study, particularly in relation to the notion of art's autonomy. Gaucheron notes that Cousin's transmission disregards the important relation to science worked out by Kant, which points to an interesting deviation on Cousin's part from the popular craze over scientific knowledge and progress.

33. Tennant writes that "historically . . . art for art's sake has often been associated with periods when, as in France of the 1830's, artistic alienation is uppermost" (Tennant, *Théophile Gautier*, p. 19). The historical and social conditioning of the notion of artistic "autonomy" receives an extremely interesting discussion in Peter Bürger's *Theory of the Avant Garde*.

34. Théophile Gautier, Préface to "Albertus ou L'ame et le péché," in *Poésies complètes*, p. 82.

35. Théophile Gautier, Preface to *Les Jeunes France*, p. 25. Further page references are to this edition and are cited in the text to *JF*.

36. Gautier is quick to expose the critic's hypocritical use of woman as the gauge of virtue in his own imitation of a "virtuous" critique—"The theater has become a school of prostitution which you tremble to enter with a woman whom you respect. You come on the strength of an illustrious name, and you are obliged to leave at the third act, because your young daughter is thoroughly upset and out of countenance. Your wife is hiding her blushes behind her fan; your sister,

your cousin, etc. (one can diversify the relationships: they just have to be female)" (*MM*, pp. 22–23). Yet, his own rhetoric simply replaces this image with the image of woman as style, if not superfluous ornament. In other words, there is little critique of the use/abuse of woman as figure. For a discussion of the way ornament has been gendered as feminine within the academy (the reverse side of the feminine as restrictedly mimetic), see Schor, *Reading in Detail,* chap. 1.

37. Ornament, by virtue of its superficial or unnecessary status, is claimed by Gautier to be the very essence of art. It is, he explains in a book review of 1858, a microcosm of creation, or the locus where the creative genius asserts itself. "In leafing through this magnificent volume, we have made a number of comments on that particular art that is called 'ornament' and that has not been granted the philosophical importance it deserves. Of all the arts, it is the one that contains the most creativity. . . . It exists alone, outside of everything, its variable forms are infinite and its precise model is nowhere to be found. Nothing is more fantastic than the world of ornament, a complete world. . . . What is most difficult in the world is to imagine something outside of what exists. Ornament tries to resolve this problem and to invent creation alongside creation" (Gautier in *L'Artiste,* 28 February 1858, quoted in M. Voisin, *Le Soleil et la nuit,* pp. 324–25).

38. It is difficult not to be reminded, by Gautier's proclamations about art and beauty, of Schiller's definition of the "living shape," the embodiment of art as a synthesis of sensuous and ideal impulses and as "play." "The object of the sensuous impulse, expressed in a general idea, is called 'life,' in its widest signification; an idea implying all material existence, and all that is immediately present to the sense. The object of the form-impulse, expressed generally, is called 'shape,' as well in a free as in a literal signification; an idea which includes all formal qualities of things, and all their relations to reflection. The object of the play-impulse, expressed in a general proposition, can then be called 'living shape,' an idea which serves to indicate all aesthetic qualities of phenomena, and in a word, what in its widest signification we call 'Beauty.' " Gautier, like Schiller, insists on the role of the material and the sensual in beauty, but at the same time, on the sublimation of that attraction to the sensual, regarded on a second level as mere reflection of the creative imagination. "A man, although he lives and has shape," Schiller continues, "is therefore for a long while no living shape. . . . He is a living shape, only when his form lives in our perception, and his life shapes itself in our understanding" (Friedrich Schiller, "Upon the Aesthetic Culture of Man in a Series of Letters," pp. 68–69).

39. Gautier, "Du Beau dans l'art," in *L'Art moderne,* p. 151.

40. Bürger, *Theory of the Avant Garde,* p. 46.

41. Priscilla Clark says something similar when she writes that, "the nineteenth century French novel was 'bourgeois' in that novelists consciously defined the genre in opposition to the bourgeoisie and bourgeois society" (*The Battle of the Bourgeois,* p. 16).

42. I disagree with Giraud, who, in "Winckelmann's Part in Gautier's Perception of Classical Beauty," states that Gautier, like Winckelmann, would "have the observer suspend, as it were, his sexual impulses" (p. 179).

43. A cult of useless beauty, influenced by Kantian aesthetics, was evident

in the eighteenth century in the admiration for such figures as Antinous, whose androgynous and useless body (particularly seen in opposition to Hercules) was considered to be the apotheosis of beauty. For a discussion, see Jean Seznec, *Diderot et l'antiquité.*

44. Gautier, "Delacroix," in *Histoire du romantisme,* p. 216.

45. Gautier, "En Grèce," in *Oeuvres complètes,* 11:229. Gautier thus reiterates the Socratic hierarchy of thought production over reproduction discussed in chap. 3, above.

46. René Girard, *To Double Business Bound,* p. ix. If we apply the terms by which Girard distinguishes among writers of the nineteenth century to the Gautier of the Preface as well as of the novel it introduces, we will find him to be, not "romantic," but "novelistic." He is the first to equate such a notion of "virginity" with a denial of historicity and with illusion. "Our innocence is quite passably sophisticated, and our virginity has gone around the town for quite a while; those are things which you don't have a second time, and, whatever we do, we can't get them back again, for nothing in the world goes faster than a virginity which is departing, or an illusion which is being destroyed" (*MM,* p. 27).

47. Geoffrey H. Hartman, *The Unmediated Vision,* pp. 164, 173.

48. Delacroix quoted in P. G. Castex, *La critique d'art,* p. 9 (my translation); Chambers, "Pour Une Poétique du vêtement," p. 27.

49. Castex, *La Critique d'art,* p. 9. No wonder, then, moreover, that he will embark on a long detailed study of the German painter Peter von Cornelius despite the fact that he finds him a lesser artist. Even while his idea, which is beautiful, "doesn't circulate from his brain to his hand," Gautier finds that when they are "told" (*racontées*), Cornelius's works seduce you. (See Gautier, "Pierre de Cornelius," in *L'Art moderne,* pp. 235–60.)

50. Richardson's translation of *Mademoiselle de Maupin* does not always convey the sexual overtones of Gautier's prose.

51. Hartman, *Unmediated Vision,* p. 164.

52. Gautier, "La Légende du gilet rouge," in *Histoire du romantisme,* p. 92.

53. Gautier quoted in Bergerat, *Théophile Gautier: Entretiens, souvenirs, Correspondances,* p. 127 (my translation).

54. For an in-depth study of the critical reception of the novel during the first half of the nineteenth century, see Iknayan, *The Idea of the Novel.*

55. Ibid., p. 71.

56. Latouche broaches the question of the suitability of different art forms in the Preface to *Fragoletta* and reveals his intention to create a new genre: "Those judges . . . believe it their right to say that any subject that has been consecrated in one art form by a masterpiece cannot be repeated in any other art form. They will add that the statuary that spreads apart the veils is more chaste than the narrative that carefully assembles them. . . . The author answers to them only by trying better to make a work of a totally different genre." Within the novel itself, Latouche touches on questions of the relation between art and historical fact and of the role of verisimilitude or illusion in various art forms. The controversy comes to a climax in the novel before Polycles' statue of the hermaphrodite in the museum of Naples, which is shocking to the Frenchman

d'Hauteville: "I don't really understand this kind of poetry or sculpture that involves such an exclusion of truth. . . . Don't you find that whimsical composition unworthy of the arts?" His Italian guide blames such a lack of imagination and lack of appreciation of beauty on his northern blood but responds civilly with a "to each his own" or "to every country its own taste." "I'll leave you the reality of all this if you will leave me its poetry" (Henri de Latouche, *Fragoletta*, pp. 51–52, my translation).

57. Cited in Frederic Ségu, *Henri de Latouche*, p. 341.

58. Gautier's hero is in line with the idealist tradition, which regards women as restricted to immanence and deprives them of the self-consciousness necessary for transcendence—"women don't understand poetry . . . they are poetry or at least the best instruments of poetry: the flute doesn't hear or understand the tune you play on it" (*MM*, p. 191). Maupin will only acquire "a sense of beauty" (*MM*, p. 280) when she takes on male attire.

59. Baudelaire, *De l'Essence du rire*, in *Curiosités esthétiques: L'Art romantique et autres oeuvres critiques*, pp. 215 ff. My understanding of this text and of Baudelarian irony draws heavily upon Paul de Man's elegant and insightful analysis "The Rhetoric of Temporality," in *Blindness and Insight*, pp. 187–228.

60. Friedrich Schlegel, "On Incomprehensibility," in *Lucinde and the Fragments*, p. 267. Gautier and Schlegel seem to manifest their irony in a similarly sexual rhetoric, one that theorists of romantic irony have not called attention to. It is as if the rhetoric of irony could answer the dream for an androgynous language that transcends sexual markings—the very dream that romantic authors like Gautier see the need to ironize. See above, chapter 2.

61. Schlegel quoted by René Bourgeois in *Ironie romantique*, p. 18.

62. In the first case, that "truth" would be the prime target for a psychoanalytic criticism; in the second, for a deconstructive and/or feminist criticism.

63. Luce Irigaray, "The Power of Discourse and the Subordination of the Feminine," in her *This Sex*, p. 76. Gautier seems to perceive, as Irigaray claims, that women have had to mime roles prescribed for them by men and thus the representations of women within male discourse are necessarily the reflected images of those "imitations" of male fantasies.

Chapter 6: "Androgyny, Feminism, and the Critical Difference"

1. Julia Kristeva, "Women's Time," p. 51.

2. Virginia Woolf, *A Room of One's Own*, pp. 108, 101, 108, 102.

3. Carolyn Heilbrun, *Toward a Recognition of Androgyny*, p. 115. Subsequent page references to this edition will be cited in the text to *TRA*.

4. Here I disagree with Toril Moi's understanding of Heilbrun's motive for distinguishing androgyny from feminism as a "refusal to draw the conclusion that feminists can in fact desire androgyny" (*Sexual/Textual Politics*, p. 14).

5. Elaine Showalter, *A Literature of Their Own*, p. 264. Future page references to this edition will be cited in the text to *LTO*.

6. Woolf, *A Room of One's Own*, p. 108.

7. Cynthia Secor, "The Androgyny Papers," in *The Androgyny Papers*, p. 139.

8. Barbara Charlesworth Gelpi, "The Politics of Androgyny," ibid., 151–60; Cynthia Secor, "Androgyny: An Early Reappraisal," ibid., pp. 161–69.

9. Daniel Harris, "Androgyny: The Sexist Myth in Disguise," pp. 171–84; Catherine R. Stimpson, "The Androgyne and the Homosexual," ibid., pp. 237–48.

10. Harris, "Androgyny," p. 173.

11. Nancy Topping Bazin and Alma Freeman, "The Androgynous Vision," in *Women's Studies,* vol. 2 (1974) pp. 185–215; Carolyn Heilbrun, "Further Notes toward a Recognition of Androgyny," ibid., pp. 143–49.

12. Bazin and Freeman, "The Androgynous Vision," pp. 185–86.

13. On the identification of woman and nature, see, for example, Sherry Ortner, "Is Female to Male as Nature is to Culture?" Many have called attention to woman's status as lack or hole within Freudian and Lacanian theory. See for instance, Luce Irigaray, *This Sex Which Is Not One,* chaps. 3, 5; Jane Gallop, *The Daughter's Seduction,* chap. 2.

14. Mary Daly, *Gyn/Ecology,* p. 387.

15. Moi, *Sexual/Textual Politics,* p. 18. Future page references to this edition will be cited in the text to *S/T.*

16. Showalter, *Literature,* p. 282.

17. Kristeva, "Women's Time," p. 52.

18. On the Derridean spelling of "différance," see the text that contains the reference to note 26 in chapter 1, above.

19. Julia Kristeva, "Oscillation between Power and Denial," and "Woman Can Never Be Defined," in *New French Feminisms,* ed. Elaine Marks and Isabelle de Courtivan, pp. 165, 137.

20. It is not my intention here to go into the role of the body in "essentialist" vs. antiessentialist" discourses. This has become a significant issue, however, in recent "returns" to essentialism that question the opposition between these two positions and whether all essentialist discourses are the same—whether those invested in antiessentialism might not also find "strategic" value in some forms of essentialism. On this debate see for example, Diana Fuss, *Essentially Speaking;* Naomi Schor, "This Essentialism Which Is Not One"; and Gayatri Spivak, with Ellen Rooney, "In a Word: Interview."

21. Hélène Cixous, "The Laugh of the Medusa," p. 254.

22. Luce Irigaray, "When Our Lips Speak Together," in her *This Sex,* p. 207.

23. Woolf, *A Room of One's Own,* p. 108 (my emphasis).

24. For an antiessentialist defense of Irigaray's figurative construction of the female body, see Jane Gallop, "Lip Service," in her *Thinking through the Body,* pp. 92–99. For discussions of her "strategic essentialism," see Fuss, *Essentially Speaking,* and Schor, "This Essentialism."

25. Mary Jacobus rightly comments that, in light of *Orlando,* "we should reread [Woolf's] famous remarks about androgyny—not as a naive attempt to transcend the determinants of gender and culture (though it is that too), but rather as a harmonizing gesture, a simultaneous enactment of desire and repression by which the split is closed with an essentially Utopian vision of undivided consciousness. The repressive male/female opposition which 'interferes with the unity of the mind' gives way to a mind paradoxically conceived of not as one, but

as heterogenous, open to the play of difference" ("The Difference of View," in her *Reading Woman: Essays in Feminist Criticism*, p. 39). Her reading of the novel/biography is directed towards rescuing Woolf not only for a poststructuralist feminism but more specifically for a feminism informed by psychoanalysis, whereby femininity, like the unconscious, is only "disclosed" as it also "discomposes" itself in writing and the linguistic play of difference (p. 24). While I agree with Jacobus's reading, I would put more emphasis on Woolf's insights into the political necessity to name and identify the woman.

26. The following discussion of *Orlando* was printed in somewhat different form in my "Aesthetics of Androgyny in Balzac and Woolf, or What's the Difference of Difference?"

27. Virginia Woolf, *Orlando*, p. 13. Future page references to this edition will be cited in the text to *O*.

28. Susan Suleiman, Introduction and "(Re)writing the Body: The Politics and Poetics of Female Eroticism" in *The Female Body in Western Culture*, ed. Suleiman, pp. 4, 24.

29. In her essays "The Power of Discourse and Subordination of the Feminine" and "When Our Lips Speak Together," Irigaray plays on various meanings of the word *indifferent*, written in French in the feminine as *indifférente*—meaning alternately, indifferent, not different, or in difference (different within). Here, I am referring particularly to that "sexual indifference that underlies the truth of any science, the logic of every discourse"—by which she implicates the falsely presumed neutrality and universality of the masculine ("The Power of Discourse," in *This Sex*, p. 69).

30. Teresa de Lauretis, "Feminist Studies/Critical Studies: Issues, Terms, and Contexts," in *Feminist Studies/Critical Studies*, ed. de Lauretis, p. 9, Nancy Miller, "Changing the Subject: Authorship, Writing, and the Reader," p. 116; Irigaray, *This Sex*, p. 76.

31. See, for example, Tania Modleski's discussion of the way that "mimesis" or mimicry works in Maya Angelou's *I Know Why the Caged Bird Sings* in "Feminism and the Power of Interpretation," in *Feminist Studies/Critical Studies*, ed. Teresa de Lauretis, p. 129. For a discussion of mimesis in a colonial context, see Homi K. Bhaba, "Of Mimicry and Man: The Ambivalence of Colonial Discourse," pp. 131–33.

32. Irigaray, *This Sex*, p. 76.

33. Donna Haraway's "Manifesto for Cyborgs" was first published in *Socialist Review*, no. 80, in 1985. It has also been anthologized with four commentaries in *Coming to Terms*, ed. Elizabeth Weed. Future page references will be to the latter edition and will be cited in the text to MC.

34. See my discussion in chap. 2.

35. See also the excellent discussion of the classical vs. the grotesque body in Peter Stallybrass and Allon White, *The Politics and Poetics of Transgression*, pp. 6–26.

36. Hayden White, *Metahistory*, p. 38.

37. Miller, "Changing the Subject," p. 119 n. 18.

38. On feminism's move to the interior of the academy, see Marianne Hirsch and Evelyn Fox Keller's "Conclusion," in *Conflicts in Feminism*, p. 379.

39. Judith Butler, *Gender Trouble*, p. x.
40. Ibid., p. 1.
41. Ibid., p. 139.
42. For an excellent discussion of the ways in which certain technologies have created new forms of surveillance, see Jennifer Terry, "The Body Invaded," p. 3.
43. Lisa G. Nash, "(Re)producing Choice, (De)constructing Bodies: Feminist Strategies for Reading Reproductive Technologies," pp. 118–19. I thank Christina Crosby for bringing this excellent thesis to my attention.
44. Christina Crosby, "Commentary: Allies and Enemies," p. 208; Nash, "(Re)producing Choice," p. 121.
45. Rosi Braidotti, "Organs without Bodies," pp. 152, 154.
46. Ibid., p. 156.
47. See Tania Modleski, "Three Men and Baby M."
48. Braidotti, "Organs without Bodies," p. 157.
49. Ibid., p. 158.
50. I am echoing Schor's remark that "more than deconstruction, *essentialism is not one*" ("This Essentialism," p. 41—original emphasis).
51. Luce Irigaray, "Sexual Difference" in *French Feminist Thought*, ed. Toril Moi, p. 119. This is a translation of the first chapter of *Ethique*.
52. Irigaray, *Ethique*, p. 133.
53. Naomi Schor borrows the term *paleonymy* from Derrida to describe this mimetic strategy that Irigaray uses in "This Essentialism Which Is Not One," p. 48.
54. Irigaray, "Sexual Difference," p. 124.
55. Derrida, for instance, describes deconstruction's phase of overturning and links it to the recognition that: "we are not dealing with the peaceful coexistence of a *vis-à-vis,* but rather with a violent hierarchy. One of the two terms governs the other. . . . To deconstruct the opposition, first of all, is to overturn the hierarchy at a given moment. To overlook this phase of overturning is to forget the conflictual and subordinating structure of opposition" (Jacques Derrida, *Positions*, p. 42).
56. Irigaray, "Sexual Difference," p. 124.
57. Irigaray, *Ethique*, pp. 174, 175.
58. Irigaray, "Sexual Difference," p. 121.
59. Luce Irigaray, "Equal to Whom?" pp. 69, 73.
60. Irigaray, "Sexual Difference," pp. 127, 128.
61. Miller, "Changing the Subject," p. 119 n. 18.
62. Irigaray, "Equal to Whom," p. 74.
63. Luce Irigaray, *Parler n'est jamais neutre* (Paris: Minuit, 1985), p. 9, quoted in Schor, "This Essentialism," p. 45.
64. Margaret Whitford, "Luce Irigaray and the Female Imaginary," p. 6.
65. On *Aufhebung*, see chap. 2, near reference for note 19, above.

Bibliography

Aarsleff, Hans. *From Locke to Saussure*. Minneapolis: University of Minnesota Press, 1983.

Abel, Elizabeth, ed. *Writing and Sexual Difference*. Chicago: University of Chicago Press, 1982.

Abrams, M. H. *Natural Supernaturalism*. New York: Norton, 1971.

Allemand, André. *Unité et structure de l'univers Balzacien*. Paris: Librairie Plon, 1965.

The Androgyny Papers. Edited by Cynthia Secor. Vol. 2 of *Women's Studies*, 1974.

Auerbach, Eric. *Mimesis*. Princeton: Princeton University Press, 1986.

Bakhtin, M. M. *Rabelais and His World*. Translated by H. Iswolsky. Cambridge, Mass.: MIT Press, 1968.

Ballanche, Pierre-Simon. *La Vision d'Hébal*. Introduction by A. J. L. Busst. Geneva: Librairie Droz, 1969.

Balzac, Honoré de. *La Comédie humaine*. Paris: Editions du Seuil, 1966.

———. *Correspondance*. Paris: Editions Garnier Frères, 1962.

———. *Lettres à Madame Hanska*. Edited by Spoelberch de Louvenjoul. Paris: Editions du Delta, 1967.

———. *Oeuvres complètes*. 24 vols. Paris: Club de l'Honnête Homme, 1968–71.

Bardèche, Maurice. *Balzac*. Paris: Juliard, 1980.

Barthes, Roland. *Michelet*. Translated by Richard Howard. New York: Hill and Wang, 1987.

———. *The Pleasure of the Text*. Translated by Richard Howard. New York: Hill and Wang, 1975.

———. *Roland Barthes by Roland Barthes*. Translated by Richard Howard. New York: Hill and Wang, 1977.

———. *S/Z*. Translated by Richard Miller. New York: Hill and Wang, 1974.

Baudelaire, Charles. *L'Art romantique*. Paris: Editions Garnier Frères, 1962.

———. *Curiosités esthétiques: L'Art romantique et autres oeuvres critiques*. Edited by H. Lemaître. Paris: Garnier, 1962.

———. "Le Peintre de la vie moderne." In his *Oeuvres complètes*. Paris: Gallimard, 1976.

Bazin, Nancy Topping. *Virginia Woolf and the Androgynous Vision*. New Brunswick, N.J.: Rutgers University Press, 1973.

Béguin, Albert. *Balzac lu et relu*. Paris: Editions du Seuil, 1956.

———. *Balzac visionnaire*. Geneva: Editions Albert Skira, 1946.

Behler, Ernst. *Irony and the Discourse of Modernity.* Seattle: University of Washington Press, 1990.

Beizer, Janet L. *Family Plots.* New Haven, Conn.: Yale University Press, 1986.

Benichou, Paul. *Le Temps des prophètes.* Paris: Gallimard, 1977.

Bérard, Suzanne. "La Spécialité: Une Énigme Balzacienne." In *L'Année Balzacienne.* Paris: Garnier Frères, 1965.

Bergerat, Emile. *Théophile Gautier: Entretiens, Souvenirs, Correspondances,* Paris: Charpentier, 1897.

Bhaba, Homi K. "Of Mimicry and Man: The Ambivalence of Colonial Discourse." *October* 28 (Spring 1984): 125–33.

Borel, Jacques. *Séraphîta et le mysticisme Balzacien.* Paris: Corti, 1967.

Borowitz, Helen O. "Balzac's Sarrasine: The Sculptor as Narcissus." *Nineteenth-Century French Studies* 5, nos. 3–4 (Spring-Summer 1977): 171–85.

Bourgeois, René. *L'Ironie romantique: Spectacle et jeu de Mme. de Staël à Gerard de Nerval.* Grenoble: Presses Universitaires, 1974.

Bowman, Frank Paul. *Le Christ romantique.* Geneva: Droz, 1973.

Braidotti, Rosi. "Organs without Bodies." *differences* 1, no. 1 (Winter 1989): 147–61.

Brenkman, John. "The Other and the One: Psychoanalysis, Reading, *The Symposium,*" *Yale French Studies* 55/56 (1977): 448–49.

Brown, Norman O. *Love's Body.* New York: Random House, 1966.

Brownmiller, Susan. *Femininity.* New York: Simon & Schuster, 1983.

Bürger, Peter. *The Theory of the Avant Garde.* Minneapolis: University of Minnesota Press, 1984.

Busst, A. J. L. "The Image of the Androgyne in the Nineteenth Century." In *Romantic Mythologies,* edited by Ian Fletcher, pp. 1–95. New York: Barnes and Noble, 1967.

Butler, Judith. *Gender Trouble.* New York: Routledge, 1990.

Butler, Ronnie. *Balzac and the French Revolution.* New York: Barnes and Noble, 1983.

Cassagne, Albert. *La Théorie de l'art pour l'art en France.* Paris: Hachette, 1906.

Castex, P. G. *La Critique d'art en France au XIXe siècle.* Paris: Centre de Documentation Universitaire, 1966.

Chambers, Ross. "Narrative as Oppositional Practice: Nerval's *Aurelia.*" *Stanford French Review* 8 (Spring 1985): 55–74.

———. "Pour Une Poétique du vêtement." In *Poétiques: Théories et Critiques Littéraires,* edited by Floyd Gray, pp. 18–46. Ann Arbor: Michigan Romance Studies, no. 1, 1980.

———. *Story and Situation: Narrative Seduction and the Power of Fiction.* Minneapolis: University of Minnesota Press, 1984.

Cixous, Hélène. "The Laugh of the Medusa." In *New French Feminisms,* edited by Elaine Marks and Isabelle de Courtivran, pp. 245–64. New York: Schocken Books, 1981.

Clark, Priscilla. *The Battle of the Bourgeois.* Paris: Didier, 1973.

Crosby, Christina. "Commentary: Allies and Enemies." In *Coming to Terms: Feminism, Theory, Politics,* edited by Elizabeth Weed, pp. 205–8. New York: Routledge, 1989.

Curtius, Ernst. *Balzac.* Translated by Henri Jourdan. Paris: B. Grasset, 1933.

Daly, Mary. *Beyond God the Father: Toward a Philosophy of Women's Liberation.* Boston: Beacon Press, 1973.

——. *Gyn/Ecology.* Boston: Beacon Press, 1990.

Delattre, Geneviève. "De *Séraphîta* à *La Fille aux yeux d'or.*" *Année balzacienne.* Paris: Garnier Frères, 1970.

Delcourt, Marie. *Hermaphrodite, mythes et rites de la bisexualité dans l'antiquité classique.* Paris: Presses Universitaires, 1958.

——. *Hermaphroditea.* Brussels: Latomus, 1966.

de Lauretis, Teresa, ed. *Feminist Studies/Critical Studies.* Bloomington: Indiana University Press, 1986.

Deleuze, Gilles. *Proust and Signs.* New York: George Braziller, 1972.

De Man, Paul. *Blindness and Insight: Essays in the Rhetoric of Contemporary Criticism.* Minneapolis: University of Minnesota Press, 1983.

——. "The Concept of Irony." Transcription of a lecture given at the Ohio State University, Columbus, 4 April 1977.

——. *The Rhetoric of Romanticism.* New York: Columbia University Press, 1984.

Derrida, Jacques. *Spurs/Epérons.* Bilingual edition. Translated by Barbara Harlow. Chicago: University of Chicago Press, 1978.

——. *Of Grammatology.* Translated by Gayatri Spivak. Baltimore: Johns Hopkins University Press, 1976.

——. *Positions.* Translated by Alan Bass. Chicago: University of Chicago Press, 1981.

——. *Speech and Phenomenon.* Evanston, Ill.: Northwestern University Press, 1973.

Des Fontaines, J. Halley. *La Notion d'androgynie dans quelques mythes et quelques rites.* Paris: Le François, 1938.

Diderot, Dennis. "Essai Sur la Peinture." In *Oeuvres,* edited by André Billy, pp. 1143–2000. Paris: Gallimard, 1946.

Dijkstra, Bram. "Androgyne in Art and Literature." *Comparative Literature* 26 (1974): 63–73.

Dillingham, Louise B. *The Creative Imagination of Théophile Gautier.* Bryn Mawr, Pa.: n.p., 1927.

Dubois, Page. *Sowing the Body: Psychoanalysis and Ancient Representations of Women.* Chicago: University of Chicago Press, 1988.

Eagleton, Terry. *Literary Theory.* Minneapolis: University of Minnesota Press, 1983.

Eichner, Hans. *Friedrich Schlegel.* New York: Twayne, 1970.

Eisenstein, Hester, and Alice Jardine, eds. *The Future of Difference*. Boston: G. K. Hall and Co., 1980.

Eliade, Mircea. *The Two and the One*. Translated by J. M. Cohen. Chicago: University of Chicago Press, 1962.

Ezdinli, Leyla. "George Sand's Literary Transvestism: Pre-texts and Contexts." Ph.D. diss., Princeton, 1988.

Felman, Shoshana. "Rereading Femininity." *Yale French Studies* 62 (1981): 19–44.

———. "Woman and Madness: The Critical Phallacy." *Diacritics* 5 (Winter 1975): 2–10.

Foucault, Michel. *Herculine Barbin: Being the Recently Discovered Memoirs of a Nineteenth Century French Hermaphrodite*. New York: Pantheon Press, 1980.

———. *The History of Sexuality*. Vol. 1, *An Introduction*. New York: Vintage Books, 1978.

Freedman, Ralph. *The Lyrical Novel*. Princeton, N.J.: Princeton University Press, 1963.

Freud, Sigmund. *Beyond the Pleasure Principle*. Translated and edited by James Strachey. New York: W. W. Norton, 1961.

———. *The Three Essays on the Theory of Sexuality*. Translated by James Strachey. New York: Basic Books, 1962.

Friedrichsmeyer, Sara. *The Androgyne in Early German Romanticism*. New York: Peter Lang, 1983.

Furst, Lilian. *Fictions of Romantic Irony*. Cambridge, Mass.: Harvard University Press, 1984.

Fuss, Diana. *Essentially Speaking*. New York: Routledge, 1989.

Gallop, Jane. *The Daughter's Seduction*. Ithaca, N.Y.: Cornell University Press, 1982.

———. *Reading Lacan*. Ithaca, N.Y.: Cornell University Press, 1985.

———. *Thinking through the Body*. New York: Columbia University Press, 1988.

Gaucheron, Jacques. "Ombres et lueurs de l'art pour l'art." *Europe* 601 (May 1979): 74–83.

Gautier, Théophile. *L'Art moderne*. Paris: Michel Levy Frères, 1856.

———. *Critique artistique et littéraire*. Paris: Bibliothèque Larousse, 1929.

———. *Ecrivains et artistes romantiques*. Paris: Plon, 1933.

———. *Les Grotesques*. Paris: Charpentier, 1897.

———. *Histoire du romantisme*. Geneva: Slatkine Reprints, 1978.

———. *Les Jeunes France*. Paris: Flammarion, 1974.

———. *Mademoiselle de Maupin*. Paris: Garnier Flammarion, 1966.

———. *Mademoiselle de Maupin*. Translated by Joanna Richardson. New York: Penguin, 1981.

———. *Oeuvres complètes*. 11 vols. Geneva: Slatkine Reprints, 1978.

———. *Poésies complètes*. Vol. 3. Paris: Nizet, 1970.

————, and Hippolyte Taine. *Honoré de Balzac.* Brussels: Librairie Internationale, 1858.

Genette, Gerard. *Figures II.* Paris: Editions du Seuil, 1969.

Giese, Fritz. *Der Romantische Charakter I: Die Entwicklung des androgynenproblems in der Frühromantik.* Langensalza: Wendt and Klauwell, 1919.

Girard, René. *Deceit, Desire, and the Novel.* Baltimore: Johns Hopkins University Press, 1976.

————. *To Double Business Bound.* Baltimore: Johns Hopkins University Press, 1988.

Giraud, Raymond. "Winckelmann's Part in Gautier's Perception of Classical Beauty" *Yale French Studies* 38 (1967): 172–82.

Gray, Ronald. *Goethe the Alchemist.* Cambridge: Cambridge University Press, 1952.

Grosz, Liz. *Sexual Subversions: Three French Feminists.* Sydney: Allen & Unwin, 1989.

Halperin, David M. *One Hundred Years of Homosexuality.* New York: Routledge, 1990.

Handwerk, Gary. *Irony and Ethics in Narrative.* New Haven, Conn.: Yale University Press, 1985.

Haraway, Donna. "A Manifesto for Cyborgs: Science, Technology, and Socialist Feminism in the 1980's." In *Coming to Terms: Feminism, Theory, Politics,* edited by Elizabeth Weed, pp. 173–204. New York: Routledge, 1989.

Harper, Mary. "Recovering the Other: Women and the Orient in Writings of Early Nineteenth-Century France." *Critical Matrix: Princeton Working Papers in Women's Studies* 1, no. 6 (1985): 1–31.

Hartman, Geoffrey H. *The Unmediated Vision.* New York: Harcourt, Brace and World, 1966.

Heath, Stephen. "Joan Rivière and the Masquerade." In *Formations of Fantasy,* edited by Victor Burgin, James Donald and Cora Kaplan, pp. 45–61. New York: Methuan, 1986.

Hegel, G. W. F. *On Art, Religion, Philosophy.* Edited by J. Glenn Gray. New York: Harper Torchbooks, 1970.

————. *The Phenomenology of Mind.* Translated by J. B. Baillie. New York: Harper Colophon, 1967.

Heilbrun, Carolyn. "Androgyny and the Psychology of Sex differences." In *The Future of Difference,* edited by Hester Eisenstein and Alice Jardine, pp. 259–66. Boston: G. K. Hall and Co., 1980.

————. *Toward a Recognition of Androgyny.* New York: W. W. Norton, 1973.

Higonnet, Margaret R. "Writing from the Feminine: *Lucinde* and *Adolphe.*" *Annales Benjamin Constant* 6 (1986): 17–35.

Hirsch, Marianne, and Evelyn Fox Keller, eds. *Conflicts in Feminism.* New York: Routledge, 1990.

Hugo, Victor. "Préface à *Cromwell*." In his *Théatre Complet*, vol. 1, ed. J. J. Thierry and Josette Mélèze, pp. 409–58. Paris: Pléiade, 1976.

Iknayan, Marguerite. *The Idea of the Novel in France: The Critical Reaction, 1815–1848*. Geneva: Librairie Droz, 1961.

Irigaray, Luce. "Equal to Whom?" *differences* 1, no. 2 (Summer 1989): 59–76.

———. *Ethique de la différence sexuelle*. Paris: Minuit, 1984.

———. *Speculum of the Other Woman*. Translated by Gillian C. Gill. Ithaca, N.Y.: Cornell University Press, 1985.

———. *This Sex Which Is Not One*. Translated by Catherine Porter. Ithaca, N.Y.: Cornell University Press, 1985.

Jacobus, Mary. *Reading Woman: Essays in Feminist Criticism*. New York: Columbia University Press, 1986.

Jameson, Frederic. *The Political Unconscious*. Ithaca, N.Y.: Cornell University Press, 1981.

Jardine, Alice. *Gynesis: Configurations of Woman and Modernity*. Ithaca, N.Y.: Cornell University Press, 1985.

Jasinski, René. *Les Années romantiques de Théophile Gautier*. Paris: 1929.

Johnson, Barbara. *The Critical Difference: Essays in the Contemporary Rhetoric of Reading*. Baltimore: Johns Hopkins University Press, 1980.

Jordanova, Ludmilla. "Natural Facts, a Historical Perspective on Science and Sexuality." In *Nature, Culture, and Gender*, edited by C. P. MacCormack and Marilyn Strathern, pp. 42–69. Cambridge: Cambridge University Press, 1980.

Josipovichi, Gabriel. *The World and the Book: A Study of Modern Fiction*. London: Macmillan Press, 1971.

Kanes, Martin. *Balzac's Comedy of Words*. Princeton, N.J.: Princeton University Press, 1975.

Kant, Immanuel. *The Critique of Judgement*. Translated by J. H. Bernard. New York: Hafner Press, 1951.

Kelly, Dorothy. *Fictional Genders*. Lincoln: University of Nebraska Press, 1989.

Kermode, Frank. *The Sense of an Ending: Studies in the Theory of Fiction*. London: Oxford University Press, 1963.

Knoop, Bernhard. *Victor Cousin's Aesthetic and Its Sources*. Chapel Hill: University of North Carolina Press, 1965.

Kofman, Sarah. *The Enigma of Woman*. Translated by Catherine Porter. Ithaca, N.Y.: Cornell University Press, 1985.

Kristeva, Julia. "Women's Time." In *Feminist Theory: A Critique of Ideology*, edited by Nannerl O. Keohane, Michelle Z. Rosaldo, Barbara C. Gelpi, pp. 31–54. Chicago: University of Chicago Press, 1982.

Lacan, Jacques. *Ecrits: A Selection*. Translated by Alan Sheridan. New York: W. W. Norton, 1981.

———. *Feminine Sexuality: Jacques Lacan and the Ecole Freudienne*. Edited by Juliet Mitchell and Jacqueline Rose. New York: W. W. Norton, 1982.

————. *The Four Fundamental Concepts of Psycho-Analysis.* Translated by Alan Sheridan. New York: W. W. Norton and Co., 1981.

Lacoue-Labarthe, Philippe, and Jean-Luc Nancy. *The Literary Absolute.* Translated by Philip Barnard and Cheryl Lester. Albany: SUNY Press, 1988.

Latouche, Henri de. *Fragoletta, ou Naples et Paris en 1799.* Paris: Les Editions Desjonquères, 1983.

Libis, Jean. *Le Mythe de l'androgyne.* Paris: Berg International, 1980.

Lock, Peter. "Melancholia, Mourning, and the Question of Symbolization" (unpublished paper).

Lukács, Georg. *The Theory of the Novel.* Cambridge: The MIT Press, 1968.

McCarthy, Mary Susan. *Balzac and His Reader.* Columbia: University of Missouri Press, 1982.

Marks, Elaine, and Isabelle de Courtivan, eds. *New French Feminisms.* New York: Schocken Books, 1981.

Matoré, Georges. *Le Vocabulaire et la société sous Louis-Philippe.* Geneva: Librairie Girard, 1951.

Miller, D. A. *Narrative and Its Discontents.* Princeton, N.J.: Princeton University Press, 1981.

Miller, J. Hillis. "The Two Allegories." In *Allegory, Myth, and Symbol,* edited by Morton Bloomfield, pp. 355–70. Cambridge, Mass.: Harvard University Press, 1981.

Miller, Nancy. "Changing the Subject: Authorship, Writing, and the Reader." In *Feminist Studies/Critical Studies,* edited by Teresa de Lauretis, pp. 102–20. Bloomington: Indiana University Press, 1986.

Modleski, Tanya. "Three Men and Baby M." *Camera Obscura* 17 (May 1988): 69–81.

Moi, Toril, ed. *French Feminist Thought.* New York: Basil Blackwell, 1988.

————. *Sexual/Textual Politics.* New York: Methuen, 1985.

Molino, Jean. "Le Mythe de l'androgyne." In *Aimer en France, 1760–1860,* pp. 401–11. Clermont-Ferrand: Actes du Colloque International de Clermont-Ferrand, 1980.

Moses, Claire Goldberg. *French Feminism in the Nineteenth Century.* Albany: SUNY Press, 1984.

Nash, Lisa. "(Re)producing Choice, (De)constructing Bodies: Feminist Strategies for Reading Reproductive Technologies." Honors thesis, Wesleyan University, 1989.

Nash, Suzanne. "Story-telling and the Loss of Innocence in Balzac's *Comédie humaine.*" *Romanic Review* 70, no. 3 (May 1979): 249–67.

Novalis. *Henry Von Ofterdingen, a Novel.* Translated by Palmer Hilty. New York: Frederick Ungar, 1964.

Nussbaum, Martha. "The Speech of Alcibiades: A Reading of Plato's *Symposium.*" *Philosophy and Literature,* 3, no. 2 (Fall 1979): 131–72.

Ortner, Sherry. "Is Female to Male as Nature Is to Culture?" In *Woman,*

Culture, and Society, edited by Michelle Z. Rosaldo and Louise Lamphere, pp. 67–87. Stanford, Calif.: Stanford University Press, 1974.

Ovid. *Metamorphoses.* Translated by Mary M. Innes. New York: Penguin, 1955.

Pacteau, Francette. "The Impossible Referent: Representations of the Androgyne." In *Formations of Fantasy,* edited by Victor Burgin, James Donald, and Cora Kaplan, pp. 62–84. New York: Methuen, 1986.

Patch, Helen E. *The Dramatic Criticism of Théophile Gautier.* Bryn Mawr, Pa.: n.p., 1922.

Perrot, Philippe. "Le Jardin des modes." In *Misérable et glorieuse: La Femme du XIXe siècle,* edited by Jean-Paul Aron, pp. 101–16. Paris: Fayard, 1980.

Picon, Gaeton. *Balzac par lui-même.* Paris: Editions du Seuil, 1956.

Plato. *Symposium.* In *The Portable Plato,* translated by Benjamin Jowett. New York: The Viking Press, 1976.

———. *The Symposium,* translated by Walter Hamilton. New York: Penguin, 1951.

Prendergast, Christopher. *Balzac: Fiction and Melodrama.* London: Edward Arnold, 1978.

Praz, Mario. *The Romantic Agony.* London: Oxford University Press, 1970.

Proust, Marcel. *Contre Sainte-Beuve.* Paris: Gallimard, 1954.

———. *Sodome et Gomorrhe.* Paris: Gallimard, 1954.

Raymond, Janice. *The Transexual Empire.* Boston: Beacon Press, 1979.

Rousset, Jean. *Forme et signification.* Paris: Corti, 1962.

Said, Edward. *The World, the Text, and the Critic.* Cambridge, Mass.: Harvard University Press, 1983.

Savalle, Joseph. *Travestis, métamorphoses, dédoublements.* Paris: Librairie Minard, 1981.

Schiller, Friedrich. *On Naive and Sentimental Poetry and on the Sublime.* Translated by Julias A. Elias. New York: Frederick Ungar Publishing Co., 1966.

———. "Upon the Aesthetic Culture of Man in a Series of Letters." In *The Aesthetic Letters, Essays, and Philosophical Letters of Schiller,* translated by J. Weiss, pp. 1–148. Boston: Little and Brown, 1934.

Schlegel, Friedrich. *Dialogue on Poetry and Literary Aphorisms.* University Park: Pennsylvania State University Press, 1968.

———. *Lucinde.* In *Dichtungen,* edited by Hans Eichner, pp. 1–96. Munich: Paderborn, 1962. Vol. 5 of *Kritische Ausgabe.* 35 vols. (1958–79).

———. *Lucinde and the Fragments.* Translated by Peter Firchow. Minneapolis: University of Minnesota Press, 1971.

———. "Über die Diotima." In *Studien des Klassischen Altertums,* edited by Ernst Behler, pp. 70–115. Munich: Paderborn, 1979. Vol. 1 of *Kritische Ausgabe.* 35 vols. (1958–79).

———. "Über die Philosophie, an Dorothea." In *Studien zur Philosophie und Theologie,* edited by Ernst Behler and Ursula Struc-Oppenberg, pp. 41–62. Munich: Padernborn, 1975. Vol. 8 of *Kritische Ausgabe*. 35 vols. (1958–79).

Schor, Naomi. "Dreaming Dissymmetry: Barthes, Foucault, and Sexual Difference." In *Men in Feminism*, edited by Alice Jardine and Paul Smith, pp. 98–110. New York: Methuen, 1987.

———. "Idealism in the Novel: Recanonizing Sand." *Yale French Studies* 75 (1988): 56–73.

———. *Reading in Detail*. New York: Methuen, 1987.

———. "This Essentialism Which Is Not One: Coming to Grips with Irigaray." *differences* 1, no. 2 (Summer 1989): 38–58.

Ségu, Frederic. *Henri de Latouche*. Paris: Les Belles Lettres, 1931.

Seznec, Jean. *Diderot et l'antiquité*. Oxford: Clarendon Press, 1957.

Showalter, Elaine. *A Literature of Their Own*. Princeton, N.J.: Princeton University Press, 1977.

Silverman, Kaja. *The Subject of Semiotics*. Oxford: Oxford University Press, 1983.

Singer, June. *Androgyny*. New York: Anchor Press, 1976.

Smyth, John Vignaux. *A Question of Eros: Irony in Sterne, Kierkegaard, and Barthes*. Tallahassee: University of Florida Press, 1986.

Spivak, Gayatri, with Ellen Rooney. "In a Word: Interview." *differences* 1, no. 2 (Summer 1989): 124–56.

Stallybrass, Peter, and Allon White. *The Politics and Poetics of Transgression*. Ithaca, N.Y.: Cornell University Press, 1986.

Stapfer, Paul. *Questions esthétiques et religieuses*. Paris: Félix Alcan, 1906.

Suleiman, Susan, ed. *The Female Body in Western Culture*. Cambridge, Mass.: Harvard University Press, 1986.

Szondi, Peter. *On Textual Understanding and Other Essays*. Translated by Harvey Mendelsohn. Theory and History of Literature, vol. 15. Minneapolis: University of Minnesota Press, 1986.

Tennant, P. E. *Théophile Gautier*. London: Athelone Press, 1975.

Terry, Jennifer. "The Body Invaded." *Socialist Review* 3 (1989): 13–43.

Tritier, J. L. *Le Langage philosophique dans les oeuvres de Balzac*. Paris: A. G. Nizet, 1976.

Tuin, H. Van der. *Théophile Gautier*. Amsterdam: N.V. Holdert & Co., 1933.

Viertel, John. "Concepts of Language Underlying the Eighteenth-Century Controversy about the Origin of Language." In *Report of the Seventeenth Annual Round Table Meeting on Linguistics and Language Studies,* ed. Francis P. Dineen S.J., pp. 109–32. Washington, D.C.: Georgetown University Press, 1966.

Voisin, Marcel. *Le Soleil et la nuit: L'Imaginaire dans l'oeuvre de Théophile Gautier*. Brussels, Editions de l'Université, 1981.

Weber, Samuel. *The Legend of Freud*. Minneapolis: University of Minnesota Press, 1982.

Weed, Elizabeth, ed. *Coming to Terms*. New York: Routledge, 1989.

Weil, Kari. "The Aesthetics of Androgyny in Balzac and Woolf, or What's the

Difference of Difference?" *Critical Matrix: Princeton Working Papers in Women's Studies* 1, no. 6 (1985): 1–24.

———. "Femino-centric Utopia and Male Desire: 'The New Paris of the Saint-Simonians.'" In *Feminism, Narrative, and Utopia,* edited by Sarah Webster Goodwin and Libby Jones, pp. 159–73. Knoxville: University of Tennessee Press, 1990.

———. "Romantic Androgyny and Its Discontents: The Case of *Mademoiselle de Maupin.*" *Romanic Review* 77, no. 3 (May 1987): 348–58.

Whitford, Margaret. "Luce Irigaray and the Female Imaginary: Speaking as a Woman." *Radical Philosophy* 43 (Summer, 1986): 3–8.

White, Hayden. *Metahistory.* Baltimore: Johns Hopkins University Press, 1973.

Will, Frederic. *Flumen Historicum: Victor Cousin's Aesthetic and Its Sources.* Chapel Hill: University of North Carolina Press, 1965.

Winckelmann, J. J. *History of Ancient Art.* Translated by Alexander Gode. New York: Frederick Ungar, 1968.

Woolf, Virginia. *Orlando.* New York: Harcourt, Brace, Jovanovich, 1956.

———. *A Room of One's Own.* New York: Harcourt, Brace, 1957.

Index

Index